VOICES *of* THUNDER

VOICES

of

THUNDER

Radical Religious Women of
the Seventeenth Century

NAOMI BAKER

REAKTION BOOKS

For Isabel and Florence

Published by
REAKTION BOOKS LTD
2–4 Sebastian Street
London EC1V OHE, UK
www.reaktionbooks.co.uk

First published 2025
Copyright © Naomi Baker 2025

EU GPSR Authorised Representative
Logos Europe, 9 rue Nicolas Poussin, 17000, La Rochelle, France
email: contact@logoseurope.eu

Printed and bound in Great Britain by Bell & Bain, Glasgow

A catalogue record for this book is available from the British Library

ISBN 978 1 83639 119 7

CONTENTS

'The secret voice of thunder hath a louder report,
than men's great cannons.'
(Anna Trapnel, *Anna Trapnel's Report and Plea*, 1654)

Textual Note

Seventeenth-century spelling has been updated for ease of reading, as has some punctuation. The titles of publications are unaltered.

New Style dating – taking the first day of the year to be 1 January instead of 25 March – has been used throughout.

Biblical quotations are from the King James Version.

Abbreviations:

CSPD   *Calendar of State Papers, Domestic*
ODNB *Oxford Dictionary of National Biography*

Timeline

1658	Cromwell dies, names son Richard successor. Mary Fisher meets Mehmed IV; Katharine Evans and Sarah Cheevers travel to Malta
1660	Restoration: Charles II becomes king. Hester Biddle, *A Warning from the Lord God of Life and Power, unto thee O city of London*
1661	Fifth Monarchist uprising, led by Thomas Venner
1662	Quaker Act requires subjects to swear Oath of Allegiance and outlaws Quaker meetings. Katharine Evans and Sarah Cheevers, *This is a Short Relation of some of the Cruel Sufferings.* Hester Biddle, *The Trumpet of the Lord Sounded Forth unto these Three Nations*
1664	Conventicle Act outlaws religious meetings of more than 5 people outside of the Church of England
1665	Great Plague kills *c.* 100,000
1666	Great Fire of London
1676	Anne Wentworth, *A True Account of Anne Wentworth's being cruelly, unjustly, and unchristianly dealt with by some of those people called Anabaptists*
1677	Anne Wentworth, *A Vindication of Anne Wentworth*
1679	Anne Wentworth, *The Revelation of Jesus Christ; Englands Spiritual Pill*
1681	Jane Lead, *The Heavenly Cloud Now Breaking*
1683	Jane Lead, *The Revelation of Revelations*
1685	James II becomes king
1688	William III of Orange and Mary to London, 'Glorious Revolution'
1689	Toleration Act grants freedom of worship to Nonconformists
1696	Jane Lead, *A Fountain of Gardens*, vol. I

Introduction

Pray you tell me, what authority this unbelieving husband
hath over the conscience of his believing wife? It is true,
he hath authority over her in bodily and civil respects,
but not to be a lord over her conscience; and the like
may be said of fathers and masters.

Katherine Chidley, 1641

I will write defiance.

Anna Trapnel, 1654

In that day shall my mouth be opened . . . and I shall speak,
and be no more reviled, nor more abused,
no more persecuted.

Anne Wentworth, 1679

Take no notice of Katherine Chidley, she is nothing more
than a 'brazen-faced audacious old woman', sneered the
Presbyterian Thomas Edwards in 1646.[1] Not only did Edwards
think that Chidley's beliefs were heretical but five years earlier
she had published a pamphlet refuting his views. Their war
of words was a skirmish within the wider battle of ideas and
beliefs taking place in Civil War England, a battle that turned
on questions of authority. Supporting the king or Parliament

was just the tip of the iceberg. Far more was at stake: to what or to whom should English people make themselves subject? Could any institution or individual – whether a priest, a father, a husband, a master or a king – command unquestioning obedience? Or was every woman and man free to follow her or his own conscience, no matter what the consequences?

For Chidley and Edwards, as for others in this era, these questions were brought into focus by their relationship with the Church of England. Edwards lamented the fact that during the 1640s there had been an explosion of independent, self-governing Protestant congregations whose members no longer showed allegiance to the established Church – or, in his mind, to any notion of stable order. As an outspoken member of one such 'gathered church', Katherine Chidley embodied his worst nightmares of the topsy-turvy world that was emerging. Not only had she abandoned the national Church, but she had taken the rare – and, for him, outrageous – step, as a woman, of publishing a pamphlet, *The Justification of the Independent Churches of Christ* (1641), in which she defended Independent congregations against his criticisms. Given that the established Church was governed by the 'discipline of antichrist', she asserted, the godly were not only free to separate from it but had no other option. In the true Church, unlike the hierarchical Church of England, 'all the Lord's people' were 'kings and priests to God'. Edwards mocked those in gathered churches for having little education and for being of a low social status, she observed. But to Chidley, 'well-meaning Christians' were

> the fittest on the earth to make churches, and to choose their officers, whether they be tailors, felt-makers, button-makers, tent-makers, shepherds, or ploughmen, or what

honest trade soever ... They are not men of so mean parts, as you would make them, but are able to divide the word of God aright by the Spirit that God hath given them.

Individual believers were in direct contact with God, she declared, making them more than capable of discerning spiritual matters for themselves, no matter what their sex or social rank.[2]

To the conservative-minded Edwards, this emphasis on spiritual equality had dangerous and far-reaching implications. Such ideas, he exclaimed, threatened to take 'away that power and authority which God hath given to husbands, fathers, and masters, over wives, children and servants'.[3] For Chidley, however, all human authority had its limits. What power does an 'unbelieving husband [have] over the conscience of his believing wife?' she questioned. He might have legal claims 'over her in bodily and civil respects' but he could not be 'a lord over her conscience; and the like may be said of fathers and masters'. 'I pray you Master Edwards,' she continued, 'would you have magistrates, and kings, and princes to have more power over their subjects than over their bodies, estates, and lives? Would you have them be lords over their consciences? I pray you where must Christ reign then? Must he sit at the magistrate's footstool?'[4] Believing herself in the end to be subject to God alone, Chidley not only left the Church of England but went on to establish a separatist congregation of her own. She ultimately became a leader of the Leveller women who petitioned Parliament in 1649 and again in 1653, insisting that their voices be heard even though 'the law took no notice of them.'[5]

Katherine Chidley exemplifies the radical spirit of the women in this book, women whose belief that they were in personal contact with God empowered them to resist the status quo. Like Chidley, these women questioned the authority of those who sought to lord it over them. Like her, too, they interrogated the legitimacy of the institutions – whether the Church, the state or marriage – that structured their lives. Above all, they envisaged 'a new order of things'.[6] Since these authors, prophets and preachers found ways, against the odds, to make their voices heard, it is time that we, too, bring them out of the shadows of history, allowing them to come centre stage so that they can tell us the stories of their audacious lives.

––––

PERSONAL EXPERIENCES ARE at the heart of this book. In it, we will hear the stories of more than a dozen seventeenth-century women, including a Colchester woman who feared that her four children – abandoned by their father – would starve to death, a woman in London who survived decades of abuse at the hands of her widely respected husband, and a former maidservant from Yorkshire who was granted an audience with the sultan of the Ottoman Empire. As well as illuminating the lives of a series of remarkable women – women who have not usually been given a prominent position in history books – this book highlights the importance of the radical Protestant beliefs held by these women. As will become apparent, they did not speak with one voice. In their writings and their actions, however, they each illustrate the enormous importance given to subjective experience within Protestantism, particularly in its more radical varieties.[7] These women were driven by a powerful sense of individual conviction, and the consequences were far-reaching.

The Protestant Reformation that swept through Europe in the sixteenth century threw into doubt long-established religious and cultural traditions, raising questions about an individual's access to truth. On what should people base their beliefs? Could they trust inherited forms of knowledge, passed down by learned authorities since time immemorial? Protestant iconoclasm stripped church buildings bare, whitewashing walls and throwing out crucifixes and statues. More significantly, however, it also stripped bare the soul of the individual believer. No longer able to rely on a priest to act as an intermediary, she stood alone before God. 'The thoughts and intents of the heart can be known to no-one but God,' said Martin Luther, at once establishing the necessity of freedom of conscience and the loneliness that came with that freedom. Another person cannot 'go to hell or heaven for me', he pointed out, and just as 'little can he believe or disbelieve for me'. It follows that 'no-one shall and can command the soul, unless he can show it the way to heaven; but this no man can do, only God.'[8] Newly disconnected from rituals such as confession, Protestants could not rely on actions or institutions to establish their spiritual status. Instead, they had to look within themselves. Faith was not something that could be inherited and nor was it a way of life. It was not even a matter of assent, in a purely cognitive sense. True belief, instead, operated at the level of individual conviction, and to be authentic it had to be rooted in the heart and the soul. Knowing about God counted for nothing; what mattered was having a personal, heartfelt experience of God.

For mainstream Protestants, God was primarily encountered through the Bible, hence the efforts made to allow people to read the Bible for themselves in their own languages. To those on the more radical wings of the Protestant movement, however, God's voice was not limited to the pages of the Bible. Margaret Fell, one of the leaders of the Quaker movement, described the moment in 1652 when George Fox (later her husband) declared that it was not enough to quote what Christ and the apostles said about God. The key question, instead, was 'what canst thou say?' Reduced to tears, Fell cried out, 'we are all thieves, we have taken the Scriptures in words and know nothing of them in ourselves.'[9] God's word was not simply that which you read. It was that which you heard within and – even more startlingly – that which you spoke. And to speak God's word was to speak from the heart: I preached 'what I felt, what I smartingly did feel', wrote the nonconformist preacher and author John Bunyan in 1666, 'even that under which my poor soul did groan and tremble to astonishment'.[10]

For many in this era, this relocation of spiritual authority away from institutions – and even away from the Bible – towards subjective experience spelled very grave danger. There was no single idea that had caused more 'evils and mischiefs' in the world than that of 'divine inspiration', lamented one observer in the 1650s.[11] Aiming to stifle the wave of 'enthusiasm' that was sweeping the nation (the term 'enthusiasm' stems from the ancient Greek term for being inspired or possessed by a god), comments such as these betray the unsettling power of the beliefs driving the women in this book. Despite the many differences between them, these women shared the conviction that God spoke to them personally. It is hard to think of anything more empowering. Anne Wentworth, for example, could face being vilified by her community for revealing the truth about her abusive husband because she believed that God had commanded her to speak out: 'the great God hath put the word of truth in her mouth,' she claimed, 'and dare you forbid her to declare it?'[12]

THE IDEA OF God speaking to individuals, including women, was not new, of course. The actions and words of the women in this book sometimes echo those of medieval mystics such as the visionaries Julian of Norwich and Margery Kempe.[13] Nor was the pressure to reform the English Church entirely novel. Since the fourteenth century, the Lollards had been criticizing aspects of Roman Catholicism and emphasizing the importance of individuals reading the Bible for themselves. By the end of the sixteenth century, however, pressure for further reform of the Church of England was becoming intense. Many felt that the Protestantism of the national Church was only half-baked, and there were fears that the changes that had been made were in danger of unravelling. Queen Elizabeth's insistence on religious uniformity – requiring ministers to wear surplices, for example – generated ever-growing rumblings of dissent. From the 1560s onwards, the derogatory term 'Puritan' was applied to those who agitated for further reform of the Church of England. Showing a disturbing propensity to 'resist the commandment of their sovereign', these individuals, according to one disgruntled observer, revealed that 'they themselves will be supreme governor in spiritual causes, and play the popes themselves.'[14]

Puritanism, by its very nature a diverse, internally divided movement, did not necessarily require its adherents to separate from the Church of England. From the mid-sixteenth century onwards, however, some dissenters began to meet outside of the established Church.[15] Dissenters at this stage were small in number, but by the early years of the seventeenth century one commentator (having himself passed through a separatist phase) warned that separatist ideas were becoming so widespread that it was 'as if the true Christ could not be found otherwise, than without in woods, mills, by-stables, barns and haylofts . . . all the speech now is, go out, go out of Babel, come into the secret places'. Such thinking, he claimed, drawing as it did on 'giddy passions and headstrong affections', was particularly widespread among 'simple women'.[16]

By the 1630s, when Archbishop Laud re-instigated what many saw as 'popish' practices in the Church of England – kneeling for communion, for instance – dissenters increasingly felt compelled to leave the established Church. By 1642, the nation, divided between those supporting the autocratic King Charles I and those backing Parliament in its drive to free the country from what it perceived to be tyrannical oppression, had lurched into civil war. At every level of society, debate raged as people set about trying to define God's blueprint for the nation. Print censorship was an early casualty of the chaos, and its absence in the early 1640s poured fuel on the fire, enabling the circulation of innovative and sometimes downright outrageous ideas. Individuals, including women, who would never previously have had a public platform from which to speak were suddenly able to broadcast their views to an ever-widening reading public, with explosive results.

The febrile political atmosphere of mid-seventeenth-century England was inseparable from a powerful sense of apocalyptic crisis. Many individuals from all walks of life believed themselves to be living in the last days of history, with the return of Christ – as predicted in the Bible – expected imminently. Many believed, moreover, that this event would inaugurate a new era – a millennium – when the 'saints', or the people of God, would reign on earth either with or on behalf of Christ. Apocalyptic expectation in this period was not simply about awaiting the end of the world, then, but often involved the anticipation of a new era in which everything would be reconstructed in alternative terms. This reconstruction would involve social and political as well as religious revolution. Everything was about to change, and no established practice or institution was sacred.

Unsurprisingly, exactly what form this new godly society would or should take was open to debate. No one assumed that it would simply take its course. God's people had to mobilize so that the barriers to the arrival of Christ's kingdom could be swept away, and they were eager to get going with the task. Instigating among themselves the principles and the practices that they believed would define life in the coming millennium – in essence choosing to live as though the kingdom of God had already arrived on earth – radical religious groups of many different persuasions burst onto the scene in London and beyond in the 1640s. Radical beliefs that had previously been whispered about behind closed doors were suddenly shouted from the rooftops as a diverse range of Protestant sects emerged into view, each claiming divine authority for their model of an ideal society. Gripped by the power of their convictions, many individuals within these sects declared themselves answerable to God alone. Centralized forms of authority began to crumble, not only within the church and state but within the family. In 1646, for instance, one bewildered citizen in London described how his 'family' of four, consisting of 'himself, his wife, a man, and a maidservant', had splintered in terms of their beliefs. He remained loyal to the Church of England but his wife had abandoned all churches, 'doubting whether there be any church or no upon the earth'. This position identified her as a Seeker (a description of some of the key radical religious groups, including Seekers, can be found at the end of this Introduction). Their maidservant, meanwhile, attended a congregation led by Paul Hobson, a radical from the parliamentary army, while the citizen's 'man' had joined a group of 'twenty or more young men, who meet together . . . but sing no psalms, abominate the hearing of our ministers, keep none of our days of fasting nor thanksgiving'.[17] No longer able to impose his views on his broadly defined 'family', this citizen was experiencing at first hand the colourful range of spiritual possibilities that had opened up for women and men of all social ranks.

Despite the ultimate triumph of parliamentary forces over the king and his supporters, many dissenters in the late 1640s and '50s viewed the religious and social reforms made by Parliament as inadequate. Feeling a godly revolution to be within their grasp and yet afraid that Oliver Cromwell would sell the nation short, radical religious groups agitated for more extensive changes. The Diggers, for example, attempted to instigate alternative, communal forms of living based on principles of shared ownership of the land, while the Levellers and the Fifth Monarchists – those who believed that a fifth and final kingdom, that of Christ, was about to arrive on earth – pushed for more far-reaching religious and political reforms. Bursting notoriously onto the scene for a few years at the end of the 1640s, the Ranters explored the possibilities unleashed by antinomianism (the rejection of moral law), advocating the use of swearing and free love as radical expressions of spiritual freedom.[18] From the 1650s onwards, the Quakers pushed the spiritual principles of radical Protestantism to an extreme, giving priority to the 'light within' over all external forms of authority. Whatever their differences, those associated with these groups all believed themselves to be participating in the unveiling of Christ's kingdom on earth. As they saw it, they were fighting not merely for their own rights or freedoms but for the spiritual fate of the nation and the world itself.

NEW 'SECTS AND schisms' are sprouting up daily, lamented Thomas Edwards – the enemy of Katherine Chidley – in *Gangraena* (1646), his multi-volumed catalogue of the 'errors, heresies, blasphemies and pernicious practices of the sectaries of this time'. But if separatism was a monstrous Hydra, multiplying in all manner of confusing directions, there was a key belief or 'great religion' underpinning all its manifestations, and that was 'liberty of conscience'.[19]

It was the Church Father St Augustine who established the idea that the conscience was the voice of God. God 'speaks in the conscience of good and bad people alike', he claimed, defining the conscience as the 'voice of truth' that speaks 'in the silence of the heart', while noting that 'truth is what God is.'[20] To the influential sixteenth-century Protestant theologian John Calvin, 'a certain feeling of the godhead' existed in everyone: God had 'planted in all men a certain understanding of his divine majesty,' meaning that everyone had 'knowledge in [their] conscience of [their] own wretchedness.'[21] If to Calvin the conscience stood 'between God and man', to many Protestants in mid-seventeenth-century England there was no meaningful distinction between ordering someone to act against their conscience and telling them to defy God. In one pamphlet published in 1650, the conscience was described as 'a little map or volume of divinity': it 'smelleth more of God . . . than the heavens, the sun, the stars, or all the glorious things of the earth'.[22] The Independent preacher Henry Walker, writing in 1641, also said that it was in the conscience that we most closely apprehend God: in the conscience the 'soul is knit to Christ, and Christ is united to the soul, and both made one'.[23]

If to be guided by one's conscience was to follow God, it also translated into being one's 'own master'. 'What hast thou to do with another man's conscience . . . or what hath he to do with thine?' asked the 1650 pamphlet: 'A man standeth or falleth to his own conscience . . . conscience's work is to make every man his own keeper.'[24] Almost six hundred works with the word 'conscience' in the title were published in England between 1640 and 1659, testifying both to the level of interest in the idea and to the role of the press in facilitating heated debates: 'the presses were more free than the pulpits,' observed one tract.[25] The stakes were high. Individuals were reassessing their relationships not only with the national Church but with all forms of authority. 'Over the soul God can and will let no one rule but himself,' Luther had insisted in 1523: 'every man is responsible for his own faith, and he must see to it for himself that he believes rightly.'[26] Calvin reiterated the claim that consciences are 'exempt from all power of men': Christ's 'death is made void', he argued, 'if we yield our selves into subjection to men.' Wary of the implicitly radical consequences of this teaching, he warned that Christians should be careful not to transfer 'wrongfully' their 'spiritual liberty . . . to the civil order', as 'though Christians were . . . less subject to the laws of men, because their consciences are at liberty before God'. But if Calvin reminded Christians to obey civil authorities, his *The Institution of Christian Religion* (English trans. 1561) emphasized that subjection to 'those men that are set over us' must always be limited: 'if they command anything against [God], let it have no place.'[27] Writing while imprisoned by the Inquisition in the 1660s, the Quaker Katharine Evans agreed. For her, those who sought to 'exalt' themselves 'over the consciences of any people, to compel them to a tyrannous law', were to be identified with Lucifer himself: no amount of intimidation could force her to act against her own beliefs.[28]

To many opponents of the radicals, including Thomas Edwards, the idea that individuals were free to follow their own sense of God's voice within threatened to unravel the entire social order. One of the many errors of the sectarians, lamented Edwards, was the belief 'that 'tis lawful for women to preach, and why should they not, having gifts as well as men?' Disregarding what to his mind was the divine law of women's subjection to men, female sectarians, seeing themselves as inspired by God, no longer felt obliged to remain silent in church, spelling an end to patriarchal order. Some sectarians, he claimed, also taught that 'all the earth is the saints, and there ought to be a community of goods, and the saints should share in the lands and estates of gentlemen, and rich men.'[29] By no means all – or even many – radical Protestants in mid-seventeenth-century England would have supported this particular principle, but Edwards's alarm reveals the radical implications of sectarian doctrines. The 'consciousness of direct relationship with God' held enormous power, as the historian Keith Thomas points out, its implicit levelling of social and gendered hierarchies making it 'a powerful solvent of the established order'.[30]

The danger posed by the emphasis on spiritual equality in dissenting circles had long been clear to the authorities. At the end of the sixteenth century, those agitating for further reform of the Church had used secret printing presses to publish colourful denunciations of the 'bishops and proud, popish, presumptuous, profane, paltry, pestilent, and pernicious prelates'. In vividly polemical language, such pamphlets encouraged their readers to 'shake off' the yoke of those who were attempting to usurp power over their very souls.[31] The revolutionary tone of this language did not go unnoticed. The 'schismatic' upstarts, who 'despise government and fear not to speak evil of them that are in dignity and authority', had decided that they were 'nothing inferior to any of their superiors', claimed the clergyman Richard Bancroft (later Archbishop of Canterbury) in 1588. Resentful of social and economic inequalities, these radicals were in 'hot pursuit' of new forms of government, he warned, claiming that they were advocating a 'desperate and dangerous' course that threatened 'the destruction and overthrow of all good rule'. For Bancroft, it was only a short step from the Puritan insistence that truth was not the sole possession of those in high office to violent revolution. 'Their tongues and pens are their own,' he lamented, 'they will write and speak what they list, and who shall control them?'[32]

Writing after the outbreak of civil war, the Church of Scotland minister Robert Baillie was also alarmed by the idea that 'every man must be absolutely at his own disposition, to believe, speak, write, do, whatever he thinks fit.' The 'great law' of the sectarians, he claimed, was this: 'let every man be fully persuaded in his own mind of the truth of what he believes without any control from any upon earth.' This emphasis on individual conviction, Baillie realized, would not remain restricted to matters of religion: if 'in religion there must be no law, but what every man in his conscience thinks to be the sense of the word of God, that is the supreme rule to him, so it must be in the state'. 'This anabaptistic root, the people's supremacy', he warned, threatened to 'overturn the whole state from the very foundation'. The so-called 'free-born people of England' had become the new 'sovereign lords and masters': even 'the poorest beggar', if the sectarians were to be believed, had an equal 'share of the supremacy, both civil and ecclesiastic . . . with the most noble, wise, able, wealthy of the land'.[33]

The desire of those smeared as 'heretics and sectaries' to do 'what seems good in their own eyes' was therefore seen by many to have 'pernicious, God-provoking, truth-defacing, church-ruinating, and state-shaking' implications.[34] The nonconformists were regularly accused of being opposed to any notion of order: 'if every Phaethon that thinks himself able may drive the chariot of the sun,' warned one observer in 1651, 'no wonder if the world be set on fire.'[35] It was a revolutionary role that some were happy to embrace: 'as for setting the world on fire', responded the Quaker Thomas Taylor, this can be understood 'in a good sense' – Jesus said 'that he came to set fire in the earth', so why should those who 'are zealous for God' do anything less?[36]

———

WHEN THOSE APPALLED by the undeniably unsettling developments in mid-seventeenth-century England sought to discredit the Protestant sects, they often did so by sneering that they were overrun with women. Lamenting the 'ridiculous' notions of those who believe 'the law hath nothing to do with a Christian,' a 1636 pamphlet, for example, associated antinomianism – or the 'doctrine of liberty' – with the women whom it claimed were its fiercest promoters. The antinomian 'front is ranked with them', it declared: since women 'are fit for word-combat, these are their intelligencers, their demi-scouts, their paper challengers, with these they discharge their invectives'.[37] But while some historians have concluded that women outnumbered men in the radical religious sects of seventeenth-century England, others have cast doubt on this claim.[38]

Whatever the precise ratio of women to men within each gathered church or radical group – figures that are impossible to ascertain with any reliability – dissenting women

were undeniably vocal. The historian Phyllis Mack has identified almost three hundred visionary women who wrote and
prophesied in seventeenth-century England.[39] Rather than
being silent or demure in the manner that seventeenth-century
women were often encouraged to be, radical religious women
were often shockingly confrontational. Two Quaker women,
for example, were arrested in 1662 for disrupting a service at
St Paul's Cathedral. Imitating the actions of Old Testament
prophets, one of them smeared her face with ashes and poured
blood over her loose hair, 'which ran down upon her sackcloth
which she had on, and she poured also some blood down upon
the altar, and spoke some words'.[40] As this dramatic display
indicates, Quaker women were particularly scandalous figures, frequently interrupting church services and preaching
disruptively in streets and marketplaces. Some even stripped
themselves naked in public 'as a sign'.[41]

If radical religious women spoke out – and acted up – fearlessly, they also wrote relentlessly. Radical religious women's
writing accounts for a significant proportion of all women's writing in England in this period. Between 1649 and 1688, more than
half of all publications by women were prophecies, notes one historian.[42] Quaker women alone published around 220 theological,
prophetic and autobiographical works between 1650 and 1699,
comprising at least 20 per cent of all texts published by women in
seventeenth-century England.[43] The writing of radical Protestant
women from this era is often inventive in form as well as in
content. Ranging from the early conversion narrative of Rose
Thurgood in the 1630s to the luminous prophetic works of Anna
Trapnel in the 1650s and the visionary publications of Jane Lead
in the 1680s and beyond, the writing of the women discussed in
this book is among the most striking and innovative of its time.

———

RADICAL RELIGIOUS WOMEN did not always operate on a fully equal basis with men within their communities. Many gathered churches continued to prohibit women from preaching in a formal capacity. Despite such remaining inequalities, dissenting congregations often enabled women to participate in both spiritual and community matters to a degree that scandalized their contemporaries. The Independent minister John Rogers, for instance, encouraged women 'to speak, object, offer, or vote with the rest' in his Dublin congregation (although women were still not permitted to preach).[44] 'Most men do arrogate a sovereignty to themselves which I see no warrant for,' he stated, an approach that led his opponents to accuse of him of giving women 'power to rule'.[45]

Until 'our days', noted the outraged Presbyterian John Bastwick in 1645, 'Peter's keys never hung at any woman's girdle.' In this allusion to Jesus giving Peter the 'keys of the kingdom of heaven' (Matthew 16:19) as a sign of his status in the Church, Bastwick associated 'Peter's keys' with male phallic power. In her publication of the same year, Katherine Chidley reworked the same symbol to the opposite effect. 'The power of the keys is as absolutely the Church's, which is Christ's wife, as the power of the keys of the family are the mistress's, to whom the husband giveth full power' when he is away, she argued. Her image of the mistress of a house having a right to its keys wrested ecclesiastical authority from a small group of men and placed it in the hands of the Church as a whole, a Church gendered female in her account. But if her argument carried the suggestion that women as well as men had the right to speak in church, Bastwick could not have disagreed more. Disregarding the 'law of God and nature' that commanded women to remain silent in church, the women 'of the new congregations . . . have their voices', he lamented. They

> make learned parts of speech in the congregation, and dispute questions and debate of matters and give their reasons *con & pro* . . . and others of them set forth and print learned treatises in polemical divinity with great applause and admiration of the Independent ministers who cite their authority, and quote them in their writings as classical authors, to the shame of the nation.

If we want to avoid the 'overthrow' of 'all government in church and state', he warned, we must put these disorderly women back in 'their places'.[46]

Despite the hostility they encountered – sometimes from within their own communities – some women, as we will see, did begin to preach publicly in London in the mid-1640s. By the 1650s, many Quakers were openly supporting the right of women to preach as well as to prophesy. 'Who is it that dares stop Christ's mouth,' asked George Fox, 'that now is come to reign in his sons and daughters, Christ in the male, and Christ in the female'? 'They are ignorant that forbid women or daughters prophesying, and women labouring in the gospel,' he continued, 'and their comparing them to Jezebel shows their ignorance.' 'We', on the other hand, 'say that all the women in Christendom that know the death of Jesus, and his resurrection . . . may freely declare it.'[47]

THE POTENTIAL FOR women to operate as leaders in the gathered churches of mid-seventeenth-century England is evident in the story of Dorothy Hazzard, the co-founder in 1640 of the first separatist church in Bristol.[48] For twenty years before that point, Hazzard had been meeting with others to pray and to discuss sermons. Continuing to run a grocer's business and to lead a godly community after the death of her husband (who had also been a leader of the group), she made a point of opening her Bristol shop on Christmas Day. Being seen sewing at the front of the shop on this day was an act of resistance, signalling the fact that she rejected the 'superstitious' observance of 'holy-days'. In the late 1630s, Dorothy married Matthew Hazzard, a minister with Puritan sympathies. Despite being the wife of a minister, she found it increasingly difficult to attend church services, experiencing what she described as a 'sore conflict' in her 'spirit' when her husband read from the Book of Common Prayer. One Sunday, unable to bring herself to go to church, she ran upstairs to her chamber. Flinging open her Bible, she was confronted with a stark warning from the book of Revelation about the dangers of worshipping 'the Beast'. The 'terror in her soul' was such that she resolved 'never to go more to hear common prayer'. From this point on, the 'Spirit of Christ in her soul' outweighed the social pressure to attend church or to play the role expected of her as the minister's wife.

In 1640, John Canne, a 'baptized man' and a printer of radical books in the Netherlands, was briefly in Bristol, possibly to smuggle books.[49] Enlisting his advice, Hazzard set up the fellowship that would become Broadmead Baptist Church (a church that continues to exist). By the civil war period (during which Hazzard was actively involved in the defence of Bristol against Royalist forces), they had around 160 members. One of these was a Black maid named Frances, a woman who when she died was carried to her grave by the 'chiefest of note of the brethren in the congregation', illustrating to another church member that the congregation operated according to the principle that 'God is no respecter of persons' (Acts 10:34). The separatists were not viewed kindly by their neighbours, who thought it a 'very strange and unheard-of thing, for people to meet in a church with a chimney in it'. On one occasion, a 'rude multitude' violently disrupted their meeting, breaking all the windows of the house in Bristol High Street where they were assembled. The fact that there were many women in the group sparked suspicions, generating rumours of 'women preachers' as well as gossip that they 'met together in the night to be unclean'.[50]

In this book we will meet many radical women like Dorothy Hazzard, women who followed their consciences even when this meant defying husbands and ministers (sometimes one and the same figure), alienating neighbours, being slandered as 'whores' or being stripped in marketplaces and whipped. These are women who overcame huge social and personal obstacles to write books, travel abroad, preach, prophesy and play leading roles in their communities, all on the basis that they were ultimately accountable to no one but God.

———

BRINGING THE LIVES and writings of seventeenth-century women centre stage, this book focuses more on specific women than it does on the sects with which they were (sometimes fluidly) associated.[51] Listening to the voices of these women – women who lived across the seventeenth century and who adhered to a range of radical religious beliefs – it is quickly apparent that they do not share identical political or even theological perspectives. One of the women in this book – Jane Lead – disagreed so strongly with another – Anne Wentworth – that she wrote in her journal about all the ways in which Wentworth was in the wrong. In their own distinctive ways, however, all these women were radical, bravely contesting widely accepted norms of thought, belief and behaviour.

Many of the women in this book penned biting critiques of the social and economic inequalities by which they and others were oppressed. Their perception that God was not only willing to speak to those marginalized by society but actively preferred to do so bolstered their insistence that spiritual authority was not the sole preserve of well-educated white men. As Katharine Evans wrote from her prison cell in Malta, 'they say, none ought to speak in the name of Jesus but the divine doctors that have received their ordinations' from universities. But the real 'Doctors of Divinity', she claimed, are those 'that dwell in the divine light of God and grow into his divine nature, and do receive their ministry by the inspiration of his divine Spirit of life and power, and do speak as they are moved, and as the Spirit gives them utterance in the will of God'.[52] To the Fifth Monarchist prophet Mary Cáry, meanwhile, it was a cause for celebration that 'not only men, but women shall prophesy; not only superiors, but inferiors; not only those that have University-learning but those that have it not; even servants and handmaids.'[53] As these statements suggest, the women in this book held fast to a principle of spiritual equality that led them to believe that they – along with other marginalized figures – had a right to be heard both within their communities and beyond. Although they did not necessarily agitate explicitly for the reform of gender hierarchies, the terms in which they expressed their spiritual equality with men had far-reaching implications, unsettling the foundational principles of the patriarchal society in which they lived.[54]

———

DESPITE THE IMPORTANT differences in doctrine and practice that existed between the mid-seventeenth-century sects, membership of these groups was highly fluid. Radical Protestants, as we have seen, were loyal to their own consciences rather than to organizations. They also tended to believe that divine revelation unfolded gradually over time, meaning that they would not necessarily remain bound to any one group. Katharine Evans, for example, was raised in the Church of England and became first a Baptist and then an Independent before she finally identified with the group that 'some Englishmen call in scorn "Quakers"'.[55]

Whichever radical religious group(s) they identified with, the women whose stories we will hear in this book were largely from ordinary backgrounds, apparently unremarkable figures who were almost guaranteed in the normal run of things to be all but invisible in the historical record. Yet their tenacious belief that they were protagonists in a divine drama translated into a sense that their lives were of momentous significance. It was this conviction that drove them to tell their stories, creating some of the earliest autobiographical accounts in English and allowing us a rare and precious glimpse of the lives and experiences of seventeenth-century women – women who were anything but ordinary.

———

BELOW, I GIVE a brief description of the radical religious groups most relevant to the women in this book.

Independents

Justifying his inclusion of the Independents as one of the 'sects and schismes' by which the nation was overrun, Thomas Edwards argued in 1646 that 'all the sectaries', in the end, 'are Independents', bent on separating from the established Church.[56] Those he labelled Independents in his *Reasons against the Independent Government of Particular Congregations* (1641) rejected what Edwards regarded to be a necessary 'dependency' on a hierarchical Church structure, arguing for autonomous congregations. Putting forward their manifesto in 1643, the ministers who became leading Independents did not advocate separation from the Church of England, making a case instead for their remodelled fellowships to exist within the national Church. The 'proud and insolent title of Independency' was designed to imply that they cultivated 'defiance', they complained, when instead they sought a 'middle' way between an 'odious' separation and 'authoritative Presbyteriall government' with all its 'subordinations'. Their congregations, they claimed, were based on a biblical model and were therefore 'the true churches'.[57] Restricting their membership to believers, these fellowships elected their own ministers, often choosing people from among their membership, regardless of formal qualifications.

Brownists

In 1581, Robert Browne set up a separatist congregation in Norwich before being arrested and fleeing to the Netherlands. For Browne, the godly had no choice but to separate from the Church of England. Browne's publications, including

A Treatise of Reformation without Tarying for Anie (1582), were printed on the Continent before circulating surreptitiously in England. Reading or distributing his books was a dangerous business: two men who did so in Bury St Edmunds in 1583 were hanged. Browne later re-entered the Church of England but 'Brownist' separatism continued to be practised. Henry Barrow, for example, led a separatist London congregation before being executed along with other separatist leaders in 1593.

Anne Stubbes, the sister of the eminent jurist Sir Edward Coke, was a notable Brownist. Writing to her brother-in-law, the theologian Thomas Cartwright, in 1590, Stubbes reminded him of the verbal sparring match they had engaged in one day in Buxton. Having refused to participate in prayers, she said she 'was commanded by the Lord to come out from amongst them that were not the Church of God'. It was a straight choice, she stated, between 'Christ or Antichrist'. Stubbes knew that Cartwright thought her ignorant, but she rejected 'man's judgement', having decided to be faithful to her version of God's 'truth so far as I know with all my heart'. If Stubbes was unshakeable in her convictions, she was not complacent, knowing that those who 'separated' were 'counted as sheep to the slaughter'.[58] Well before the end of the Elizabethan era, then, women as well as men were prepared to risk their lives to practise dissent.

The Family of Love

The Family of Love was a Dutch sect founded by the sixteenth-century merchant Hendrik Niclaes. Niclaes believed that the Bible should be interpreted allegorically. The 'coming of the kingdom of God' was not 'with outward appearance', he claimed, but took place 'inwardly, within us'.[59] He also taught that it was possible to be united with God in a state of sinless perfection. Believers, he wrote, become 'godded with God, or incorporated to God, in all love. With whom also God in one being and power of his Holy Spirit is hominified or become man.'[60] The group, whose followers were known as 'Familists', were particularly threatening to the authorities because of the elusive nature of their dissent. For Familists, all that mattered was what was 'inward in the heart': they had no qualms about faking an 'outward reverence' for established forms of religion even while they were 'keeping their hearts to God'.[61] They therefore took to an extreme the Protestant emphasis on the inward nature of faith, severing the link between inner belief and outward practice.

Familists were active in England, particularly in East Anglia, from as early as the 1550s. In the 1570s, books promoting their beliefs were translated into English and smuggled into the country. Stealthily, they made their way from hiding places behind benches and in kitchen chimneys into the hands of those who knew that they were risking their lives just by reading them.[62] Women played a 'crucial but largely invisible part' in the 'the Family's development and sustenance', notes the historian Christopher Marsh.[63] Despite attempts by the authorities to stamp them out – efforts that included a royal proclamation in 1580 – their doctrines continued to circulate in England into the seventeenth century. A pamphlet published in 1608, for example, presented a caricature of a Familist, one who was said to 'comprehend far greater revelations of the Spirit' in the space of fifteen minutes than most people do in a lifetime. But he ultimately seemed more interested in kissing a 'wench', playing up to popular perceptions of the group as licentious.[64]

Antinomians

Familism overlapped with antinomianism, a position frequently adopted by radicals in the 'puritan underground' in the decades preceding the civil wars, as the historian David Como demonstrates. Although not a formally organized sect, antinomians formed a 'densely interwoven subculture' in pre-civil war England. They argued that Christians, who lived under grace, had been released from the moral law. Emphasizing the transformative impact of conversion – conversion, that is, from a 'dead' form of religious observance to a 'living', experiential faith – they stressed the contrast between the desperate human condition in advance of conversion and the joyous state that followed it, when the believer enjoyed an unremitting sense of 'assurance' or confidence in his or her salvation. For the most radical antinomians, believers were so utterly transformed by God that to all intents and purposes they became divine.[65]

William Walwyn (later a Leveller leader) presented antinomian ideas in his tract *The Power of Love* (1643). Mainstream religion, he argued, was characterized by wealth, corruption and the abuse of power; true believers, instead, shared 'all things [in] common'. Godliness, for Walwyn, was demonstrated by concern for the poor. As well as confronting social and economic inequalities, Walwyn addressed the problem of spiritual suffering, specifically the misery inflicted by people's inability to believe that salvation did not require 'our labour, industry, study, and watching'. If salvation involved 'work', he stated, the effort was all Christ's and had already been 'perfected': 'no performance at all' was required on our part.[66]

Seekers

Seekers rejected all forms of institutional or organized religion, declaring that no true Church existed on earth. They were 'seeking' for God's kingdom, the arrival of which was imminent. In the meantime, they refused to participate in religious institutions, rituals or meetings, none of which to their minds offered the possibility of an authentic encounter with God. As Alec Ryrie points out, they were not so much a sect as an anti-sect.[67] Often depicted in their own time – and since – as nihilists who had lost their way, Seekers took seriously the idea that God dealt with individuals on a personal basis, obviating the need for a religious community.

George Fox's account of his lonely wandering in Derbyshire in 1647 captured the Seeker experience: walking 'in solitary places many days', he 'went and sat in hollow trees, and lonesome places, till night came on'. 'All this time', he noted, 'I was never joined in profession of religion with any, but gave up myself to the Lord, having forsaken all evil company . . . I kept myself much as a stranger, seeking heavenly wisdom, and getting knowledge from the Lord; and was brought off from outward things, to rely wholly on the Lord alone.'[68] Elizabeth Avery also described how for several years during the 1640s she rejected all forms of religious community, relying solely on God's 'teachings within me . . . for I had his Spirit, his voice speaking within me, and God alone was with me'.[69]

Baptists

Baptists derived their name from their belief that baptism should be reserved for adult believers, arguing that the infant baptism practised in the Church of England was a meaningless ritual. Faith, they asserted, was not passed on by the family or nation of one's birth but was an individual matter. Critics often slurred them with the name 'Anabaptist', a term suggesting that they were being baptized twice.

The label 'Anabaptist' carried huge stigma in seventeenth-century England. The group known as the Anabaptists emerged in continental Europe in 1525, becoming a loosely defined separatist movement with multiple Swiss, German and Dutch subsets. In one much-publicized instance in Münster in the 1530s, an Anabaptist group violently imposed highly unorthodox doctrines, including the Old Testament practice of polygamy.[70] Regarded as posing an extreme threat, Anabaptists in Europe were heavily persecuted: 2–3,000 Anabaptists were executed in the sixteenth century, around a third of them women.[71] English authorities were quick to clamp down on any members of the group discovered in their communities. In April 1575, for example, 27 Dutch Anabaptists were arrested in a London house, four of whom only avoided being burned at the stake because they recanted. The next month, ten female Anabaptists alongside a male member of the group were also 'condemned to be burned', although one of the women subsequently 'converted' and the rest were ultimately banished. In July of the same year, two Anabaptists were burned at Smithfield.[72]

Perceptions of Anabaptists as dangerous heretics persisted in seventeenth-century England. In his tract *Anabaptism, the true fountaine of Independency . . . and most of the other errours which for the time doe trouble the Church of England* (1647), Robert Baillie declared that Anabaptists mistake 'their enthusiasms and revelations for God's express commandments'. In Switzerland in February 1526, he claimed, one Thomas Skyker,

BEING
A True
RELATION
OF

The great and bloudy Murder, committed by *Mary Cham-pion* (an Anabaptist) who cut off her Childs head, being 7. weekes old, and held it to her husband to baptize. Also another great murder committed in the North, by a Scottish Commander, for which Fact he was executed.

Presbyterian   Anabaptist

Printed in the Yeare of Discovery, *Feb.* 13. 1647.

Representation of the 'Anabaptist' Mary Champion from the anonymous pamphlet, *Bloody Newes from Dover: Being a True Relation of the Great and Bloudy Murder, Committed by Mary Champion (an Anabaptist)* . . . (1647).

'having spent the whole night with a company of Anabaptists in their religious exercises', had been 'filled with an enthusiasm, and before his father, mother, and whole company, he commanded in the name of God his . . . brother Leonard Skyker to kneel before him, and . . . cut off his brother's head, avowing he had an express warrant from God so to do'.[73]

If male Anabaptists were widely feared to be violent anarchists, female Anabaptists had an even worse reputation. In 1647, for example, one tract (with a gruesome title page image) accused an Anabaptist of decapitating her own child in response to her husband's wish to have the baby baptized, confirming assumptions of the 'unnatural, disorderly femininity' of those in the sect, as Rachel Adcock observes.[74]

Despite merging with Anabaptists in the popular imagination, English Baptists were not directly related to these earlier European groups.[75] The first English Baptist church was established in 1612 in Spitalfields, London, by Thomas Helwys. Helwys had been baptized as an adult by John Smyth after the two men had been forced into exile in Amsterdam in the first decade of the seventeenth century. After splitting from Smyth's group, Helwys and some other members of the Amsterdam fellowship returned to England to set up their own congregation. Helwys's pamphlet, *A Shorte Declaration of the Mistery of Iniquity* (1612), contains a note in the flyleaf reminding King James that he is 'a mortal man and not God, and therefore hath no power over [the] immortal souls of his subjects'. The tract, which contains over forty references to the conscience, makes an impassioned case for freedom of belief. Helwys asks the king whether there be so unjust a thing, and of so great cruel tyranny, under the sun as to force men's consciences in their religion to God, seeing that if they err, they must pay the price of their transgression with the loss of their souls. . . . men should choose their religion themselves, seeing they only must stand themselves before the judgement seat of God to answer for themselves, when it shall be no excuse for them to say, we were commanded or compelled to be of this religion, by the king.[76]

Clearly the king did not agree with his reasoning, as Helwys was almost immediately arrested, dying shortly afterwards.

Helwys's congregation were General Baptists, believing that Christ died for all. In the 1640s, another group – the Particular Baptists – emerged. These congregations were established by former members of Independent fellowships who held Calvinist beliefs (that only those chosen as God's 'elect' would be saved). Baptists appointed their own ministers and lay members were actively involved in their congregations. To their fierce critic Thomas Edwards, Baptist meetings were characterized by 'such a confusion and noise, as if it were a play; and some will be speaking here, some there'.[77] To Baillie, English 'Anabaptists', as he termed them, were characterized above all by their zeal for a 'self-destroying and God-provoking liberty'. Despite his claim that they encouraged 'she-preachers', women were not usually permitted to preach within Baptist congregations. They have been described as 'the most conservative of the radical Puritan movements in their attitudes to women'.[78] Female prophets such as Sarah Wight were nevertheless high-profile members of their communities.

Ranters

The Ranters were a group of libertines who were active in the late 1640s and early 1650s. Working through the implications of the belief that they were under grace and not law – and reaching some extreme conclusions – they rejected the notion of sin and embraced sexual freedom as well as swearing and other forms of behaviour that disregarded the moral law. Although they were not an organized group, Ranters were nevertheless an 'identifiable body of interconnected individuals sharing a common heterodox religious language', as Nigel Smith demonstrates.[79] No female Ranter voices have been preserved in the archive: the sexual libertinism associated with the group, as Smith points out, meant that any woman publicly identifying with them would have seen her reputation destroyed.

Levellers

All men and women 'that ever breathed in the world . . . [are] all equal and alike in power, dignity, authority and majesty', insisted the Levellers. Led by John Lilburne, Richard Overton and William Walwyn, they emerged in the mid-1640s and were active until the end of the decade. Their belief that no one had the right to lord it over anyone else led them to emphasize the principle of government by the consent of the people. As the Leveller Thomas Rainsborough declared so potently in the Putney Debates, 'the poorest he that is in England has a life to live as the greatest he; and therefore . . . every man that is to live under a government ought first by his own consent to put himself under that government.'[80] The Levellers petitioned for constitutional reform, including the abolition of the monarchy and the House of Lords, as well as for legal reform (including the use of English) and for freedom of conscience in matters of religion. The Levellers also argued for an extension of the franchise, demanding that all men over the age of 21 be given the vote (except for a few groups, including servants and those who had fought on the side of the king). Despite the name by which they became known (which they disliked), they insisted that they 'never had it in our thoughts to level men's estates'.[81] Although Katherine Chidley and other women were actively involved in the movement, petitioning Parliament with Leveller demands, the Levellers did not argue for women to be given the vote.

Fifth Monarchists

The Fifth Monarchists were a millennial religious and political group who emerged in the early 1650s. Their name derives from a prophecy in Daniel 2:44, in which four kingdoms – usually taken at this time to be Babylon, Assyria, Greece and Rome – were said to be followed by a fifth and final kingdom – that of Christ – that would 'endure forever'. The Fifth Monarchists, who were largely drawn from Independent and Particular Baptist congregations, believed that King Jesus was about to return and that he would reign on earth either alongside or in the form of his saints. This new era, they declared, would be one of social as well as spiritual transformation, including the over-turning of oppressive social and economic hierarchies. Fiercely critical of Oliver Cromwell after he became Lord Protector at the end of 1653, Fifth Monarchists believed him to be blocking the reforms required for Christ's kingdom to unfold on earth. (Accused of being on the side of Antichrist, an exasperated

Cromwell complained that Fifth Monarchists tended to 'fix the name of antichristian upon anything'.)

When John Rogers, an Independent turned Fifth Monarchist, was imprisoned in February 1655 for being a 'raiser of sedition', around 250 Fifth Monarchists accompanied him to Whitehall for his audience with Cromwell. The group included large numbers of women: Rogers was asked why there were 'so many women, and what they meant'. The Fifth Monarchist report of the occasion accused the prison guards of assault, 'slashing and striking in a most violent manner, calling us rogues, damned rogues'. Rogers scoffed that 'a few white aprons' had been enough to make the guards 'fly to [their] swords'. Rejecting Cromwell's accusation that they 'intended a tumult' and insisting that his supporters were armed only with Bibles, Rogers nevertheless openly challenged the Lord Protector's authority: 'I regard your laws in matters of my God no more than straws,' he stated.[82]

Fifth Monarchists declared themselves ready to inaugurate the reign of the saints by force.[83] In *A New and More Exact Mappe* (1651), Mary Cary claimed that 'the Beast' spoken of in the book of Revelation had begun to lose its power in 1645, although it would be 1701 before 'complete deliverance' occurred. The saints were therefore living in a critical phase of history: 'these are the saints' rising times,' she declared, 'wherein they shall rise higher and higher.' In such circumstances, it was 'warrantable for saints under the gospel to fight': 'it is nowhere said that now in the latter days, when the time of the saints' deliverance cometh, that they shall not by the sword ... subdue the enemies of God, which are also their enemies.' God had promised to 'strike through kings in his wrath; but what instruments shall the Lord Jesus use in doing these things, he being at the right hand of God?' The 'saints', she declared, 'are and shall be the Lord's instruments . . . and they shall be willing in this day of Christ's power'.[84]

In line with such rhetoric, Thomas Venner organized two armed insurrections on the streets of London in 1657 and 1661, the second of which, involving around fifty people, led to four days of violence. The vast majority of Fifth Monarchists, however – a conservative estimate suggests that the group had around 10,000 members – did not participate in these plots. Unique among the sects 'in claiming the right and indeed the duty of taking arms to overthrow existing regimes and establish the millennium', as the historian Bernard Capp observes, in practice 'the violence of most of the saints was strictly verbal.'[85]

Fifth Monarchists put forward detailed proposals for social, legal and political reform. In July 1653, for example, Mary Cary published twelve 'humble proposals' for the 'Parliament of Saints' to consider. In order to 'give the world a taste, what it is to have Jesus Christ to reign', she advised, you should

> lay to heart the condition of the poor, and make it your care to provide for the supply of their wants . . . before any rich man's case whatsoever be taken into consideration . . . for certainly the crying of the poor, and the sighing of the needy, maketh a louder noise in the ears of the Lord of Sabbath, than the complaints of any rich man whatsoever.

It is a 'great scandal' that 'so many beggars go up and down in all parts of this nation', she continued, proposing a 3*d*. stamp on letters to raise money for poor relief. The universities should 'be new modelled', she stated, so that those without 'vast estates' would be able to attend. The justice system also needed a radical overhaul, because currently 'the rich man's cause is heard before the poor.' 'Great and tedious volumes of law ... serve for no other end but to enrich the lawyers and impoverish others,' she noted, arguing for old and incomprehensible laws to be replaced by 'some plain brief general rules, which all men may be acquainted with'. It should no longer be the case, meanwhile, that 'the richest men of the places where they live' – 'though they be very dunces' – be given all the positions of power.[86] For radicals like Cary, then, the kingdom of God was not limited to religious matters but involved revolutionary change at all levels of society.

Quakers

The Society of Friends, as they called themselves, were labelled Quakers by hostile observers because their members would sometimes manifest their experiences of the Holy Spirit by trembling all over. George Fox was their most influential early leader, but women such as Elizabeth Hooton operated alongside him from the outset. Quakers, a group described by Phyllis Mack as the 'most receptive' of the sects to the 'spiritual authority of women', encouraged their female members to prophesy, to preach, to travel and, above all, to write. Analysing the writing of hundreds of visionary women from the 1650s, Mack noted that two-thirds of these works were by Quakers.[87]

Leaving his home in Leicestershire in the mid-1640s on a quest to discover truth, George Fox initially detached himself from all religious institutions. Both the 'priests' and the 'separate preachers', he said, failed to speak to my condition. And when all my hopes in them, and in all men was gone, so that I had nothing outwardly to help me ... then I heard a voice, which said, 'There is one, even Christ Jesus, that can speak to thy condition': and when I heard it, my heart did leap for joy.

In 1649, Fox travelled to Nottingham, where he caught sight of a 'great steeplehouse', a church building that to him was a 'great idol'. Making his way to the church, he heard the priest instruct the congregation that 'they were to try all doctrines, religions and opinions' by the Scriptures. These words incensed Fox, who 'was made to cry out, and say; "Oh no, it is not the Scriptures". But I told them what it was, namely the Holy Spirit.' The Quakers, as this episode suggests, emphasized personal inner revelation above all else, demoting even the Bible to an 'outward' entity that could not compare with the inner light that was within every individual. 'Friends' confronted 'earthly' forms of authority while simultaneously presenting themselves as the passive instruments of divine truth: when Fox described the showdown in the Nottingham 'steeplehouse' – for which he was put in 'a nasty, stinking prison' – he wrote that he was 'made to cry out' and 'commanded to tell' in obedience to the light within.[88]

Fox, Hooton and other early Friends travelled in 1652 to the north of England, where Quakerism soon spread like wildfire. Thousands were 'convinced', including Margaret Fell, the wife of a judge, who became a key leader of the movement. Fell's home, Swarthmoor Hall, near Ulverston, became the Quaker headquarters.[89] From 1654 onwards, Friends spread their message across England and into Wales, Scotland and Ireland. They were highly successful: by the end of the decade, there were around 60,000 Friends, a membership exceeding that of any other radical religious group.[90] Female Friends travelled even more extensively than did their male counterparts.[91] Both Oxford and Cambridge, for example, were first introduced to Quakerism by itinerant female preachers.[92]

Belief in the levelling effect of the 'light within' led Quakers to disregard differences of sex and social rank to the point of scandal. They addressed social 'superiors' with the familiar forms of 'thee' and 'thou', and on occasion both female and male Friends would strip themselves naked in public places as a sign of spiritual equality, among other things.[93] Walking 'cheerfully over the world', in the words of Fox, they also as Catherine Gray observes 'used print and manuscript to turn a national community into a transnational, potentially global one'.[94] As we will see, women were at the forefront of this effort.

Part One:

'Mine own experience'

I

Rose Thurgood

That which I have written is out of mine own experience,
which the Lord hath wrought in me by his Holy Spirit,
and not by traditions of men.

Rose Thurgood, 1636-7

In the last decade of the twentieth century, a scholar on a brief
visit to the John Rylands Library in Manchester made a sensational discovery.[1] Opening the blandly titled *English Manuscript
875* in the cavernous reading room of the neo-gothic library, he
found not just one but two previously unknown autobiographical narratives, both dating to 1636–7. Both accounts were by
women. The narrative of Rose Thurgood (b. *c.* 1602) was a particularly thrilling discovery. Nowhere else in the writing of the
era are we given such a powerful and extended insight into the
experiences of a woman struggling with the devastating effects
(physical, emotional and spiritual) of what she termed 'extreme
poverty'.[2] Watching helplessly as her four children were tortured by illness and hunger, Thurgood was driven to the brink
of despair. 'I began to rage and swell at God himself,' she admitted, 'saying to myself, what a God is this? What doth he mind
to do with my children? Surely they will die.' Deciding that
she could not 'abide this life any longer,' she told a neighbour
that she would 'not live to see [her] children starve'. Her threat

to leave her 'bad husband' shocked her neighbour into silence, 'for I used not to speak such words.'

As well as giving us a unique glimpse into the mind of a woman enduring desperate poverty in the early decades of the seventeenth century, Thurgood's account – alongside that of Cicely Johnson in the same manuscript volume – is one of the earliest known English conversion narratives, and therefore a very early example of autobiographical writing in English. The fact that such a remarkable narrative was written by a woman living with a 'hard and hungry' stomach is truly startling. Thurgood and Johnson were both from Colchester, and they both moved in radical religious circles. Their accounts shed light on unorthodox and elusive forms of Protestant belief in England in the early decades of the seventeenth century. Departing dangerously from mainstream Protestantism, those within these circles adhered to radical doctrines – including antinomianism – that were too risky to be endorsed openly, making it difficult to find traces of such beliefs in the archives. For multiple reasons, then, these narratives, carefully copied into a manuscript volume by an unknown scribe, were an explosive find.

———

ROSE THURGOOD'S CONVERSION narrative initially appears to be a letter written to her mother, from whom she has been absent for ten years. As her account proceeds, however, she refers to it as her 'book', one that she addresses to her 'loving mother, sisters, and friends or whatsoever thou art', indicating that she has a wider audience in mind. Entitling her work 'A Lecture of Repentance', she ultimately addresses 'all that have ears to hear God's promises to every particular soul', echoing Jesus's claim to speak to all who have 'ears to hear'

A Lector of
Repentance
Lo, the Co=
pie of a
Letter pen=
ned by
R. The

(o de íse)

My love remembred to you lovinge mo=
ther, And not forgetting my love to
my brothers & sisters with the rest
of my frends. || Loving mother it is a vie
greable to mee when I consider of those
times past which I have bene from you,
But though I be absent from you in body yet
I am present with you in spirit, for God is
my witnes whom I serbe in my spirit, that I
make mention of you in my prayers to God. There
fore loving mother it is my desire that you
should know in what condition I have lived
since I was with you, and estate now I live in,
which by Gods helpe I will relate to you in my
complaints. || Loving mother to trouble you with
a long discourse of my outward being it
would be teedious to you, But my desire is you
should understand how & in what manner the
Lord, out of his love, hath done for my soule. first
how hee wounded mee, And then how hee gaue
mee a salue to cure my wounded soule. || But
loving mother, it greeveth mee when I call
to mynd how disobedient a child I have bene to
you in former tymes in not obeying you as I
am commanded by God himselfe, which saith
honour thy father & thy mother. Therefore
I am not onely a disobedient to you loving
mother, but also I am guilty of the breach
of Gods comandement. || Now loving
mother, there remayneth two pardons for mee
to get, one at Gods hand, the other at you. ||
But loving mother, take this for your comfort
God hath forgiven mee my synnes past And
hath given mee a full assurance of his love in

(hee)

Christ

1. fol. D.

[heart] lee firke & so my eyes ended. And my —
heart, mee thought was lightned. But I
could not beleeve assuredly that there was
a God, for I sawe my selfe in a damnable —
estate, & no hope of mercie for mee, because —
that I did not beleeve there was a God. Then I
wished in my heart, o that I could beleeve that there
were a God, & that I were but as I was before I
fell sicke, for then I could praise God with all
my heart, and I lay all day before I was assured of Gods love in Christ. But on the morrowe
after, which was the day before the Gunpow-
der treason day, about eight of the clocke, as
I lay sicke in my bed, mee thought I felt a —
sweet-flash roming over my heart, & suddenly
withall theise wordes were pronounced in my
heart: Thy name is written in the booke of Life:
thou hast that white stone & a newe name.
Then I cryed aloud & said: now God is my
God, Christ is my Christ, and all the devills in
hell cannot take Christ from mee. And thus I
still cryed with such joy & gladnes of heart that
I am not able to expresse the joy which I felt —
at that tyme. So my neighbours hearing mee
rejoyce in such aloud a manner, they thought I
had byn in some fitt, they came hastely in to mee,
and prayed mee to be patient, for God was

fol. 14 .

mercifull

Rose Thurgood, 'A Lecture of Repentance', 1636–7.

(Matthew 11:15). Thurgood's description of her account as a 'lecture' not only identifies it as a form of instructive counsel but aligns it with the sermons delivered outside of regular church services that were popular with Puritans in her time. Her narrative, she claims, serves a spiritual purpose, providing her readers with a 'pattern, how [they] may get the love of God'. Thurgood's 'A Lecture of Repentance' is a rare surviving example of one of the manuscripts that circulated secretly among religious radicals in this era, forming a 'lively underground of clandestine tracts', in the words of David Como.[3] Such manuscripts often took the form of pastoral letters or polemical tracts. Thurgood's work – a highly unusual example from this period of antinomian sentiments being expressed by a woman – illustrates their potential to be both at the same time.[4]

If Thurgood harbours no doubts about the importance of her 'lecture', she knows all too well that her readers are likely to be sceptical. 'Why but you will say to me, that you know these things as well as I can tell you,' she notes, imagining her readers calling her a 'fool'. It is true that 'I am a poor woman,' she concedes, and 'a weak woman, and you see no scholarship in me, neither in writing nor inditing, so you may scorn to be catechised of me'. For Thurgood, however, the assumption that her sex and her low social status undermine the authority of her words is misguided. 'Do not despise me for my love, nor scorn my counsels for my poverty,' she warns. If you do, you will be rejecting the words of God, which he often delivers through unlikely instruments. When the biblical prophet Elijah was hungry, God fed him 'from the mouth of ravens', suggesting that God tends to use agents we might think of as unworthy (1 Kings 17:4–6). Think of me as nothing other than 'base carrion', she continues; inherently worthless, perhaps, but deployed

– as were the ravens – on a divine mission. If the apostles could 'be sent to the crane and the swallow for instruction, and by your leave to the poor pismire [ant] to learn of her to labour ... I am in good hope you will accept of this my *Lecture of Repentance*, and take no distaste of my words, though they be a woman's writing.' The Bible made it clear, after all, that God hid his revelations from 'the wise and prudent', granting them instead to 'babes and sucklings' (Matthew 21:16). Thurgood therefore makes a virtue of the fact that she is one of 'those babes', insignificant in the eyes of the world and yet chosen by God to speak his truth.

Despite Rose Thurgood's efforts to deny that her social position devalues her writing, it is evident throughout her account that she has struggled to come to terms with her traumatic fall into poverty. In her youth she was 'brought up to London to live ... with them that belonged to the king's court'. Associating with 'knights and ladies of great account', she learned to 'work fine works' with her needle and dressed in fashionable clothes. But those days were long gone. Her 'bad' husband, she writes, sold his land and living (she prayed for him to amend his life, but 'the poorer he was the worse he was'), leaving her and her four small children with 'nothing to live on' but her 'poor labours'. Despite knowing that her husband is to blame for their hardship, Thurgood assumes at first that God is punishing her for her sins, particularly for her pride. But as she writes about her devastating experiences, she begins to find alternative ways to make sense of her losses. 'What though God hath taken from me my wealth and sent me poverty', she comments, 'yet hath he given me Christ, and through him I receive all fullness.' Not only is the spiritual 'fullness' offered by Christ a compensation for her daily deprivations, but her loss of worldly goods is presented as a prerequisite for her spiritual inheritance. Drawing reassurance from the parable in Luke's gospel where a sore-encrusted beggar named Lazarus was said to be received into heaven while the rich man who was indifferent to him was cast into hell (Luke 16:19–25), Thurgood celebrates the fact that God welcomed 'the beggar in his rags and with his scabs, before the rich glutton in his perfumed robes'. Studying the story in forensic detail, she notes that the rich man, unlike the beggar, is unnamed: 'he is called nothing but glutton.' From a divine perspective, she concludes, a worldly 'somebody' is a spiritual nobody while a social outcast is precious, giving her 'great comfort' that 'though I were a poor woman, yet God would hear me.' 'A Lecture of Repentance' therefore gives us insight into the mind of an early seventeenth-century woman wrestling with the emotional and spiritual implications of poverty. As Thurgood tells her story, she begins to reconcile herself to her painful experiences. By the end of the narrative, her 'poor estate' is no longer a source of 'dismay': 'for though the world hate it, yet God love it.'

As far as we know, Rose Thurgood never escaped her poverty. Towards the end of her account, she acknowledges that 'as yet the Lord is pleased to let me and mine to pasture on bare commons, and feed near, with hard and hungry stomachs.' While she and her children continue to suffer, telling her story has helped her to counter some of the shame associated with her poverty, enabling her to reverse the significance (in spiritual terms, at least) of her losses. The wealthy may appear to be enjoying God's blessings, but those who are allowed to 'run in pasture knuckle-deep' are being 'prepared for the day of slaughter' – literally, it seems, being fattened for the kill. The 'hard and hungry stomachs' of her family, meanwhile, suggest that they are destined for eternal blessings. Her 'good and quiet conscience will do [her] more good in the Day of Judgement than a full purse', she remarks, implying that it is a straight choice between the two, for 'riches prevails not in the day of vengeance, but righteousness and peace delivereth from death.'

―――

THURGOOD NOT ONLY reinterprets the significance of her own poverty in her narrative but draws on her experiences to mount a sharp critique of the injustices pervading her society. Her concern with the plight of the poor reflects the focus on social justice in the writing of those influenced by antinomianism during this period. In *The Power of Love* (1643), for instance, William Walwyn – uniquely willing to identify himself as an antinomian – draws attention to the suffering of the poor and to the indifference to their anguish displayed by many so-called Christians.[5] 'Look about and you will find in these woeful days thousands of miserable, distressed, starved, imprisoned Christians,' he notes: 'see how pale and wan they look: how coldly, raggedly and unwholesomely they are clothed? Live one week with them in their poor houses, lodge as they lodge, eat as they eat, and no oftener, and be at the same pass to get that wretched food for a sickly wife, and hunger-starved children.' If you did, he suggests, you would no longer tolerate the behaviour of 'religious people' in church with 'their silks, their beavers, their rings', those who betray through their disregard of the poor that 'the love of God they have not'.[6]

Unlike Walwyn, however, Rose Thurgood speaks about poverty from personal experience. It is an all-too-familiar thing to see 'rich worldlings' pursuing their own interests, she observes, but God will punish anyone who fails to 'hear the cry of the poor'. In her account, the wealthy merge seamlessly with the defenders of established religion who do little to challenge injustice. Many of 'our ministers', she declares scathingly, teach their congregations that 'they may lie upon beds of down and go to heaven.' Unsurprisingly, the message that righteousness is compatible with luxurious living goes down well with the rich and powerful, 'and thus the shepherd and the flock are agreed together, and so without God's mercy they shall go singing you know whither.' But if the wealthy are confronted with their viciousness, 'they will say, what a Puritan fellow have we gotten here? And . . . they will pinch him of his lecture money.' Seeking to speak truth to power, Thurgood distinguishes herself not only from the women who 'shriek and squeak at the leaping of a frog, but will not shrink an inch for all the curses in the Bible', but from a mainstream religious establishment that she accuses of perpetuating social injustice. Turning her poverty into a sign of her lack of complicity with corrupt social and religious structures, she positions herself as an alienated prophetic speaker of truth. Others may appear to have the advantage, possessing the 'brain knowledge' that stems from education, but they are merely parroting the words of others. What she has written, on the other hand, is 'out of mine own experience, which the Lord hath wrought in me by his Holy Spirit'.

Thurgood's narrative is a very early example of an English conversion narrative, a genre that would allow many other apparently unremarkable women and men to tell their stories. She is driven to record her 'own experience' – as were many after her – because she grasps the significance of the Protestant teaching, heavily emphasized within radical religious circles, that the knowledge that counts is not academic learning – of which she has none – but 'experimental' or subjective experience. If God deals with individuals without regard for social standing – in Thurgood's account even showing a preference for the poor over the rich – and if what is important above all is personal experience, then the lived experiences of a 'poor', 'weak' woman (as Thurgood describes herself) carry the same weight as the pronouncements of the most revered religious authority. For Thurgood to speak of her 'own experience' is for her to testify to the workings of God. Who, then, can question the significance of her story?

———

ROSE THURGOOD WAS influenced by two self-proclaimed prophets, the Colchester weavers Richard Farnham and John Bull. Claiming to be the 'two great prophets that should come in the end of the world', they later moved to London, where their disciples were said by hostile observers to consist mainly of 'deluded' women.[7] Both men were ultimately imprisoned, with Farnham being sent to Bethlehem Hospital, even though he insisted that he was 'not mad', as his doctors later agreed.[8] He was nevertheless convicted of bigamy, having expressed his sense of liberation from the law by marrying a woman while her husband was away at sea – in imitation, he claimed, of the biblical prophet Hosea and his 'wife of whoredoms'.[9] Farnham and Bull both died of the plague in January 1642, although their followers kept faith with Farnham's prediction that he and Bull would be raised from the dead in order to continue their messianic mission abroad.

Thurgood details her conversations with the pair, with whom she discusses prayer. Stressing the extreme passivity of humans before God in a manner reminiscent of antinomian teachings, Farnham and Bull instruct her that she can do nothing to influence God: any blessings you receive are due to God's mercy

A True Difcourfe of the Two infamous upſtart Prophets, *Richard Farnham*
Weaver of *White-Chappell,* and *John Bull* Weaver
of *Saint Butolphs* Algate, nowPriſoners, the one in *Newgate,*
and the other in *Bridewell* : with their Examinations
and Opinions taken from their owne mouthes *April* 16.
Anno 1636.
As alſo of *Margaret Tennis* now Priſoner in Old Bridewell, with the
Hereticall Opinions held by her, *at the ſame time Examined.*

Written by T. H.

Printed at *London* for *Thomas Lambert,* and are to be ſold at his Shop at
the ſigne of the Horſe-ſhooe, neare the Hoſpitall-gate in *Smithfield.* 1636

Title page, T. H. [Thomas Heywood], *A True Discourse of the
Two Infamous Upstart Prophets . . .* (1636).

and are not the result of your prayers, they insist.[10] 'You shall
never make me believe that,' Thurgood retorts. She nevertheless
comes to accept their teachings. Richard Farnham – mocked
by one of his critics for being a 'shuttle-witted fellow' because
he had the temerity as a 'plain' weaver (and therefore 'understanding nothing') to set himself up as a prophet – reminded
Archbishop Laud in a petition that God gave 'wisdom to the

poor base despised ones of the world'.[11] Articulating sentiments echoed in Thurgood's narrative, Farnham accepted that he was 'no scholar' but declared that 'a poor man or woman that can read never letter in the book, if the Lord have wrought the work of conversion in them, and endued them with his sanctifying Spirit, has more saving knowledge than the greatest learned man, if the work of regeneration be not wrought in him.'[12]

In line with antinomian teachings, Farnham and Bull taught that true conversion was always accompanied by a sense of 'assurance', or certainty of one's salvation.[13] Thurgood accepted this unorthodox teaching. Unlike other conversion narratives from the seventeenth century, in which conversion is often presented as a drawn-out process, her account is structured around a single moment, the unforgettable point at which 'God gave me my assurance that my name was written in the book of life' and 'all doubting [flew] away.' Her narrative builds to this climactic experience – the personal nadir that becomes her spiritual apotheosis – through a detailed description of her suffering. Her whole family was struck down with a 'burning fever' and lay ill for a month, during which time her 'children sometimes were so hot in their fits, that none could quench their [thirst]'. Terrified that they would die, she was 'driven to watch with them', even though for three weeks she could not sit up herself without fainting. Just as the family seemed to be recovering, they fell ill again, leaving her to 'rage and swell at God' until she began to doubt his very existence. Knowing herself to be sinning by harbouring such doubts, she added a guilty conscience to her other torments. She was haunted by horrifying images: an 'angry God' seemed to glare down at her, while she imagined 'hell open for me, and a garrison of devils gaping with open mouth for me ... all laying hot battery against my fainting soul.' Her combined physical and spiritual helplessness increased until she was 'very weak and not able to fight any longer, for I had fought myself weary'. Crying as though her 'heart would have burst', she raged against her terrible situation and against the God who seemed indifferent to her pain: 'shall I always have the whip on me? What, shall I cry and thou wilt never hear me?' Her children, lying ill nearby, were terrified by the sound of her weeping, causing her to cry 'louder, to think of their misery and mine'. At this precise moment – 8 a.m. on 4 November, four months before she wrote her narrative – she felt 'a sweet flash coming over my heart, and suddenly . . . these words were pronounced in my heart: "Thy name is written in the book of life."' An event that happened to her rather than her own decision, Thurgood's conversion generated an instantaneous sense of certainty that she was saved: 'Then I cried aloud, and said, now God is my God, Christ is my Christ, and all the devils in hell cannot take Christ from me.' She celebrated so loudly that her neighbours came running, thinking she was having 'some fit'. She could not stop 'rejoicing': 'For lo, I was now become a new creature, and all things were become new to me.'

———

IN THIS HARROWING account of an early seventeenth-century woman's conversion, we can see the radical implications of the Protestant belief that personal experiences carried supernatural significance. It was this belief that preserved the voice and story of a woman on the brink of starvation, a woman who was able to overcome the historical invisibility almost guaranteed by her social position through her conviction that her story mattered. She had the 'same Spirit', after all, 'which the apostles had', putting her description of her own experiences on a par with the divinely inspired words of the Bible. 'If thou sayest the Lord caused me to write this book, you say the truth,' she declared. Her 'book' may be plain old 'barley bread' rather than 'fine manchet' (good quality wheaten bread), but it offered life-giving sustenance, 'wholesome both for your souls and bodies'. Unable to feed either herself or her children, Rose Thurgood wrote an account whose words both in their content and the very fact of their existence countered some of the agonies of her situation, securing for herself as she did so a pivotal position in the history of autobiographical writing in English.

2

Testimonies

When I take a view of my life upon the stage of this world,
I may very well compare it to a comical tragedy,
or a tragical comedy.

'M. K.', 1653

Those wanting to join Independent congregations in
mid-seventeenth-century England and Ireland were often
asked to give an account of their 'faith and experiences'. In
the first published anthology of these testimonies, *Spirituall
Experiences of Sundry Beleevers* (1653), a woman identified only
as 'D. M.' describes how she searched her soul to pinpoint the
'real evidences' of her salvation, while 'I. B.' states that she was
relieved to find 'testimonies of [her] conversion' within, in the
form of her 'sincere love to God'. Women spoke in their testimonies about the suicidal feelings they had experienced after
giving birth, the agony of burying much-loved children, and
their fears for children who had left home. With sometimes
startling openness, they admitted to having favourite children,
to appreciating a daughter only after losing a son, to being
overly in love with their husbands and even in one case to
plotting a murder.[1] The speakers of these testimonies were 'prac-
titioners of a new autobiographical form', one that allows us to
'hear for virtually the first time in print the new public voices

of women', as Kathleen Lynch observes.[2] *Spirituall Experiences* includes 61 testimonies. Those speaking are identified only by their initials, but of the 44 testimonies where the sex of the speaker is identifiable, 25 are by women.

The preface to *Spirituall Experiences* was written by the Welsh Fifth Monarchist preacher Vavasor Powell, but the collection was probably compiled by Henry Walker, an iron-monger who became an Independent preacher and an editor of parliamentary newsbooks. Several of the accounts refer to him, and his own testimony is possibly included in the collection.[3] In the early 1650s, Walker was the minister of a congrega-tion in Knightsbridge, London, but the accounts in *Spirituall Experiences* do not necessarily originate from a single congre-gation. Another volume of testimonies, *Ohel; or, Beth-shemesh* (1653; a title referencing Hebrew terms for places where people met with God), was published later in the same year. Most of the testimonies in this second collection were delivered to the gathered church meeting in Christ Church Cathedral, Dublin, whose minister, the Independent and later Fifth Monarchist John Rogers, organized their publication. Of the 38 testimo-nies in this anthology, 17 are by women. Taken together, then, the two volumes allow us to hear the voices of more than forty mid-seventeenth-century women, all of whom chose to bare their souls in public, giving us a rare glimpse into lives and experiences to which we would not otherwise have access.

————

WITHIN RADICAL PROTESTANT communities, the Church was not a building but was the people of God, his living 'body' on earth. 'Those that enter into church fellowship' need to 'have some knowledge of each other,' explained *Spirituall Experiences*, so that they can be sure they are all 'fit materials to make a church'.⁴ Looking to demonstrate the genuine nature of their belief, those giving their testimonies knew that it would be pointless to cite the moral character or the religious dutifulness that fell into the category of meaningless 'works'. The only evidence that carried weight was a confession of the truth of their inner being, one in which their heart as well as their mind was demonstrated to be in 'union with God'.⁵

In his preface to *Spirituall Experiences*, Powell defines an authentic spiritual experience as that which is 'written by the Spirit of God upon the hearts of believers'. It is 'the inward sense and feeling, of what is outwardly read and heard; and the spiritual and powerful enjoyment of what is believed'. The believer, in other words, does not merely possess 'brain knowledge' about God, but has personal 'heart knowledge'.⁶ Like Rose Thurgood, whose response to the 'sweet flash' of her conversion was to cry out 'now God is my God, Christ is my Christ,' the woman identified in *Spirituall Experiences* as 'D. R.' knew that she had to be able to 'say (in particular) that God was my God': only when she had felt 'the love of God in Christ Jesus unto [her]' could she be sure of her salvation.

Searching for signs of the necessary 'inward sense and feeling', women such as 'D. R.' were following the lead of the eminent Calvinist theologian William Perkins, who wrote in 1592 that God imprinted 'certain marks' on the hearts of his chosen people. Do you 'truly feel that you are persuaded of the truth of the Gospel'? Do you feel 'such a love towards [God] ... that you do hate and detest whatsoever is against his glory'? If so, these feelings attest to the presence of authentic belief: 'as long as thou feelest these effects in thy self, albeit very slender, and greatly languishing: yet assure thy self, thou art endued with true faith.'[7] The fact that the necessary emotions could be so 'slender' and 'languishing' as to be almost imperceptible nevertheless led Perkins to reassure his readers elsewhere that feelings were not foolproof. 'We must not live by feeling but by faith,' he cautioned – someone 'may be the dear child of God' even though they feel 'nothing but his wrath and indignation'.[8] Despite such warnings about the potential unreliability of feelings, the careful self-analysis of emotions was a central feature of spiritual testimonies in this era. If you want to know your spiritual standing, advised Rogers, look within. All the necessary information is written in 'the records in thy heart': to find answers about the state of your soul, ask yourself, 'how is it with thy heart?'[9]

———

THOSE GIVING TESTIMONIES before gathered churches in the 1650s sought to answer this question, 'pour[ing] out their experience' and thereby providing the 'experimental experiences of the work of grace upon [their] soul (for the church to judge of)'. There was no correlation, of course, between salvation and eloquence, and Rogers was quick to acknowledge that God's grace was not the sole preserve of 'such as can word it well, and speak, and act zealously'. Some 'maids', he observed, were particularly 'bashful' and 'very unable to speak in public'. On one occasion, he recalled, a woman had been questioned about her testimony by the Dublin congregation and had answered 'very fearfully, and uncertainly', leaving some members 'unsatisfied'. It was suggested that the decision about whether to admit her to the church be postponed until the next meeting, causing the woman to 'burst into tears bitterly, before the church.' 'The Word hath called me, and Christ hath called me, and bid me come,' she declared, and so 'I must come, without any worthiness in myself; and shall I now be put by?' Only last week, she exclaimed in 'weeping words', Rogers had preached that 'Christ called us freely, without any such qualifications first; and that he said . . . that those that come to him, he would in no wise put by, and upon these promises I am come.' Struggling to speak through her tears, the woman's 'bold challenge of the promise' had a powerful impact on the congregation, who allowed her to join on the spot.

Rogers placed particular emphasis on 'extraordinary' revelations, such as dreams, trances and visions, but he acknowledged that many also heard God's voice through more ordinary channels such as 'preaching, praying, reading, writings or such like'.[10] This more cerebral means of encountering the Holy Spirit recalls John Milton's description in 1644 of the people of England avidly reading by their 'studious lamps', 'musing, searching, revolving new notions and ideas . . . others as fast reading, trying all things, assenting to the force of reason and convincement'. For Milton, the refinement of belief enabled by the free circulation of books enabled 'all the Lord's people [to] become prophets', able to know and to speak the truth for themselves.[11] Not everyone shared Milton's faith in 'the force of reason', but the sense of the Church as a body of individuals, all of whom heard God speaking to them personally, was at the heart of radical Protestantism in this era. But many of those delivering their testimonies to gathered churches in the mid-seventeenth century did not have the luxury of encountering divine truth in a cosy room lit by a 'studious' lamp. 'M. W.', whose account appears in *Spirituall Experiences*, had to content herself with reading a 'piece of an old Bible' in the barn in which she, her 'wounded child' and her 'little daughter' had taken shelter after running for their lives during the Civil War. She had been 'stripped and wounded' in Liverpool – 'it was thought I could not live' – and had seen her husband and another child die before her eyes. Fearing that she was about to lose her mind, she ultimately found 'much settledness' through reading the 'holy word', even if she only had access to a ragged fragment of text.[12]

———

'M. W.' WAS not the only woman to speak bluntly about her traumatic experiences. Another to do so was 'E. R.', who gave her testimony on 18 July 1652.[13] Brought up within a 'godly' Protestant home, 'E. R.' believed herself to have committed a 'detestable sin' at the age of eleven, when she falsely accused her sister of something she had done herself. Three months later, in a 'fit of sickness', she was overwhelmed with guilt, becoming convinced 'that the horrors of hell-fire would seize on [her] soul and body.' She had compulsions to 'hang [her] self, or cut [her] throat, or take the bed-staff to thrust down [her] throat': that was how 'an ox died', after all, and she felt that she deserved no better. Terrified to hear her saying that she was 'damned' and 'must go to hell', her parents searched her bedroom to remove the 'instruments' with which she planned to kill herself. Deprived of other means, 'E. R.' resorted to pulling apart her pillow, picking out 'the feathers to swallow them down'.

After the doctor had been and gone, 'E. R.''s parents arranged for two ministers to come to the aid of their daughter's troubled soul. She met with 'Mr Newstubs, a minister in Edmunds Bury, and one Mr Rogers, another minister of Dedham, who took great pains with me'.[14] John Knewstub was a prominent puritan preacher in Suffolk while 'Mr Rogers' possibly refers to Richard Rogers, a puritan minister in Essex and a friend of Knewstub. Rogers often sought to comfort those in despair. His diary entry on 17 November 1587, for example, records his visit to a 'woeful creature' who sounds much like 'E. R.'. Describing her as a tormented girl who refused to believe in God's mercy, Rogers laments the fact that his words fell on deaf ears and she remained resolved to 'hurt herself'.[15] Rogers's nephew, John Rogers, was nevertheless also a puritan minister whose theatrical sermons – on one occasion he simulated the suffering of the damned by roaring from the pulpit – drew crowds in Dedham, Essex.[16]

'E. R.''s account of her meeting with the ministers evokes the question-and-answer format of the catechism, in which a child would be asked a series of theological questions and would reply with set answers. 'E. R.' nevertheless turns this didactic form of religious instruction on its head, refusing to answer the ministers with anything other than the truth of her own subjective convictions. When she is asked if she believes in God, for example, she responds that she believes 'in God that he would damn me'. And when she is asked if she has repented of her lie, she agrees that she is sorry, as well she might be, since she 'must be damned for that sin'. The ministers reassure her that she has been forgiven, but she retorts that they have no way of knowing the condition of her soul. Their words carry no weight when set against her powerful sense that 'Christ never died for such a one as I was, neither could his mercy save me.' They describe her as a 'beloved Christian, a dear Christian', and yet she tells them 'no . . . I was born to be damned, and must be damned.'

Frustrated, the ministers berate 'E. R.' for having the presumption to sit in judgement on her 'own soul'. But this, she believes, is exactly what she must do. Capturing the terrifying experience of believing yourself to stand alone before God, 'E. R.''s testimony illustrates the extent to which Protestants could look to their feelings to ascertain the state of their souls. When 'E. R.' is asked why she is so sure that she will be damned, she points to her turbulent emotions as evidence. In her heart, she insists, there is 'nothing but death, and hell, and confusion', causing her to sigh, weep and groan over the fate of her soul.

Thankfully, 'E. R.' ultimately achieved a more optimistic perspective. After suffering from insomnia for weeks, she fell asleep and had a dream of Christ in the figure of a child, leading her out of hell. Waking disorientated, she asked the friends who were keeping watch over her if she was 'in hell or . . . redeemed out of hell?' Almost immediately, she realized that their answers meant nothing, for 'how could they tell? Had they been there? For I told them that I had newly been there.' It was only because she had 'been there', experiencing her own salvation in the form of a vivid dream, that she was finally able to believe in the authenticity of her faith.

Personal experiences of the kind 'E. R.' describes were produced within specific communal contexts and did not originate within the individual alone. The two anthologies of testimonies published in 1653 exhibit the influence of the ministers who transcribed and published them, demonstrating the role played by external factors – including male religious authorities – in the shaping and presentation of women's testimonies.[17] The communities within which these women were operating nevertheless gave them a public platform from which to tell their stories, providing a context in which even the most shocking thoughts and feelings were able to be expressed.

———

AN ENCOUNTER WITH God such as the one 'E. R.' describes in her dream was believed to be transformative. A conversion experience, declared Rogers, instigated 'a great change' in 'judgement, will, and affections'. For some, this change was sudden and abrupt. They were violently 'cut to the heart, pierced to the quick', as the Spirit of God fetched 'blood from the soul'. For others, it was a slow and gentle process: their souls were melted by 'love, cherries, promises, warm tenders of the blood of Christ'. Either way, conversion involved radical change: 'O! What a great alteration there is now in them!'[18] It was this sense of a significant transformation of the narrator's innermost being that conversion narratives sought above all to demonstrate.

'D. M.' structured her dramatic testimony around the unforgettable moment when God spoke to her, instantaneously transforming her suicidal despair into rapturous joy. Forty years ago, she testified, she was besieged by sorrows as if by 'an armed man'. Having 'too much loved her husband in a fleshly love, making an idol of him', she was appalled to see him becoming an 'enemy to goodness'. She 'doted on him' but he abandoned her, causing her to lose her 'goods, and all'. Like Rose Thurgood, 'D. M.' worried that her loss of 'creature-comforts' was God's punishment for having 'loved the world too much'. Gripped by 'despair' and 'fear', she cried herself 'almost blind', finally deciding to 'drown [herself] in a pond near Leeds in Yorkshire'. Arriving at the lake with her 'young infant' – for whom she had a 'great love' – in her arms, she was struck by the horror of what she was about to do: 'what, shall I destroy myself and my poor child?' This was the moment when she heard God speak to her soul, telling her to trust in him. Walking away, she experienced 'much joy': believing herself to have found 'the favour of God', she never returned to a state of despair.[19]

———

EVEN IF A believer could identify the precise moment of her conversion, however, the soul-searching went on. The soul could be saved in one 'sweet flash', but sanctification, or the process of spiritual refinement, was the work of a lifetime. Every day, spiritual lessons were waiting to be learned through apparently mundane experiences. Isaac Ambrose, a dissenting clergyman in Leeds, Preston and Garstang, wrote in 1649 that it was crucial to 'sort our experiences, as the apothecary sorteth his drugs'. To keep track of daily events was to acquire a treasure trove of experiences: we learn by this means 'to mark things which fall out, to observe the beginnings and ends of matters, to eye them every way, on every side, that they may stand us in stead for the future.' Paying close attention to daily experiences enables us to see 'the breathings, movings, stirrings, workings of a soul towards Christ, or of Christ towards a soul', he claimed. For Ambrose, God's truth was so closely entwined with 'the story of our own lives' that the more we examined our lives, the more we would 'see and feel and taste of God'. To Ambrose – and to the women in this book – the will, imagination and feelings of the individual were worth nothing in and of themselves – they were 'base and unworthy marks to be aimed at'. Paradoxical as it seems, those keeping close track of their experiences were not primarily aiming for self-understanding but were seeking to 'taste God to be good': turning their gaze within, they were not searching for themselves but were looking for God.[20]

Testifying before the Dublin fellowship, Mary Burrill insisted that she 'rested on Christ Jesus alone! And on nothing of self!' 'M. W.', whose account was published in *Spirituall Experiences*, claimed meanwhile to have 'nothing but emptiness' in herself, forcing her to rely on 'the fulness of Christ'. Self-renunciation for these women paved the way for the construction of an alternative sense of being. 'I thought myself to be something,' 'D. R.' admitted sorrowfully, until 'when being seriously weighed, I became nothing.' Becoming 'acquainted with an emptiness in [herself], and an inability of [her] own to do any good', she was able to reach an alternative understanding of herself: 'I am, in and through God's free grace, what I am; not for anything in me, or that I could do'. 'D. R.''s repetition of 'I am' in this passage (a reiteration of Paul's statement in 1 Corinthians 15:10, which itself contains an echo of God's identification of himself as 'I am who I am' in Exodus 3:14) emphasizes the paradoxical nature of the identities that are presented in these testimonies. Claiming to be 'empty' or 'nothing' in and of themselves, the women nevertheless align themselves with revered biblical figures. For 'D. R', the 'death' of her 'worldly' self represents not defeat but triumph: 'I shall become (over sin, Satan, self, and all things opposite to grace) more than a conqueror through him that hath loved me.'[21] Once again appropriating Paul's words, 'D. R.''s statement uses the language of Romans 8:37 to express her own experience. To abandon her individuality is to identify herself with a leading apostle, allowing her voice to become inextricable from the words of the Bible.

The voices that speak in these testimonies are therefore complex and multiple. Women tell their stories, but they do not necessarily see themselves as the authors – or even, in simple terms, the subjects – of these stories. Samuel Petto, an Independent minister in Suffolk who published some testimonies in *Roses from Sharon* (1654), described believers as the 'epistle[s] of Christ': it was God who wrote the script, leaving individuals not as the authors but as the readers of the stories of their lives.[22] If God wrote the script of a life, however, all the events in that life were charged with divine meaning. Even terrible experiences such as the death of a child – an all-too-frequent tragedy in this era – could be understood as part of a coherent narrative. If God displaced the self as the author of a life, moreover, this placed the individual centre stage in a divinely authorized drama. While testimonies often present their speakers in self-denying terms, the genre also therefore encouraged spectacular displays of self-dramatization, as the astonishing account of 'M. K.' illustrates.

———

'WHEN I TAKE a view of my life upon the stage of this world,' begins 'M. K.'s testimony, 'I may very well compare it to a comical tragedy, or a tragical comedy.' Her story lives up to this claim.[23] Born one of twelve children to 'very godly and honest parents' – members of the gentry – she was her mother's favourite child. Showered with attention, she was taught to read and was encouraged to discuss spiritual issues with her mother from a young age. Describing herself as a serious child, 'M. K.' resolved early on to be Christ's 'faithful soldier', a metaphor that recurs throughout her account. Despite her spiritual efforts, however, she soon concluded that her heart was 'a sink of sin, a cage of unclean birds, a den of thieves, a place for dragons, for the screech-owl, and the satyr'.

When 'M. K.' was twelve years old, her mother died. With no time to grieve, she was immediately required to act as her father's 'housekeeper' and 'right hand' woman. Abruptly becoming 'a mother to ten children' and a 'mistress over six servants' while still a child herself, she might have been expected to feel overwhelmed. Instead, however, she was exultant, taking a 'joyful pride' in her advancement. Then, out of the blue, her father also died. This second bereavement precipitated an intense period of grief, during which she permitted herself to mourn for both of her parents.

Consumed with sorrow, 'M. K.' needed to understand why she had suffered these losses. Having examined her heart, she concluded that she was being punished for having 'sinned against God': her innocent 'brothers and sisters [had been] made fatherless and motherless' because of her shortcomings, she decided, particularly her idleness. The guilt that followed was severe. 'I refused all comfort for the space of half a year,' she stated, 'crying out continually, my sins, my sins, woe is me, my sins!' Others sought to reassure her, pointing out that apart from anything else she was not yet old enough to have committed sins of this magnitude. But 'M. K.' believed that she was 'old enough to offend God'. Having 'wearied' her friends and family with her 'excessive sorrow', she was sent away to London, a move to which she agreed because 'the word of God was more plentifully preached there.'

After some time had passed, 'M. K.' married the son of a preacher's widow and began a new life in Westminster. She had every intention of being 'honest', but her husband, it seemed, had other plans. She watched in dismay as one of his friends led him astray, encouraging him to waste his time drinking. Believing their life together to be in 'imminent danger', 'M. K.' begged her husband 'upon [her] knees with tears' to reform his life. Failing to prevail, she upped the drama, resolving abruptly to murder her husband's friend. Shortly afterwards, she had a vivid dream, in which she was sitting at a table 'covered with a green carpet, upon which lay all manner of instruments which

proclaim death'. Seeing the hated man approach, she took up a
weapon and was about to 'commit the horrid act of murder upon
his body' when God intervened, saying 'vengeance is mine.' In
the early part of the dream, she was in a scene reminiscent of the
revenge tragedies popular on the London stage at the beginning
of the seventeenth century. But the scene suddenly changed,
and her murderous plot was abandoned.

'M. K.' might not have gone through with the murder, but
she had allowed her heart to become a 'nest of most diabolical and wicked intentions' and was consequently guilt-stricken.
Obsessed with thoughts of hell, she imagined devils hiding
'behind every door', waiting to 'snatch [her] away'. She thought
herself to be 'a firebrand of hell, a child of perdition, a limb of
Satan', and believed that she did not deserve to 'live ... upon the
earth'. Thinking that she had reached her 'last night ... on earth',
she said goodnight to her family and went to bed, 'inviting the
devils to come and take their due'. In the middle of the night,
something landed on her bed. 'M. K.' screamed, convinced 'it
was the devils' who had come to 'snatch [her] away'. Happily,
however, 'it was the dog, and not the devil.' Having described
her situation in terms reminiscent of the terrifying final scene
of Christopher Marlowe's *Doctor Faustus*, where devils drag the
protagonist off to hell, she suddenly found herself in a farcical
comedy. 'Surely there was a God that had preserved me all this
while,' she concluded: only God could keep turning the tragic
drama of her life into a comedy with a happy ending.

Having been in 'grievous agony' all night, 'weeping' and
sweating so 'that the water ran off from every part of my body',
she decided to go 'into the highest room that was in the house'
so that she could look out of a window and 'see God'. In the
seventeenth-century theatre, hell was often represented by a

space beneath the stage, so that 'M. K.''s movement from a lower to an upper part of the house, when understood within the highly theatrical terms of her account, is suggestive of her journey towards God's grace. Moving from the brink of hell up towards the sky, she asked God to reveal himself. When he did so, however, it was not reassuring: 'Then I saw the Lord but with a frowning countenance[.] He looked upon me as if he had said, Thou has displeased me, and I will not hear thee, and turning his back went from me.' Earlier in the night, 'M. K.' had presented herself in terms reminiscent of Faustus, but now she aligned herself with the confused and grief-stricken Hamlet, looking on the 'frowning countenance' of an angry ghostly father. Feeling 'a dart thrust through [her] soul for the space of half an hour', she resolved to do whatever it took to obtain God's favour. It was a long time, 'M. K.' confessed, before she could believe that her sins were forgiven. But having played many different roles in the drama of her life, in the end she claimed to have found stability and peace of mind.

———

IT WAS CRUCIALLY important to those delivering testimonies that they gave an honest account of the 'records' of their hearts. For testimonies to mean anything, they had to be authentic: testifiers had to allow themselves to be 'seen in [their] naked-ness' and 'known in [their] weakness'.[24] As a result, some women who told their stories were honest enough to admit that they had not yet arrived at anything approaching either happiness or inner peace.

'A. A.', whose account was published in *Spirituall Experiences*, was one of many women to speak about harrowing experi-ences.[25] Two years previously, when she was eight months pregnant, her husband had been wounded and her children had fallen 'sick together of the smallpox'. Just as she thought they were recovering, one of them suddenly died. But this was not the end of her tragedies. Three months before she gave her testimony, her son – the 'chief comfort that [her] heart was fixed upon in this world' – had also died. Having lost her favourite child, she was left with a daughter – a child who at the time she 'did not so much value' ('but now I do', she added). 'I have slept few nights quiet since,' she admitted, thinking 'never to have comfort in this world again'. Believing 'the hand of God was against' her in her losses, she voiced her darkest fear: what if 'I was the death of my children'? Terrified that her children had died as a punishment for her sins, 'A. A.' did not conclude her testimony on a note of triumph. She still had 'many fears', she confessed. Sometimes she even had 'low thoughts of God'. It was only when she was weeping or was with the church community that she felt any relief. She hoped that in 'time [she would] be comforted' but this was not yet her experience. 'A. A.''s testimony traced God's hand in the events of her life, but for the time being at least this perspective offered her little in the way of reassurance.

While many of the testimonies included in these collections share features in common, less neatly resolved accounts such as 'A. A.''s are a reminder that we should not overstate the formulaic nature of these narratives. Rogers spoke of the testimonies in his volume as 'flowers' that he was gathering 'to present to the saints in other places; and though some appear in their weakness as well as in strength . . . the variety of the flowers, and of the colours . . . gathered together into one, give a glorious lustre . . . like the rainbow of many colours'.[26] If the women who testified were seeking to create a rainbow – or a treasure trove – of personal experiences for the spiritual benefit of themselves and others, this resulted in them giving us insight not only into the lives of 'ordinary' mid-seventeenth-century women but into their innermost thoughts and feelings: speaking from the heart about their experiences, those testifying created an intimate record of women's lives to which we would otherwise have no access.

Part Two:

'The prophetical stage'

3

Elizabeth Poole

The prophetical scene or stage upon which all apparitions
were made to the prophet, was his imagination ... there all
those things which God would have revealed unto him were
acted over symbolically, as in a masque, in which diverse
persons are brought in, amongst which the prophet
himself bears a part.

John Smith, 1660

God raised up women prophets to honour that sex,
and to help his people, and the devil raises up women
to spread lies ... Satan imitates God, if he will have he
or she prophets, the like will he have.

William Greenhill, 1650

The Lord hath a controversy with the great and mighty men
of the earth, with the captains, and rulers, and governors ...
For as you are the potsherd of the earth, he will surely break
you to pieces, till there be not a shred left to carry coals on.

Elizabeth Poole, 1649

One Sunday during Lent in 1526, throngs of people made
their way to the village of Court-at-Street, Kent. They
were hoping to see a miracle. A young servant, Elizabeth

Barton (*c.* 1506–1534), had been ill for months, unable to eat or drink.[1] Lying immobile, she had seen visions of heaven and hell. Rumours were flying that she possessed prophetic powers – she was said, for instance, to have described the meal a hermit was eating on the other side of the village. Hearing that she had predicted that she would be healed at the Chapel of Our Lady, thousands of people, including 'many ladies, gentlemen and gentlewomen of the best degree', flocked to the church, determined to see for themselves.

Elizabeth Barton walked through the village, a noisy train of people singing hymns and reading aloud from the Bible trailing behind her. As she arrived at the chapel, a musical chant rang out. Making her way inside, she halted before an image of Mary. Then, to the astonishment of everyone present, she fell abruptly to the floor, her face 'wonderfully disfigured, her tongue hanging out, and her eyes being in a manner plucked out and laid upon her cheeks'.[2] She was in a 'marvellous passion', during which she began to speak in 'metrical and rhyming' verse. Eerily, her voice appeared to come not from her mouth but from 'within her belly'.[3] For more than three hours, her audience listened, spellbound. When she spoke of 'the joys of heaven' they were 'ravished with the hearing thereof', and when she warned of the horrors of hell they fell into 'a great fear'.[4] Then came the promised miracle: suddenly, she was 'quite recovered'.[5]

Not long after this dramatic episode, Elizabeth Barton moved to Canterbury to become a nun. Every December, around the time of the 'conception of Our Lady', she would take to her bed for several days, unable to eat or drink. In her presence, it was said, candles would light spontaneously. It was also reported that she could make dried-up milk flow once more in women's breasts.[6] She told strange tales. The Devil, she said, had come into her cell and asked her to marry him. When she refused him, he spat in her face with saliva 'as black as soot and as stinking as carrion'. He continued to visit her, as was signalled by the 'great stinking smokes' that would sometimes emanate from her cell. Sometimes he appeared in the shape of a deformed bird. At other times, he would stage pornographic displays. Once, he set her veil alight (its charred remains subsequently became a relic). But alongside this unwelcome Satanic activity, Barton also received a heavenly letter – inscribed with golden words – from Mary Magdalene herself.[7]

The sensational story of the 'holy maid of Kent', as published by her supporters (all copies of which were later destroyed), drew pilgrims from all levels of society to visit her.[8] 'She has raised a fire in some hearts that you would think like the operation of the Holy Spirit in the primitive church,' claimed one observer: 'if you saw with what frequent tears some bewailed their transgressions!' But Barton's spiritual authority made her dangerous, enabling her to challenge those in power. It was so risky to associate with her that Gertrude Courtenay, Marchioness of Exeter, disguised herself as a servant (with her servant taking her place) when she visited Barton in Canterbury. Barton also visited her in her home, an event that provoked the fury of King Henry VIII. She and Barton were not plotting against him, the marchioness told the king. She had suffered multiple stillbirths, and simply wanted the 'holy maid' to pray that her current pregnancy would have a happier outcome.[9] And 'thus Elizabeth Barton was advanced from the condition of a base servant to the state of a glorious nun,' remarked one sixteenth-century account.[10] But her moment in the sun did not last long.

If for some Barton had a miraculous aura, others regarded her as either a witch or a fraud – or both. 'This wicked woman', spat Thomas Cranmer, Archbishop of Canterbury, had 'devilish' acting skills. She could 'feign herself to be in a trance, disfigure her face, draw her mouth awry toward the one ear, feigning that she was thus tormented of Satan for the sins of the people'.[11] John Foxe, another champion of Protestantism, also claimed that it was 'by false dissimulation' that Barton appeared to have 'marvellous alteration of her visage, and other parts of her body, as if she had been rapt or in a trance'. Her trances, he said, were 'feigned . . . by false hypocrisy (as though she had been inspired of God)'.[12] For those such as Foxe who were seeking to discredit Roman Catholicism, Barton's pretended visionary powers betrayed the fraudulence of the 'old faith', which, in the words of Cranmer, relied on 'many wonders and strange miracles' such as 'visions of angels' and 'apparitions of the dead', all of which were either Satanic or 'feigned and counterfeited'.[13]

Barton, to Cranmer, was merely the latest in a long line of Catholic 'holy maids', all of whom were highly dubious. A decade before Barton appeared on the scene, the twelve-year-old daughter of Sir Roger Wentworth of Essex, perhaps named Jane, had also fallen into trances during which she prophesied. She was taken to the shrine of Our Lady of Ipswich, where she had convulsions, anticipating the scenes played out by Barton. Being 'laid before the image of our blessed Lady', Wentworth was 'in face, eyes, look, and countenance so grisly changed, with her mouth drawn aside, and her eyes laid out upon her cheeks, that it was a terrible sight to behold', wrote Thomas More. On this occasion, the girl's collapse was believed to result from Satanic torment: the 'great and open miracle' celebrated by More was neither Wentworth's ability to prophesy nor her 'alienated and raving' condition but her abrupt cure, one that led her, like Barton, to enter a convent.[14]

At the beginning of the sixteenth century there had also been a 'holy maid of Leominster', who lived enclosed within a priory. Supposedly eating no food, she claimed to be sustained by 'angel's food' in the form of the host, which ('as it seemed') would shoot miraculously into her mouth during Mass. In an elaborate scheme worthy of the later playhouses, she and the prior (said to be lovers) wove strands of her hair to form an invisible wire, enabling the host to 'fly' through the air.[15] For Cranmer, the 'holy maid of Leominster' had a predilection not only for deceptive theatre but for illicit sex, in both respects prefiguring the 'holy maid of Kent', herself described by another critic as a 'hypocritical harlot' said to have lived 'carnally and filthily' with her confessor.[16]

If the not-so-holy maid of Leominster used theatre for her own immoral purposes, Elizabeth Barton's drama – labelled a 'tragedy' in one contemporary account – was even more troubling.[17] Elizabeth's prophecies, initially relatively orthodox, began over time to shift from heavenly concerns to matters of state. Shockingly, she used her public platform to condemn the king, Henry VIII – 'that infidel prince of England', as she called him. An angel, she said, had told her that the king must 'take his old wife again, or else' something too 'naughty' to write down would happen to him. Elsewhere, her threat was made explicit: she had 'sure knowledge by revelation' that if the king divorced Katherine of Aragon and married Anne Boleyn 'he should not live six months after'.[18] Such was the status given to prophecies in this era that Barton's warnings, in Cranmer's view, had the power to delay if not to ruin the king's marriage plans.[19] Barton claimed that her words had indeed prevented the marriage to Anne Boleyn taking place – for a while at least.[20] If Barton was theatrical, then, her performances possessed rare power.

Harnessing the authority of prophetic speech to intervene in national debates, she demonstrated that the role of a prophet gave women unique access to the public political realm. Because she was claiming to speak the words of God, a woman who was once a maidservant had been able to threaten 'the state of the realm so deeply and so perversely as tended to the overthrow of all together'.[21] The king 'might have lost his crown' because of her, remarked a historian in the following century, noting that these troubling events prompted Thomas Cromwell to remind people 'to use great caution before extraordinary things should be received or spread about as revelations, since otherwise the peace of the world should be in the hands of every bold or crafty impostor'.[22]

Perhaps unsurprisingly, Elizabeth Barton was charged with treason, standing accused along with her male associates of threatening 'the peace and tranquillity of this realm'. The charge sheet was long and its contents vicious. Having suffered illness in her youth and knowing how to dissimulate the 'ecstasy and extremity' of sickness, Barton, it declared, did 'falsely practise, use and show unto the people diverse and marvellous sudden alterations of her . . . body, craftily uttering in her said feigned and false trances diverse and many virtuous and holy words'. The illusion that she was 'rapt by almighty God from the affections of this world', experiencing revelations 'with heavenly lights, heavenly voices [and] heavenly melodies', deceived her audience into believing that she was 'a very holy woman inspired with God'. Accused of being the pawn of those who were 'maliciously' set against Henry's marriage to Anne Boleyn, she was charged with being 'a diabolical instrument to stir, move, and provoke the people of this realm' against the king.[23] And so on 20 April 1534, Barton, still a young woman, was executed. She suffered the 'very shameful death' that she had predicted for herself, becoming the only woman in history to have her head impaled on a spike on London Bridge.[24]

———

RIGHT TO THE brutal end of her short life, then, Elizabeth Barton was the protagonist of a prophetic and a political drama in which both her words and her body played important roles. She was a forerunner of several fasting – and sometimes 'rhyming' – female prophets in this book, women who, like her, recognized no distinction between the prophetic and the political. Speaking, they believed, on behalf of God, they did not hesitate to denounce the most powerful men in the land. Like Barton, these female prophets posed a genuine threat to those in power. Maligned by their enemies as witches, lunatics and 'whores', they were perceived by others to be the instruments of God, granting their words an authority that was not easy to dismiss.

While Sarah Wight and Anna Trapnel – whose stories we will hear in the coming chapters – were Protestants living a century after the Roman Catholic Elizabeth Barton, their similarities with her – as well as with medieval prophets such as Hildegard of Bingen, St Bridget of Sweden and St Catherine of Siena – suggest that female prophets in seventeenth-century England placed themselves in a transhistorical, transnational and transconfessional tradition of divinely inspired women.[25] So obvious were the connections that a newsbook printed in 1654 overtly likened Anna Trapnel to Elizabeth Barton. Trapnel was going from 'one good town to another to vent her prophecies, and thereby disaffect the people to the present authority', it reported, calling to mind 'the old story of Elizabeth Barton', who was similarly 'made use of' by the men around her to 'foment seditious humors against the government'.[26]

There are important differences between earlier female prophets and their seventeenth-century successors, but their commonalities – including their illnesses, trances, visions, ecstatic speech, fasting and association with miracles – have led some critics to conclude that gender played an important role in the way they presented themselves as prophets. Diane Purkiss, for example, highlights the 'unsettling' implications for women prophets of 'the female body being a mere cover for the masculine voice'.[27] To Sarah Wight and Anna Trapnel, however, prophecy was not reducible to the articulation of a disembodied – or a masculine – divine voice. Rather than involving the 'dislocation of the voice from the body', prophecy was an expression of divinely inspired truth that occurred in and through the entire being of the prophet.[28] Emulating biblical models of prophecy, these women put the spotlight on their bodies, harnessing the power of physical performance to broadcast God's message, which they believed was conveyed through symbolic acts as much as through spoken or written words. If for periods of time they refused to eat or drink, this was not simply to denounce their 'flesh' but to demonstrate that both their bodies and their spirits were sustained by God. Every dimension of their lives reverberated with divine truth: so overtaken were they by the Spirit that it was not always possible to distinguish the prophet from her prophecy. Prophecy was not simply a speech act but was a form of life, one that was lived in its entirety as a performance of God's word.[29]

———

PROPHECY IS USUALLY understood today to involve predictions about the future, but in the seventeenth century – as in the Bible – it referred to any statement inspired by God.[30] Writing in 1650, the Independent minister William Greenhill claimed that the Old Testament prophets 'saw through the clouds, they saw into the heavens, they saw into the very counsel of God'. Functioning as 'the mouth of the Lord' (a role distinct from being the 'eyes of the Church', or knowing the future), they spoke 'to the people whatsoever the Lord himself did make known to them'.[31] John Smith, a Cambridge Platonist philosopher and the author of a substantial work on prophecy published in 1660, defined it as the 'copying forth' of divine mysteries. God 'flows in upon the minds' of prophets, he wrote, and 'conveys truth immediately from himself into them'.

How, though, could God communicate with mortals? If God 'should speak in the language of eternity', mused Smith, 'who could understand him, or interpret his meaning?' Since God was determined to talk to the 'idiotical sort of men', he had to do so 'in the most idiotical way'. Tailoring his message to his audience, God abandoned the language of pure reason and resorted to theatre: he set up 'the stage of prophecy' in the prophet's imagination, where 'all those things which God would have revealed unto him were acted over symbolically, as in a masque.' The prophet not only witnessed God's drama but was given a role to perform within it.[32] He 'must, as the other actors, perform his part, sometimes by speaking and reciting things done . . . sometimes by acting that part which in the drama he was appointed to act . . . and so not only by speaking, but by gestures and actions'.[33] Ezekiel, for example, was told to eat a scroll, to create a miniature siege, to bake bread with dung, to shave his head, to throw his hair to the wind and to lie immobile on his side every day (Ezekiel 3:1, 4:1–3, 4:12, 5:1–2, 4:4–8). He was also required to restrict his consumption of food and drink (Ezekiel 3:26, 4:10–11). These bizarre actions, argued Smith, were theatrical shows designed to enact approaching forms of judgement. Lasting for years on end, Ezekiel's prophetic roles became indistinguishable from his identity: 'I have set thee as a sign unto the house of Israel,' God instructed him, leading Ezekiel in turn to tell his audience: 'I am your sign' (Ezekiel 12:6,11).[34] Unsurprisingly, he was thought to be 'out of his wits', as Greenhill noted in a 1650 Bible commentary. But 'God's command makes a thing holy': if Ezekiel could be told to eat impure bread and Hosea could be commanded to marry a 'wife of whoredoms', then 'God's command legitimates anything.'[35] On the stage of prophecy, where shock tactics featured heavily, all limits were off.

———

WHEN SEVENTEENTH-CENTURY PROPHETS behaved outrageously, however – as they did, in the eyes of many – how were their contemporaries to distinguish those delivering an authentic prophetic performance from those gripped by what Smith terms 'mistaken enthusiasm' or the 'storms and tempests' of insanity? Smith works from the assumption that legitimate prophets are male. It is only when he turns to the 'crazed minds' of those who lack genuine inspiration that he begins to reference female 'prophets'. The sibyl 'noted by Heraclitus', for example, spoke 'ridiculous and unseemly speeches with her furious mouth', while the Pythian prophetess was 'filled with inward fury', uttering 'her oracles in a strange disguise with many antic gestures, her hair torn, and foaming at her mouth'. Making a shocking display of themselves, these women, to Smith, were

Jacob Matham, *Hannah*, 1588, engraving.

self-evidently devoid of the 'divine breathings of the prophet-ical spirit'.[36] The astrologer John Gadbury, writing in the same year as Smith, also treated the notion of female prophecy with contempt. Referring to the Fifth Monarchist Anna Trapnel as one of the 'silly wretches' who aspired to be a prophet despite being a 'melancholy, distempered, crack-brained creature', he poured scorn on the very idea that 'addle-headed women' could be God's mouthpieces. For any man to 'give heed' to women's 'predictions, or twirling stories, as prophecies or oracles', he pronounced, 'is the greatest argument of imbecility or weakness that can be'.[37]

Within some radical religious circles, however, it was a very different story. Greenhill, an Independent who visited Anna Trapnel during one of her prophetic trances, argued that female prophets had the full backing of the Bible. 'The promise of the spirit of prophecy was to women as well as men,' he declared. God 'raised up women prophets to honour that sex': it was only because God 'will have he or she prophets' that the Devil sometimes used 'women to spread lies'. Greenhill observed that women who were 'esteemed prophetical' were able to 'per-suade more powerfully' than other women, recognizing the rare opportunity for authoritative speech offered to women by the prophetic role.[38] George Fox, the Quaker leader, also chal-lenged those who could not 'endure a daughter to prophesy', pointing out in 1661 that no one in the biblical account of 'old Hannah the prophetess' was offended at her speaking, yet 'if an old woman should come and prophesy' today 'you would cry to the stocks with her, or to prison with her, and hail and persecute her.' Collapsing the distinction between prophecy and preach-ing – both of which, in his view, involved speaking through the inspiration of the Holy Spirit – he emphasized that 'it was

Mary that first declared Christ, after he was risen.' 'Everyone receiving the light that comes from Christ' receives 'the spirit of prophecy', he concluded, meaning that 'we are not against such prophetesses, though many of the peevish priests are.'[39]

Paul's instruction that women must 'keep silence in the churches, for it is not permitted unto them to speak' (1 Corinthians 14:34) was said by the defenders of female prophecy not to apply to the 'daughters' described in the Bible as the recipients of the Spirit of God.[40] Those who are 'offended' at Anna Trapnel's words, declares the preface to one of her publications in 1654, should ask themselves 'if they know what it is to be filled with the Spirit, to be in the mount with God, to be gathered up into the visions of God'. If so, 'then they may judge her, [but] until then, let them wait in silence, and not judge in a matter that is above them'. The authority to speak is not contingent on the sex of the speaker but is determined by spiritual experience, the preface argues: it is the spiritually ignorant, not women, who must 'wait in silence'.[41]

'Grand mutations and extraordinary revolutions ... are even at the door, and ready to break in upon the princes and upon the people of the whole earth,' exclaims Christopher Feake, a Fifth Monarchist, in his preface to Mary Cary's *A New and More Exact Mappe* (1651). The 'revolutions' being brought about by God's Spirit are evident in the fact that women are prophesying, Cary among them. 'Many wise men after the flesh have been (and now are) much offended, that a company of illiterate men, and silly women, should pretend to any skill in dark prophecies, and to a foresight of future events,' he notes. But there are 'many hundreds of those silly and illiterate ones (so called)' who are 'wiser than their enemies, wiser than their teachers, wiser than the ancients'. The 'neglected, despised, reproached ones, both men and women . . . understand and perceive many precious truths', we silence them at our peril.

———

FOR MANY IN seventeenth-century England, these debates were beside the point, since prophecy, to their mind, was quite literally ancient history. Prophecy might not have ended with the Bible, according to John Smith, but if it extended beyond the biblical era it was only by 'a little'.[42] For other Protestants, however, especially those in the radical sects, the Holy Spirit continued to unveil new layers of truth. 'Prophecy ceased not, nor the Spirit (as the world would have it) totally is quenched' but is still 'directed to our seventeenth century', asserted Lady Eleanor Davies in 1647. (Herself a prophet, she liked to sign her publications with an anagram of her name, 'Reveale O Daniel'.)[43]

Believing that they were living in the final days of history, radical Protestants expected to experience ever-increasing levels of spiritual activity. In the end times, the Bible declared, God would pour out his Spirit on 'all flesh', and both sons and daughters would prophesy (Joel 2:28). This is 'a day of the power of God, a day of wonders, of shaking the heavens and the earth, and of general expectation of the approaching of the Lord in his temple', proclaims the preface to Trapnel's *The Cry of a Stone* (1654). In such a time, 'a witness, a voice, or a message from God to this nation' should not come as a surprise and must not be dismissed on the grounds that it 'is administered by a simple and unlikely hand'. On the contrary, the 'shaming, confounding, and casting out of all wisdom and power' – that is, of established forms of authority – is a sign that the end times have arrived: if we see prophecies 'put forth either in sons or daughters, in handmaids or servants, let us rejoice . . . for the summer is nigh at hand'.

This is the moment when 'Jesus Christ will have his secrets declared,' Mary Cary exclaims in 1647. It is 'not possible' for God's 'instruments to be silent, nor to sit still, when God hath spoken to them, and given them commission to do his work': 'if the Lord have spoken they cannot but prophesy.'[44] Confirming the impression that the prophet was rendered helpless by the prophetic experience, Sarah Wight and Anna Trapnel claimed that God spoke to them while they were lying immobile in trances. Their dramatic displays of being physically over-whelmed by God's Spirit have been interpreted by some critics in gendered terms: Diane Watt, for example, argues that female prophets presented themselves as physically weak because of their perception of the 'disjunction between the prophetic voice and the sinful female flesh'.[45] Yet male prophets in the Bible were also depicted as being incapacitated by their encounters with God. Ezekiel fell on his face and could not stand up after seeing visions (Ezekiel 1:28, 3:23), and when John of Patmos saw a vision of Christ, he 'fell at his feet as [though] dead' (Revelation 1:17). Wight's and Trapnel's visionary experiences are particularly reminiscent of those of Daniel (the prophet whose prediction of a fifth, everlasting kingdom was founda-tional to the Fifth Monarchist movement). After fasting for several weeks, Daniel had a 'great vision', causing him to col-lapse: 'there remained no strength in me,' he said (Daniel 10:8). God spoke to him while he was 'in a deep sleep' with his 'face toward the ground' (8:18, 10:9), and one of his visions so 'aston-ished' him that he 'fainted, and was sick' for several days (8:27). In his discussion of biblical prophecy, John Smith explains that the 'extraordinary impression of divine light or influence' acts powerfully on the prophet, entering his 'mind as a fire, and like a hammer that breaks the rock in pieces . . . it is even like a thing that burns and tears him', leaving the 'natural strength and spirits exhausted'. The 'strength and vigour of the perception', stupefying the senses, is one of the markers that a prophet is having an authentic spiritual experience, he suggests.[46] Wight's and Trapnel's displays of weakness during their visionary episodes therefore place them in a biblical tradition, authenticating their status as prophets, as both their bodies and their words testify to the proximity of God.

For other seventeenth-century prophets, however, prophecy was a less dramatic affair. The revelations experienced by the Fifth Monarchist Mary Cary occurred not during trances but when she was studiously applying herself to the 'frequent reading, and hearing of the Word of God, waiting for the coming in of the Spirit in it'. From the age of fifteen, she had been inspired 'by the Spirit of God' to study the Bible. It was because of the depth of her biblical knowledge that she was able to make prophetic pronouncements about current events, claiming, for instance, that the 'power of the Beast over the saints' was coming to an end. For Cary, a prophet was not a passive cipher for God's words but was a figure who was intellectually as well as spiritually and emotionally engaged in a search for truth. Unfolding the 'mysteries of the gospel' and the 'truths of Christ', the prophetic role in her writing merged with that of a preacher: to prophesy was 'to speak the word of exhortation, and information, to the confirming of saints in the truth'.[47] 'Every saint', moreover, 'may be said to be a prophet', because a prophet was someone 'to whom God discover[ed] his secrets', and if 'the Lord did not reveal his secrets unto poor souls, it would not be possible for them to be saints.' To be a prophet, then, was no more than to be a Christian: 'as the soul is made a saint, it is made a prophet.' Everyone who had a personal experience of God would 'give vent to the bubblings of Christ upon [their] heart' (even though some could 'do it far more excellently than others').[48] Cary's understanding of prophecy was grounded in the Reformation principle articulated by Martin Luther that 'all Christians are priests,' meaning that 'women are priests.'[49] No longer the preserve of a small group of elite men, prophetic and priestly roles were open to all: 'all saints that have the testimony of Jesus', emphasizes Cary, 'have the spirit of prophecy.'[50]

The authority bestowed by the right to speak prophetically meant that prophecy was 'the single most important genre for women in the early modern period', according to the literary critic Elaine Hobby. 'With God's permission,' she notes, 'a woman could write, and, for a while at least, could insist on having a hearing.'[51] One female prophet who quite literally insisted on 'having a hearing' was Elizabeth Poole, to whose astonishing story we now turn.

———

IN THE FINAL days of 1648, as the fate of the king – and the nation – hung in the balance, Elizabeth Poole (b. 1622) took herself into the heart of the political action. Marching into the council chamber at Whitehall, she confronted the commanders of the army – including, on this occasion, Oliver Cromwell – who were debating the second version of the Levellers' *Agreement of the People*. They were also weighing up the implications of the trial and execution of the king that they were in the process of instigating. As the men sat in the chamber reformulating the very structure of the state, Elizabeth

Poole announced that she had a message for them from God. Fully aware of the enormity of the decisions they were taking, the officers were all ears. It was not until a week later, however, that Poole mustered the courage to deliver her message in its entirety.

Born in 1622, Elizabeth Poole was baptized at St Gregory's by St Paul's in December of that year. In her teens, she joined William Kiffin's Baptist congregation in London. Her enraged father, Robert Poole, accused Kiffin of 'seducing my children and servants into your errors'.[52] Elizabeth was later expelled from this congregation, after Kiffin accused her of 'scandalous evils'. She relocated to Abingdon, where she joined the Baptist church of John Pendarves, becoming particularly friendly with his wife. Seeking to clear Poole's name, Thomasine Pendarves reminded Kiffin that her friend 'hath no livelihood amongst men, but what she earns by her hands': to ruin Poole's reputation was to destroy her ability to work as a seamstress.[53] Well connected in radical terms, Poole moved in the same circles as the Ranter Abiezer Coppe, the publishers Giles and Elizabeth Calvert, and the mystic John Pordage.[54] Whatever her associations, however, she operated as a prophet in her own right.

In her first appearance before the Council of Officers on 29 December 1648, Elizabeth Poole presented herself as an ally of the army. Just like them, she declared, she wanted to save the nation from itself. 'I have been . . . a sympathiser with you in your labours,' she said, suggesting that she and the army had jointly suffered 'the pangs of a travelling [or labouring] woman' as they sought to give birth to new forms of political and religious life. To assist with this process, she claimed, she had a vision to share containing vital information about how the army should proceed. She had seen the figure of a man representing the army alongside a woman with a 'crooked, sick, weak and imperfect' body, who signified the 'weak and imperfect state of the kingdom'. It would be no easy task saving this woman, she elaborated. The army would only succeed, in fact, if it was guided by Poole. She would not 'stagger', she assured them, and implored them in turn not to be 'slack' in their actions.

Vindicating the role of the army in seizing control of events, these words went down well with the officers. When Poole declared that 'the Lord hath a controversy with the great and mighty of the earth, with the captains and rulers,' they had no reason to think that this was anything other than a statement in support of their campaign against a tyrannical king. 'I see nothing in her but those [things] that are the fruits of the Spirit of God,' commented the Commissary-General Henry Ireton, the leading figure in the Whitehall Debates and ultimately one of those to sign the king's death warrant.[55] When pressed about the specific direction the army should take, however, Poole – for the time being – held back.

A week later, on 5 January 1649 – just weeks before Charles I was executed – Poole returned to the Council. This time, her message was less agreeable. Do not betray the trust that has been placed in you, she warned the leaders of the army. Then she handed over a document, on which she had written an elaborate argument against the execution of the king. Her objection worked from the principle that subjects must relate to the king in the same way that a wife relates to her husband. 'The king is your father and husband,' she told the officers, 'which you . . . are to obey in the Lord'. As Katherine Chidley had pointed out earlier in the decade, however, even God-ordained hierarchies had their limits. What if an ungodly husband tried to command a godly wife against her conscience? In such a situation, Chidley had argued, a woman must be loyal to God rather than to man. Poole, likewise, was alive to the reality that a monarch, like a husband, could fail to live up to his role, freeing his subjects from their subservience, 'the yoke taken from [their] necks'.

Like the army commanders in the Whitehall Debates to which she contributed, then, Poole carefully considered the question of whether it was ever justifiable to execute a divinely appointed king. For Poole, though, unlike the army, the answer was no. Likening the people to an unhappily married woman, she agreed that there were limits to what they must endure. A wife was free to hold down the hands of a husband who was a 'terror to her flesh' so that he could not 'pierce [her] bowels with a knife or sword to take [her] life'. But even in such an extreme situation, she was not permitted to kill her abuser. Instead, she should appeal to God to enact justice on her behalf. Charles I, despite all his failings, should likewise be left to God. Feel free to bring him to trial, she advised, but you must spare his life.[56]

Dismayed to hear their plans being called into question, the army officers challenged Poole's 'revelation'. Had this message been 'dictated to her by the Spirit'? It was obviously the case, claimed Colonel Rich, that 'for the highest breach of trust' there could be a 'forfeiture of life': 'natural reason', in his view, supported the execution of the king. Poole's statement, he insisted, would only carry weight if it was indeed, as she claimed, an 'extraordinary revelation from God to you, and from you to us'.

At this critical moment, then, with the life of the king in question, everything turned on how to know whether a 'prophetic' statement was divinely inspired. No one doubted that God could have sent a woman to reveal his will to the army. But was Poole's argument against Charles's execution genuinely inspired? Could she provide a 'demonstration or token' to prove that she was God's spokesperson? If God had indeed sent 'a messenger', argued one officer, he would also create 'an impression upon their hearts [that are] to receive it': the subjective conviction that God was speaking, in other words, would be experienced not only by the prophet but by her audience. In the absence of agreement, Poole would have to provide some form of 'proof', something she admitted she was unable to do. The message, she stated, would have to 'bear witness for itself'. I 'saw no vision, nor no angel, nor heard no voice', she clarified, 'but my spirit being drawn out about those things, I was in it. So far as it's from God I think it is a revelation.'[57]

Poole therefore presented a nuanced understanding of prophecy. Her spirit had been 'drawn out' concerning the fate of the king, leading her to 'think' that she had a 'revelation' from God. This was not a prophet who saw herself as a passive vehicle for divine words. She 'saw no vision' and 'heard no voice' in relation to Charles I's execution but put forward her own rational argument. As Marcus Nevitt observes, her message was 'very much her own'.[58] Yet this does not mean that she did not understand her words to be prophetic. Prophecy, for Elizabeth Poole – as for Mary Cary – did not require the bypassing of her own voice or intellect. Instead, it was a collaborative process, one in which God's close communion with an individual could enable the development of an argument – at once divinely inspired and logically constructed – against the killing of a king.

———

POOLE'S ARGUMENT AGAINST Charles I's execution alluded to the biblical character of Abigail, whom Poole cited as the ideal wife. I Samuel 25 tells the story of David's anger with Abigail's husband Nabal, who failed to recompense David for his protection. Having decided to march with his band of men against Nabal, David was diverted from his violent course of action by Abigail, who provided David with the provisions and, crucially, with the gratitude that her husband had refused to offer. Praised in the biblical narrative not only for being beautiful but for being a woman of 'good understanding' (I Samuel 25:3), Abigail acted on her own initiative, thwarting a massacre. Early modern conduct books, as Brownlee and Gallagher demonstrate, tended to venerate Abigail as a model of unswerving devotion, regarding her intervention to save her 'churlish' husband as an example of heroic loyalty.[59] Stressing that she went behind her husband's back, the biblical narrative could nevertheless just as easily be interpreted as the tale of a resourceful woman defying the husband whom she knew to be foolish. Although David was charmed into abandoning his mission, Abigail's actions did not ultimately save Nabal. Quite the opposite: he was so shocked when he discovered what she had done that he dropped dead on the spot. Whatever the nature of her relationship with Nabal, however, Abigail was not just a wife. She was also a prophet, one who offered advice to the future King David.

When Poole referenced Abigail in her speech to the army, the implications of her allusion were not straightforward. On one level, she argued that the army should emulate Abigail in continuing to respect the king – their 'husband' – despite his shortcomings. On another level, though, as Thomasine Pendarves noted approvingly, Poole was presenting herself as a type of Abigail.[60] Like the biblical character, she was bravely

Lambert Jacobsz., *Abigail and Nabal*, 1625–37, oil on panel.

going out on a limb to prevent a violent and, in her view, self-defeating act of revenge. Like Abigail, Poole aspired to be an eloquent and persuasive woman, a prophet who took her own initiative and displayed her 'good understanding' as she delivered her message to the most powerful men in the land.

———

TO SOME OF those observing the unprecedented scenes in Whitehall, Elizabeth Poole had very seriously overstepped the mark. According to one anonymous tract published in 1651, Poole was nothing short of a 'monstrous witch', one deployed by the 'grand impostor' Oliver Cromwell for his own nefarious purposes. Wanting to unite the Council of Officers behind his plots, Cromwell, the tract suggested, had 'provided' a witch 'full of all deceitful craft'. Having dressed the 'witch' in 'brave clothes', Cromwell, the pamphlet claimed, provided her with a script: she was to say that 'she was a lady that was come from a far country, being sent by God to the army with a revelation.' When she entered the room the officers were astonished to see 'her strange postures, expressing high devotion'. Most of the officers tried to suppress their laughter, the tract continued, while Cromwell and Ireton wept theatrically, leading Poole also to weep as she spoke her so-called 'revelations'.[61] To another mocking commentator, Poole was one of the Leveller John Lilburne's 'doxies' (sex workers). Calling her Lilburne's 'girl' and his 'handmaid', the report described Poole as having the 'spirit of a lion' as she claimed to be an 'ambassador from the Lord of Hosts'. She was allowed to 'vent the flames of zeal', sneered the author, for fear that she would otherwise make a scene and 'shake the dust off her petticoats against the Council'.[62]

Vilified in these terms, Poole also had to endure the participation of her one-time friends in a public smear campaign. Her former minister William Kiffin reportedly stated that 'she brought a delusion for a vision of God.' His words, Poole wrote, 'made long furrows in my flesh, and lashed me sore'. Her participation in the Whitehall Debates led to her being hounded 'by them that are called saints', she claimed, 'pursued' by those who wanted 'to shoot me to death at the General Council of the army, not regarding the babe Jesus in me'. The 'pretended church and fellowship of saints in London', she elaborated, was doing its best to 'render' her 'odious' by accusing her of going 'about seducing'. While she retained the support of friends such as Thomasine Pendarves, Poole was therefore accused of being

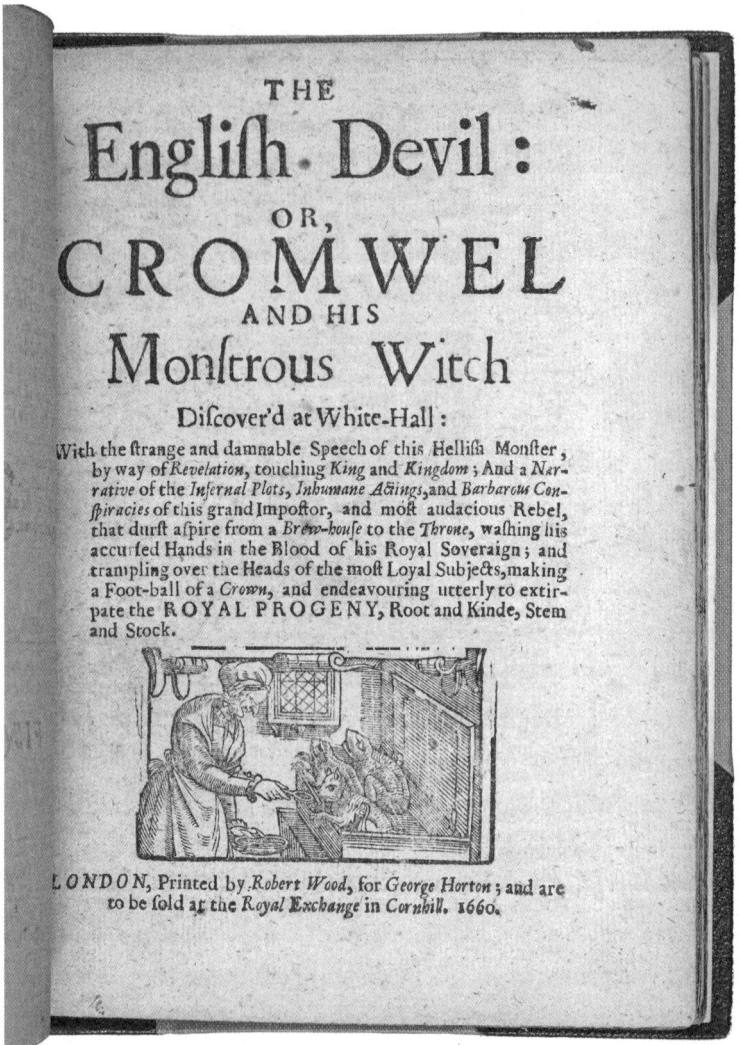

THE

Englifh. Devil :

OR,

CROMWEL

AND HIS

Monſtrous Witch

Diſcover'd at White-Hall :

With the ſtrange and damnable Speech of this Helliſh Monſter,
by way of *Revelation*, touching *King* and *Kingdom* ; And a *Narrative* of the *Infernal Plots*, *Inhumane Actings*, and *Barbarous Con-
ſpiracies* of this grand Impoſtor, and moſt audacious Rebel,
that durſt aſpire from a *Brew-houfe* to the *Throne*, waſhing his
accurſed Hands in the Blood of his Royal Soveraign ; and
trampling over the Heads of the moſt Loyal Subjects, making
a Foot-ball of a *Crown*, and endeavouring utterly to extir-
pate the ROYAL PROGENY, Root and Kinde, Stem
and Stock.

LONDON, Printed by *Robert Wood*, for *George Horton* ; and are
to be ſold at the *Royal Exchange* in *Cornhill.* 1660.

Title page of *The English Devil; or, Cromwel and His Monstrous Witch Discover'd
at White-Hall* (27 July 1660).

a witch, a fraud and a 'whore'. Such ferocious verbal assaults
illustrate the alarm caused by a woman of 'low' social status
presenting herself as a prophet, one moreover who contributed
to political debates at the very highest level.

———

UNFAIRLY DERIDED IN her lifetime – as she has been since – as nothing more than the pawn of powerful men, Elizabeth Poole was no one's passive instrument, not even God's. Her intervention in the Whitehall Debates is a reminder that prophecy, in this period, was an intensely political genre.[63] Female prophets had unique opportunities to intervene in the political sphere: as Manfred Brod observes, 'the very few women who walked the corridors of power in their own right' in this era 'were prophetesses'. As he notes, though, 'of these it is only Elizabeth Poole who is known to have participated directly in discussions of high policy.'[64]

Poole's appeal to the army was of course unsuccessful, and on 30 January 1649 Charles I was beheaded. Shortly after the king's execution, Poole published her response, a pamphlet in which she denounced those who had ignored 'the word of the Lord at my mouth'. Opening her tract with a lengthy quotation from the book of Ezekiel, she pronounced judgement on those who had 'not regarded the word of the Lord': 'I have seen your carcasses slain upon the ground,' she declared. Referring back to her first visit to the Council of Officers, she elaborated on the meaning of her words: 'said I not to you when I was at your Council with you, that as you were the great and mighty men of the earth, the Lord's controversy is with you, the day is hastening upon you, behold it is at hand'? Her claim to be God's messenger had ultimately been ignored. Yet Poole used the printing press to ensure that she got the last word. You thought I meant the king, she said, but 'yourselves remain the mighty men of the earth that shall be given to the fowls of the air, and beasts of the earth for prey'.[65]

———

HOWEVER VICIOUS THE attempts to undermine her, Elizabeth Poole was not easily silenced. The last time we hear of her is in 1668, when she petitioned for release after being imprisoned for publishing radical books on a private printing press at her home in Southwark.[66]

Poole's verbal echoes of Ezekiel as well as her allusions to Abigail illustrate the extent to which female prophets in this era modelled themselves on biblical figures, both male and female. Like Ezekiel, these prophets regarded their bodies and their minds, as well as their mouths, as the sites through which divine truth was revealed.[67] This all-encompassing model of prophecy was expressed powerfully by the two visionary women – Sarah Wight and Anna Trapnel – to whom we shall now turn.

4

Sarah Wight

I am not only filled with the Spirit, but, if one may say it,
drunk with the Spirit, it overcomes me.

Sarah Wight, 1647

One Monday evening at the beginning of March 1647, two
men were walking across Lambeth Marsh, a boggy area
south of the Thames that had yet to be drained and developed
into what is now the South Bank. Picking their way past the
many watery ditches that lay hidden beneath the green frogbit
floating on their surfaces, they were surprised to see a small
figure huddled on the ground.[1] There, sitting in the mud, her
eyes tightly closed, was a fifteen-year-old girl. Her stricken face,
wet with tears, told its own story. 'I am not well,' she blurted
out: 'I am as sad a creature as any on earth. I see my condemnation, and nothing else. I cannot be well, until I have taken
away my life.'[2] Momentarily confounded, the men – who were
ministers – asked where they could take her, saying 'this is not
a place for [you] to sit in.' Mr Carter was preaching that night,
she told them, so they made their way together over London
Bridge to Fish Street Hill, where the Independent preacher
was giving one of his popular weekday sermons. The men had
no way of knowing that the desperate girl walking alongside
them that evening was about to become a renowned prophet.

Detail from Wenceslaus Hollar, *Long View of London from Bankside*, 1647, etching.

Earlier that day, the girl, whose name was Sarah Wight, had encouraged her mother to attend William Carter's sermon, saying that she would be safe with a neighbour. Her mother had good reason to worry, as the previous month Wight had made a serious attempt on her own life. Waiting until her mother was asleep, she had crept out of a window onto the roof of their house in Laurence Pountney Lane, determined 'to do like Judas' and 'cast herself down'. Inching close to the edge of the roof, she was about to leap when she saw a 'fire, and Satan as a roaring lion in it'. A voice spoke to her, saying, 'thou shalt not fall down, and burst asunder, as Judas did, and so dishonour God

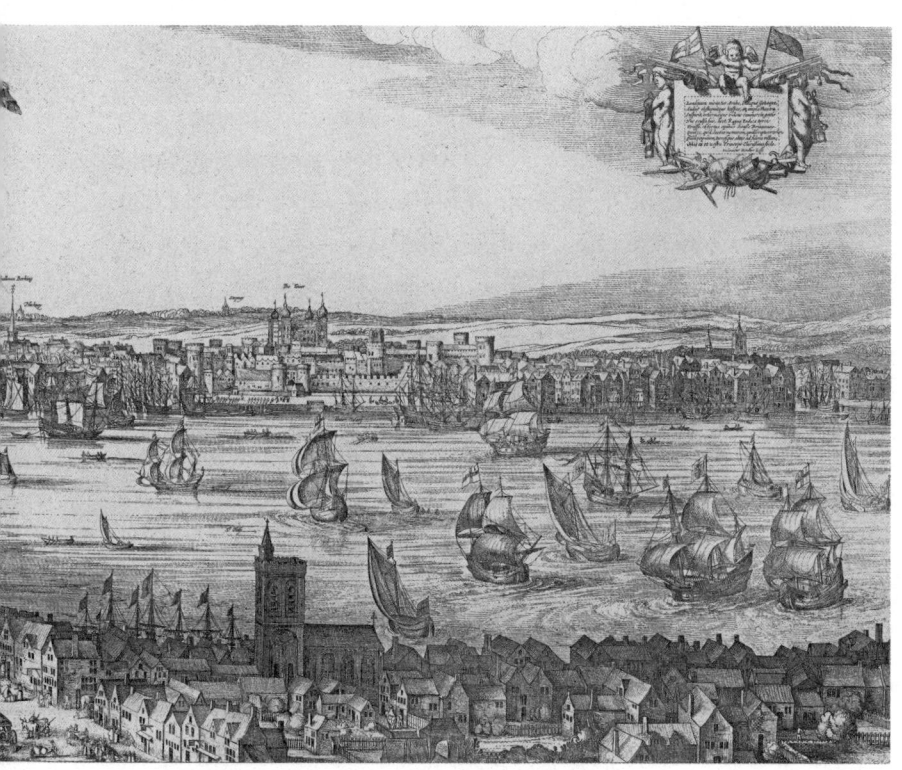

Detail from Claes Jansz. Visscher, *View of London*, 1616, engraving.

that made thee.' Thwarted, she sat down by the chimney, beating her 'head against it, till it swelled abundantly'. Having realized what was happening, her mother attempted to rescue her, but Wight fell off the roof, severely injuring her head and eyes.

Over the following weeks, under her mother's watchful gaze, Wight's mood seemed to improve. But she was in fact planning her next move. When she had left home and crossed the Thames earlier that Monday evening she had been carrying a knife, determined to use it to 'despatch herself'. The trees on Lambeth Marsh, still bare after a long winter, seemed to represent her 'dry' and barren soul. It was only because she had paused to pray before drowning herself in a ditch that she had been discovered. As she retraced her steps with the ministers that evening, she was already coming up with a new plan. Later that night, she decided, she would go 'to the doghouse . . . in Moorfields, there to offer herself to the dogs to eat her up, that her mother might never hear of her more'. Once deposited at William Carter's lecture, however, she was unable to hide from her mother, who took her safely home.

———

SARAH WIGHT'S TROUBLES had begun years earlier. Her father died when she was young and her mother endured her own period of 'deep terror and distraction', beginning when Sarah was around five years old. As a result, she lived for some time with her grandmother. Returning to her mother when she was nine, within a few years she began to suffer from extreme anxiety. When she was twelve, she was forced to obey a 'superior' about a 'small' matter even though it went against her conscience, leading to 'a great trembling in her hands and body'. Soon afterwards, she lost her hood, lying to her mother that it was at her grandmother's house. Stricken with guilt, she became convinced 'that she was shut out of heaven, and must be damned, damned, damned'. Wight's conviction that there was 'no heaven, and no hell, but what she felt within her' – an unorthodox belief reminiscent of Familist teaching – led her to decide that she 'was damned already', worsening her terror. Feeling 'as one in hell already', she made repeated attempts 'to destroy herself, as by drowning, strangling, stabbing, seeking to beat out her eyes and brains, wretchedly bruising and wounding herself'. Once, she rode a horse to an inn in Shrewsbury without holding the bridle, hoping that it would 'throw me in a ditch and kill me'. On arrival – after landing in at least one ditch – she was so 'weary of life' that she sat in her wet clothes, refusing to dry herself.

Continuing in this desperate state of mind for four years, Wight felt 'shattered to pieces'. By Tuesday, 6 April 1647, one month after she was found on Lambeth Marsh, she had reached a point of total collapse. No longer able to stand up, she lay in bed trembling. Her hands were 'clenched up together, and so were her feet, as if it were by the cramp, and her mouth was drawn up, as a purse, and her eyes were with the eyelids folded up and closed, and her hearing was taken from her, and she had no motion'. She stopped eating. On Saturday, 10 April, after days of lying asleep – 'or as in a trance' – she began to speak in 'a low voice', chanting, 'this is the faith, believing a full Christ, to a nothing creature, a full Christ, to a nothing creature, a full Christ, to a nothing creature.' Later, she spoke of this moment as a turning point: having seen a vision of Jesus on the cross, she was finally convinced that her sins were forgiven.

For the next eleven weeks, Wight remained in her bed, 'unable to eat at all' and taking just a sip of water every few days. Word began to spread that this young girl had become 'the earthly vessel' of spiritual treasures, capable of unfolding 'gospel-mysteries'. She kept bursting into ecstatic forms of speech, pointing to her experiences to declare that God could save even the most helpless of sinners. Curious and awestruck members of her community – including some high-profile figures – began to visit. While most of those who crowded into her bedroom believed her to be inspired by the Holy Spirit, now and again a visitor questioned her more sceptically. Her words, spoken quickly and brimming with biblical references, were scribbled down as accurately as possible by Henry Jessey, the Independent-Baptist minister of her congregation. Wight's mouth, he wrote, had been 'opened' to utter truth 'in a humble, melting manner', even as it had been 'opened to her . . . when her bodily eyes and ears were held [shut]'. But the sensational impact of her prophecies resulted more from the arresting manner of their delivery than it did from their content. Testifying to the mesmerizing power of her performance, Jessey acknowledged that the words 'cannot affect so much in hearing [them] at second hand, as if you had heard herself, with such brokenness of heart uttering [them]'.

―――

SARAH WIGHT'S OUTBURSTS were transcribed and published by Jessey as *The Exceeding Riches of Grace advanced by the Spirit of Grace, in an Empty Nothing Creature* (1647). This work, which as Kate Chedgzoy notes is 'the most extensive single document of female adolescence to survive from early modern England', presents Wight's account of her experiences as well as transcriptions of her prophetic speech and accounts of her dialogues with the many visitors who subsequently sought her counsel.[3] Although often attributed to Jessey, the work was co-authored: Wight makes it clear early on that she wants her words and experiences to be published to a wide audience.[4] A multi-vocal text, in which Wight's statements are interspersed with Jessey's commentary, it was published at a volatile political moment. Following the end of the first Civil War, Presbyterian parliamentarians were seeking to clamp down on their more radical former allies, including the Independents, generating a sharp sense of betrayal in the religious circles in which Wight moved. As she was lying in her bedroom, the radically minded New Model Army, aggrieved that their sacrifices had not led to the social and religious freedoms for which they had fought (and disgruntled over a lack of pay), began to march towards London. Later that summer, they would arrive in the city, insisting that radical MPs be allowed to return to Westminster and agitating for further reforms.[5]

Appearing at this moment of high tension among the 'saints', *Exceeding Riches* advertised the fact that God's Spirit was active among the Independents. Serving a political purpose that was inextricable from its spiritual focus, the publication, as Susan Wiseman observes, 'sought to clarify the place of the gathered churches in the power struggle'.[6] The work presented Wight as a prophetic example 'of what shall be' in the millennial period of social and political transformation that many radicals believed to be on the horizon.[7] Christ will shortly be bringing 'down every high thing', proclaimed Jessey in the preface, as was being demonstrated by the fact that Sarah Wight, a young woman, had been chosen to prophesy and to minister to her community. The text repeatedly emphasized the fact that the old hierarchies had had their day. When 'a noble lady sat on the bed' by Wight, for instance, she was suitably unimpressed. Being told 'that this was a great lady: she answered, it's no more to me, then if it were such a one, naming a meaner woman troubled in spirit, that oft came to her'. Here in Wight's bedroom, then, was a preview of the utopian era to come, one in which the 'meaner' sort – women as well as men, young as well as old – would operate on a spiritually equal basis with those who were said to be 'great'.

Catching the interest of a public fascinated by tales of the strange and the marvellous, the publication was widely read. Going through multiple editions (including a Dutch translation), it continued to be cited by ministers and other authors for decades after its publication.[8] When Timothy Rogers concluded his account of melancholy at the end of the seventeenth century, for instance, it was the well-known story of Sarah Wight and her inspirational return from despair to which he turned.[9] Despite the fact that she had hardly left her bedroom, Wight had become a celebrity.

———

SARAH WIGHT'S OUTPOURINGS, heavily informed by the Bible, have been characterized by some historians as relatively mainstream statements of Calvinist Protestantism. The fact that she was quizzed about her beliefs – about whether believers 'have need of the law', for example, or about why she held 'out to all that come troubled to [her], that Christ hath redeemed them' – nevertheless suggests that her contemporaries were far from convinced of her orthodoxy.[10] Her account turns on the contrast between her own extreme incapacity and the overwhelming power of God's grace, and this aspect of her story together with her instantaneous sense of assurance after a visionary moment of conversion recalls features of Rose Thurgood's antinomian-influenced conversion narrative.

Whatever Wight's specific blend of Protestant theology, though, it was the context in which her utterances were delivered that generated widespread fascination. How is it possible that 'one so young . . . should be able to speak?' marvelled Jessey. Yet the Bible taught that divine wisdom came from the 'mouth of babes and sucklings', leading him to conclude that it was surely 'the Lord's work'. If the disparity between Wight's youth and her wisdom suggested her prophetic status, her apparent ability to survive without food was an even more decisive sign of the presence of the supernatural. As the seventeenth-century philosopher John Smith observed in his discussion of prophecy, in order 'to believe a prophet is inspired, [some] might need to see a miracle', an 'altering [of] the course of nature, which indeed was the way by which the prophets of old ordinarily confirmed their doctrine, when they delivered anything new to the people'.[11] To Jessey, Wight's survival without sustenance was just such a miracle: 'the power of God [appeared] therein wonderfully to the beholders, in upholding her full 75 days without one crumb of bread or meat, and with so little drink.'

Initially, Wight 'could not eat, nor drink' because of all-consuming fears: 'in my trouble, I oft could not eat,' she reported, 'I fed on terror, that was my meat.' Referring to 1 Corinthians 11:29, where those who take part unworthily in the Lord's Supper – or communion – were said to bring judgement on themselves, she presented her food refusal as an expression of her guilt: 'I thought it was to me, as to some at Sacrament, that I did eat and drink my damnation.' Later, when a 'maid in deep despair' confessed to her that 'if I eat, I am terrified for it,' Wight could relate to her feelings. 'If I did eat, I was terrified for it,' she told her visitor, elaborating that 'sometimes I durst not drink in a whole week together, because I judged, it was a cup of devils, and I drank to devils, if I drank, and if I did eat, I thought I did eat my own damnation.' Food and drink were therefore caught up in the moral code by which Wight felt condemned. To consume, in a garbled version of the Corinthians passage, was to participate in an impure act that would confirm her eternal condemnation. At this stage of her narrative, then, Wight presented her refusal of food as a symptom of her distress. Starving herself was an aspect of her guilt-ridden cycle of self-harm: 'I beat my head oft against the wall, and took my flesh in my teeth . . . And when I had an opportunity against my life, and did not take it, then I beat myself for it most of all . . . Or if I spake anything that was offensive to any with me, or did that I should not, when it was brought to mind afterward, then I abused my body for it.'

After being assured of her salvation, however, Wight continued to be unable to eat. 'I would, if I could,' she insisted, 'but I cannot, it makes me sick to think of it.' Those around her, including Jessey as well as her brother, urged her to take some food, but she refused, claiming to be 'full': 'I am so full of the creator, that I now can take in none of the creature. I am filled with heavenly manna.' To Wight's mind, she was no longer punishing her body but was being sustained by an alternative source of nourishment. 'Do you think I do not eat?' she asked. 'How do you think I live?' Asked to explain, since no one had seen her eat for over three weeks, she replied that 'no eye of man sees it, but the eye of God. None could taste of the sweetness of the manna, by looking on it, none but they that eat of it.' 'Jesus Christ feeds me,' she continued, 'God hath given me Christ to feed upon: and his flesh is meat indeed; and his blood drink indeed.' If previously to eat had been to confirm her damnation, her renewed being now required only the spiritual 'flesh' and 'blood' of Christ to thrive. Jessey confirmed that this was the case: 'she looks better now than she did seven or eight weeks ago,' he wrote on 19 May, after she had gone 53 days with 'no outward sustenance at all'.

———

WIGHT'S INSISTENCE THAT she no longer needed to eat or drink placed her in an established European tradition of 'miraculous maids'. In the early years of the seventeenth century, for example, word had spread of a 'strange wonder' in the form of Eve Fliegen, a Dutch woman who had reportedly lived for fourteen years without consuming any food or drink. Fliegen had been born into poverty and had spent her youth looking after pigs. Tormented by an 'extremity of misery' – in her case agonizing hunger rather than struggles of the soul – she prayed for relief. Her prayers were answered not with food but with the loss of the need for it: every other day, she claimed, a bright light would appear, accompanied by the taste of an 'extraordinary delicate sweetness'.[12] Unable to eat anything other than this light, the consumption of even a single cherry left her ill for months. Fliegen was visited by thousands of people and her fame spread as far as the English stage. In the early seventeenth-century play *Love's Cure* by Fletcher and Massinger, for example, she was referenced as the 'miraculous maid' who was said to live 'without any other sustenance than the smell of a rose'.[13]

Fasting, of course, was not the sole preserve of women. Coming up with a list of people across time who had 'abstained from all manner of food' in his 1678 publication on prodigies, the clergyman Nathaniel Wanley identified multiple examples of fasting men as well as women. Martin Luther, he noted, abstained from food for days on end, while John Scot, said to be a man with no discernible good qualities, refused to eat purely out of 'discontent'. One king of France, meanwhile, stopped eating for fear of being poisoned. Wanley's examples of fasting women, meanwhile, consisted mainly of young girls who were able to live 'only upon air' while maintaining an appearance of good health.[14] Derived in part from the medieval tradition of fasting women but also departing from that precedent in important ways (most seventeenth-century 'miraculous maids', as Matt Williamson points out, present themselves as unable to eat rather than as choosing to fast), a particular model of the 'marvellous' spiritual young woman had taken hold.[15] Opinions about these women varied widely, and they were just as likely to be denounced as fraudsters as they were to be venerated as saints. One thing, however, was clear: the fascinated public could not get enough of their stories.[16]

Positioned within this tradition, Wight's inability to eat carried multiple symbolic meanings. In *Exceeding Riches*, the health of the body cannot be separated from that of the soul. When Wight was consumed by guilt, she was unable to nourish her body, whereas her spiritual renewal was associated with her physical recovery, even though this occurred by supernatural means. She did not see herself as fasting: 'I do eat,' she insisted repeatedly, 'but it's meat to eat, that the world knows not of; but those that taste of it.' Her body, she claimed, was not deprived, but was instead saturated with God. Rather than enacting a split between her starving body and her flourishing spirit, then, Wight's survival without food enabled her to present herself in miraculous terms as a human being wholly overtaken by God. After fasting for forty days and nights in the wilderness Jesus had insisted that 'man shall not live by bread alone, but by every word that proceedeth out of the mouth of God' (Matthew 4:4). Wight – who cited this verse – was determined to emulate his example. Lying prostrate on her bed, eyes bandaged, before her enraptured audience – for whom her youth and gender were likely to accentuate the impression of her innate frailty – her supernaturally sustained body was being presented as a compelling prophetic sign. Her words and her simultaneously starving and satiated body therefore came together to proclaim her central message, that a 'full Christ' could possess 'an empty creature'.[17]

———

AS SOON AS she began to emerge from her prolonged state of immobility, Sarah Wight became a renowned counsellor and minister, offering spiritual and emotional support to those in distress even before she had fully recovered herself. Seeking to demonstrate to despairing women that their situations were not as hopeless as they feared, her startling openness about her own struggles at times seemed almost competitive. Her tendency to view her own suffering as exceeding that of all others had long been apparent. At a 'lecture', or sermon, during the time of her despair, for example, she had seen another 'young gentlewoman', identified only as 'Mistress A' (possibly the soon-to-be-infamous Anna Trapnel), looking visibly distressed.[18] Mistress A told Wight that she was in 'as sad a condition as ever was any', to which Wight replied that 'none is in a condition like to mine.' Mistress A elaborated that she 'must be damned', causing Wight to retort, 'I am damned already, from all eternity, to all eternity, it's not to do, but 'tis done already.' 'I know it shall be well with you,' ventured Mistress A. 'As well as it was with Judas,' said Wight, '[who] hanged himself, which I must do, before I shall be free from these torments.' The conversation having nowhere else to go, Mistress A walked away, noting in parting that 'I shall perish ere I see you again.' ('Yet the Lord spared her,' added Jessey, his tone hard to read.)

Later, however, Wight's refusal to varnish over her suffering was aimed at reassuring her visitors that they were not alone in their torments, while demonstrating that it was possible for even the most despairing of individuals to regain a hopeful state of mind. The publication of her experiences, Jessey stated, would serve a similarly therapeutic function: 'How desirable is it to one, and to the friends of one, that is in great extremity of misery, bodily, or spiritual, to hear of another, that was just in the same condition, that now is cured?' Wight put a lot of effort into her pastoral role: if the visitor was 'silent and slow to speak, she put out fit questions to her, and so gained in, upon her answers'.

On 12 May 1647, while Wight was still 'very weak and spent', an 'afflicted woman' came to see her. The woman's husband had died nine months earlier, leaving her stricken with guilt for her 'perverse words to him, when he was faulty'. 'One morning, after I was awake,' she continued, 'I thought, the room was full of smoke, and suddenly a fire went in at my mouth, and went down hot into my belly, and there went flutter, flutter. Then (said the woman) I suddenly flew out of my bed, into the midst of the room, and a voice said within me, to my heart, Thou art damned, damned.' Smelling brimstone, she 'thought the house was full of devils. Then for six or seven weeks together, I never slept at all, I was so terrified, and have been out of hopes, ever since.' Wight replied that she, too,

> could see nothing but hell, and wrath . . . I felt myself, soul and body in fire and brimstone already. If all the

fire and brimstone in London, and all the pitch and tar, should all be in one fire, and I walking in the midst of that fire; this was my condition . . . Had you seen my condition that I was in, as I saw it, you would believe, he may as soon show mercy on you, as show mercy to me, and sooner too, by far.

Two weeks later, a woman in the early stages of labour claimed that the 'pangs' of childbirth were 'as nothing to the pangs and terrors her soul was in'. Telling Wight that 'legions of sins are before me,' the woman was reassured by Wight that 'legions of devils were within me, not before me, but within me. Yet he hath clothed me, and cast out Legion.'

Wight's last recorded consultation was with a maid who 'was not born in England', who was also suffering 'both in soul and body'. She told Wight that she felt suicidal in part 'because I am not as others are, I do not look so, as others do'. As Imtiaz Habib comments, it is possible that this maid was 'Dinah the Blackmore', one of the visitors to Wight's bedside listed at the beginning of *Exceeding Riches*.[19] Jessey noted that while he struggled to follow the woman's speech, 'mistress Sarah' was able to understand her. Attempting to offer comfort as she counselled the maid that all souls are 'black and uncomely' before Christ makes them 'fair', Wight stated that 'many nations must be blessed in him . . . why should you exclude yourself?' Despite the apparent egalitarianism of her response, Wight's language, as Chedgzoy points out, gave a 'racially charged inflection' to the biblical imagery she was deploying, perpetuating the association of blackness with ugliness and sin that appeared to be one of the causes of the maid's distress.[20] If this maid was Dinah, Jessey's attempt to give her story a happy ending was premature. Habib identifies Wight's visitor with 'Dinah the Moor' who came before the Court of Aldermen in Bristol twenty years later in a desperate attempt to fight her mistress's attempt to sell her to a man who planned to take her to the plantations. The 'peculiar manner' of the court record, according to the nineteenth-century historian John Latimer, suggested that she 'had been captured on the African coast and had lived as a slave in Bristol', providing a 'curious example of the practice of kidnapping human beings for transportation to America'.[21] Although the Bristol court ordered a temporary reprieve, nothing further is known of Dinah's fate.

———

TOWARDS THE END of *Exceeding Riches*, Wight recounts a dream, one that caused her to quake in terror so that 'the bed did shake.' She felt herself being 'violently hurried down a very steep hill', the same hill down which demon-possessed pigs fled in the biblical account of the exorcism of a man possessed by 'Legion' (Mark 5:1–13). Horses in apocalyptic colours of 'red and white and black' charged ahead of her. Knowing herself to be heading into a bottomless darkness, she cried out to God. 'Instantly', one with 'the appearance of a man (but the glory of him was so great, I cannot express it) . . . came and took me in his arms'. Carrying her down into 'the lowermost hell' before lifting her up to the top of the hill, he indicated that the initial descent as well as the final deliverance were under his control. Waking with her cheeks 'wet with weeping', Wight was left pondering the 'exceeding riches of his grace' (Ephesians 2:7), providing the title of the publication. In this dream, as throughout her account, she depicts herself in passive terms, as a helpless sinner rescued by an all-powerful God.

Wight was drawn to a disturbing passage in the book of Ezekiel where the prophet described Israel in metaphorical terms as an abandoned female baby, covered in its own blood and left without pity in an 'open field' (Ezekiel 16:5). God rescued the infant: 'I saw thee polluted in thine own blood, and I said unto thee, when thou wast in thy blood, thou shalt live' (Ezekiel 16:6). Taken up, cleansed and nourished by a divine saviour – God subsequently fed the girl with meat (Ezekiel 16:19) – the neglected baby represented those whom God loved despite their abject state. Wight identified strongly with this infant, whose abandonment by its parents, physical helplessness and apparently 'polluted' nature seemed to evoke for her aspects of her own being. Looking back on the moment of her collapse, she used the words of this passage to describe her anguish: no 'eye pitied thee', God said of the infant (Ezekiel 16:5), while Wight stated that 'mine own eyes ... pitied not myself, and just then was the time of love'.[22] Reading her suffering as well as its cure into the passage, she transformed her experiences into an allegory, one in which she, like the metaphorical infant, embodied the 'freeness of his love ... that undertakes all, when the creature is in the blood, as in Ezekiel 16'. Ventriloquizing a prophetic text to make sense of her own experiences, she endowed both her despair and her account of this despair with prophetic power. If she was the abject baby in the Ezekiel narrative, she was also the inspired prophet telling the story of this baby, displaying her miraculously sustained body as a spectacular sign of her chosen status.

———

BEFORE SARAH WIGHT was even out of her bed, rumours were spreading that there was another 'miraculous maid' in London.

Once again, a young woman's 'great enjoyments of God' were being accompanied by a miraculous ability to survive without food and drink. Despite not taking 'in a crumb or sip … for full six days together', it was said, the woman remained 'in bodily health'. Unlike Wight, however, this new prophet was declaring things that 'seemed strange' to Jessey. The prophet herself was no stranger, though: the woman who was beginning to steal the limelight had recently been at Wight's bedside. No longer willing to remain in the audience, Anna Trapnel was about to come centre stage.

5

Anna Trapnel

Thou wilt bring them into thy territories above, into thy
sweet walks, how wilt thou hang them about with honey-
suckles? Not like the honey that is of the earth, that is
clogging, but pure honey that is reviving. Thy Ezekiels that
behold thee by the river Chebar, oh what sights, what glories,
what rivers, what springs do they enjoy!
Anna Trapnel, 1654

May not I speak in my chamber, and sing on my bed, and
pray on my knees? Doth the Lord forewarn me, doth
Scripture forbid me? Or will the general assembly of the
firstborn reprove me, or the particular church I walk with,
will they be offended?
Anna Trapnel, 1654

When God first spoke to Anna Trapnel (b. 1620), his voice
was so distinct that she thought someone was speaking
behind her on the street. Throughout her life, she experienced
the supernatural in highly sensuous terms. In her visions she
was transported to heavenly territories to walk with God: 'oh
how glittering, and how glorious . . . what sparklings are there!'
She not only saw the luminous 'fabric of glory', but smelt it:
sermons left a 'fragrance upon [her] spirits' and God's words

were 'spices' that all who had 'their senses open' could 'smell
thereof'. Her tastebuds, sharpened by the Holy Spirit, could
taste spiritual blessings in food: 'Oh now, every bit of bread
I ate, how sweet it was to my taste! Christ sweetened every
creature to me, oh how sweet was the feasts of love . . . I had
feasts full of marrow and visions full of glory.' She could hear
heavenly sounds, too: 'sometimes the golden trumpet sounded
higher, and sometimes lower, yet it still was sounding, and
caused an echo to follow it.'[1] If 'earth was now gone, and heaven
come,' this opened a richly satisfying realm of existence, one
that rendered everyday experiences transcendent. The smell of
nutmeg evoked Christ 'when he is grated upon the spirits . . .
oh what sweet fragrant smell comes into every faculty of the
soul'. In bright red cherries, meanwhile, she saw 'the blood of
my saviour'. Trapnel's perception that the world was saturated
with the Spirit of God generated prophetic statements of rare
sensual power. In her visionary accounts – which anticipate
the 'sparkling' descriptions of the spiritual order penned by the
mystic Jane Lead later in the century – we encounter a dazzling,
technicolour universe, vibrating with spiritual meaning.[2]

Words – sometimes spoken, sometimes sung – poured out
of Anna Trapnel. Within the space of a single year – 1654 – four
works were published under her name. Two pamphlets transcribed her public prophecies (*The Cry of a Stone* and *Strange
and Wonderful Newes from White-Hall*), while the other publications related details of her life (*Anna Trapnel's Report and
Plea* and *A Legacy for Saints*). Within a few years, two further
collections of her prophecies were also published, one of which
is almost 1,000 pages long.[3] In all these works, the spiritual is
inseparable not only from the sensual but from the political: the
glorious 'sights' spoken of by Trapnel might reveal a heavenly

order but they do so in order to unveil a manifesto for social and political as well as religious revolution.

——

BORN THE DAUGHTER of a shipwright who died when she had just turned one, Anna Trapnel was raised in Poplar, Stepney, by her godly mother. A zealous teenager, she struggled with fears of damnation. Echoing Sarah Wight's experiences, she writes that she was 'strongly tempted to destroy myself, which had not divine power prevented, I had been a murderer of my own life, and of their lives that I loved most entirely'. She sometimes took hold of a knife 'for this very purpose'. Overwhelmed with feelings of guilt, she fasted obsessively while compulsively attending church meetings. Alarmed, her mother warned her against fasting 'day after day'. But Trapnel was convinced that she was better for 'hearing so much, and praying and fasting'. In the end, she looked so 'ghastly' that her friends were frightened by the very sight of her. 'Oh what a knotty piece was I for the great Jehovah to work upon!', she later remarked.[4]

On 1 January 1643 came a breakthrough. She was listening to a sermon by John Simpson – later to become a leading Fifth Monarchist – when the heavens suddenly opened. 'I knew not where I was, nor how to get out of the place where I sat,' she claimed: 'I apprehended nothing but a clothing of glory over my whole man.' Just a few days later, her mother died. Her mother's final words, repeated three times with 'much eagerness', were 'Lord! Double thy spirit upon my child.' Trapnel's aunt pushed home the message, instructing Trapnel that she must 'now labour to be married to Christ'. 'Great ravishings of spirit' followed, including a vision of an angel that left her with a 'perfume' in her 'spirits all that night'.[5]

In the summer of 1646, Trapnel became ill with a fever, during which she experienced a 'flood of divine excellency'. So powerful were her visions that she felt physically assaulted by them: lying in bed, her eyes were 'forced open' to see beams of light, and she was 'pulled' by the shoulder to be shown an image of Christ. Although she longed to die – to be 'swallowed up in glory' – God told her that after two days she would be 'raised'. Appropriating the words of the biblical prophet Hosea, who spoke of being 'torn' and 'smitten' by God before being revived on 'the third day' (Hosea 6:1–2), she interpreted both her illness and her recovery as evidence of her prophetic calling. Describing herself as 'like a dead carcass', with 'the scent of dead skulls turned out of the grave . . . in my nostrils, and my body like unto a clod of earth', she felt 'lifted up by the power of the most high God from my bed'. This experience heralded great things. 'I will make thee an instrument of much more,' God told her: 'for particular souls shall not only have benefit by thee, but the universality of saints shall have discoveries of God through thee.'⁶

The following year – the year of Sarah Wight's trance – Anna Trapnel was again shown 'great things and visions'. Told by God that the army was approaching London – 'I not knowing anything of it before' – she asked a maid what was happening. She was warned to keep to her room, since there were 'great fears amongst the citizens'. For Trapnel, however, the 'defiance' of the army, in their attempt to force through social and religious reforms, was in line with God's purposes. While others retreated behind closed doors, she threw open her window before rushing excitedly into the city, eager to be part of the action. She then fasted for nine days, during which time she had 'many great visions', culminating in a glimpse of the army's peaceful arrival at Southwark 'some weeks' before this happened. To many of her friends, however, including the leader of her congregation, she was behaving suspiciously. Rather than seeing her as inspired by God, they judged her 'to be under a temptation for not eating'. Forced to defend her 'singular' experiences, Trapnel insisted that God was providing for her 'in body and spirit'.[7]

Increasingly alienated from her Baptist congregation, Trapnel soon fell back into despair. By 1653, she felt once again that she would be better off dead. She later described how she was 'forced by Satan' to 'walk up and down' in fields and to 'lie in ditches' far into the night, and she considered throwing herself into a well. She 'took knives to bed' so that she could 'destroy' herself (strangely, when she reached for them they had vanished). She stopped eating, 'because it was said to me, if thou dost, thou worshippest the devil'. In one particularly dark moment, she threw herself on the ground, crying, 'Lord, there is no recovery, I shall surely go out like a snuff.' But she saw a light and heard a voice that said 'arise, why liest thou upon thy face, pray and eat, this day is salvation come to thy house.'

During this period, Trapnel resolved 'never to come among the saints again'. But the Seeker principle that an individual could 'find the presence of God in reading and praying' without being a member of a congregation soon seemed to her misguided, so she rejoined her former church fellowship at All Hallows-the-Great. Led by John Simpson, this was 'one of the most radical Baptist congregations in London', so much so that Oliver Cromwell kept it under close surveillance.[8] In 1654 one of his spies attended a meeting, sending back a report that 'the congregation is crowded, the humours boiling', with the preacher echoing the words of Revelation 19:18: 'the time was at hand when they should feed on the flesh of kings and great men.' Whatever the exaggeration of such reports, the authorities had good reason to fear these radicals. Along with other Fifth Monarchists, Anna Trapnel not only expected the imminent arrival of Christ's kingdom but was eager to play her part in overthrowing 'Babylon', or the antichristian principle that to her mind included Cromwell's Protectorate. While some Fifth Monarchists ultimately took part in violent uprisings to inaugurate the reign of the saints, Trapnel's weapon of choice was her voice, raised up – like that of the biblical prophet Habakkuk – as the 'cry of a stone' to sing 'forth Babylon's fall, and the ruin of those which endeavoured to be nurses and rockers to Babylon's brats'.[9] It is perhaps not surprising, then, that she was regarded by the authorities as a 'dangerous seditious person', one 'maliciously intending the peace, tranquillity and felicity of the good people of this commonwealth of England to disturb' and one who threatened to 'raise discord, rebellion and insurrection among the good people of England'.[10]

———

SIXTEEN FIFTY-THREE WAS a rollercoaster year for the Fifth Monarchists. In the spring of that year, Cromwell dismissed the Rump Parliament for being inadequately radical, appointing in its place a Nominated Assembly which included Fifth Monarchist members. Known as the 'Parliament of Saints' (or 'Barebone's Parliament', after one of its members), it raised hopes among radical religious communities that their demands for far-reaching social and legal reforms would finally be met. Despite the best efforts of the Fifth Monarchists, though, Cromwell and others blocked the full implementation of their visionary programme: the national church and the tax system of tithes, along with other detested legal institutions, remained in place. When Anna Trapnel was asked one day in Newgate market what she thought of the recently appointed Parliament, she could only shrug: 'little good should be done to the nation by their sitting,' she believed. It was nevertheless a bitter blow when Cromwell dissolved the Nominated Assembly and was appointed as the quasi-regal Lord Protector in December 1653. Just over a year later, John Rogers, by then a leading Fifth Monarchist, told Cromwell that the controversy was 'now between Christ and you (my Lord), Christ's government and yours'. Reportedly referring to the Protector as 'that great dragon that sits at Whitehall', Rogers accused him of wielding 'absolute power' and of losing sight of his principles: you once promised 'that the poor should be maintained and put to work . . . that we might have no beggar in England', he reminded the 'great man'.[11]

In the aftermath of the dissolution of the 'Parliament of Saints', another Fifth Monarchist, the Welsh preacher Vavasor Powell, also made no secret of his fury at Cromwell's betrayal of the cause. Using a sermon on the book of Daniel to comment on political developments – 'in a most pernicious manner', according to state papers – he asked his audience whether God would 'have Oliver Cromwell or Jesus Christ to reign over us?'[12] Powell was arrested, and in January 1654 was brought before the Council of State. Accompanying him to Whitehall for his hearing, Trapnel was sitting in a side room by a fire when she was 'seized by the Lord' and 'carried forth in a spirit of prayer and singing from noon until night'. Losing all 'her natural strength', she was taken to a room in a nearby inn where she remained for twelve days, eating nothing for the first five days and only a tiny amount each day thereafter. 'Lying in bed with her eyes shut, and her hands seldom seen to move,' she spoke and sang prophecies for hours each day, drawing crowds comprised of 'many eminent persons'.[13]

The event was sensational enough to be reported in newsbooks. One report identified her as 'Hannah, whom some call a prophetess', describing how 'many hundreds' came to see her each day in her trance. Despite her prolonged fast, she was said to look 'well in flesh in her hands and face', seeming 'lusty and strong'. Most of the time she appeared to be asleep but each afternoon she would alternate between praying and singing: her words, said the report, were 'excellent' and 'well placed', although definitely 'not ordinary'. Trapnel divided opinion. Some said that she was under 'a mighty inspiration' while others thought 'her to be of a troubled mind', accusing her of playing to the crowd that was 'flocking to her'.[14] Many simply did not know what to make of her. One witness spoke later of his confused response to her words: believing that she had some form of 'communion with God', he could not bring himself to describe her as a prophet since she seemed to have prior knowledge of the things she declared. But his doubts about her authenticity were dispelled by her extraordinary appearance: she was 'so stiffened in her body that were she not warm one would think her dead', he observed. After fasting for long periods, moreover, she was neither 'weak' nor 'faint'.[15] As had been the case with Sarah Wight, it was the inexplicable strength rather than the bodily weakness of the prophet that most impressed her audience, pointing, it seemed, to a miraculous force at work.

An account of Anna Trapnel's Whitehall prophecies was swiftly published under the title *Strange and Wonderful Newes from White-Hall* (1654). It was clear from the title page that Trapnel's words were aimed at the highest powers in the land, 'the government of the commonwealth of England, Scotland, and Ireland' including 'his Highness the Lord Protector, and the army'. If Cromwell were not 'backslidden, he would be ashamed of his great pomp and revenue, whilst the poor are ready to starve', she stated in *The Cry of a Stone,* published the same year: 'tell him, Lord, thou art come down to have a controversy with him; oh sin will lay thee flat to the earth.' To one of Cromwell's informers, Trapnel's eye-catching performance was part of a treacherous Fifth Monarchist plot. She 'does a world of mischief in London, and would do in the country', he advised the Protector, since they plan to 'print her discourses and hymns, which are desperate against your person . . . and the government', and 'to send her all over England, to proclaim them'. It would be foolish to underestimate the danger she posed, he warned, since 'the vulgar dote on vain prophecies.'[16] Seemingly confirming the truth of this warning, a letter from Cornwall in April 1654 complained that the failure of the authorities to respond when Trapnel 'tranced it at Whitehall' had led to the 'staggering of many a spirit in Cornwall' after she travelled there. Seeking to 'vent her prophecies' from town to town, Trapnel, the informant claimed, was part of a wider plot to 'disaffect the people to the present authority'.[17]

———

ANNA TRAPNEL'S 'MIGHTY visions' conjured up political and military scenes in cinematic detail. She vividly evoked specific events, imaginatively placing herself in the centre of the action with the immediacy of an eye-witness account.[18] In advance of the Battle of Dunbar in 1650, for example, she 'saw [her] self in the fields, and beheld our army, and their General, and [heard] this voice, saying, "Behold Gideon and the lapping ones with him.'" Referring to Cromwell as the biblical figure Gideon, her prophecy not only mapped the battle onto a biblical story but identified herself as a key player in the action. Two nights before Cromwell became Lord Protector, she had a particularly arresting vision. Seeing 'a great darkness in the earth, and a marvellous dust, like a thick smoke ascending upward from the earth', she described strange figures looming out of the dark, a 'great company of cattle' with 'faces and heads like men', echoing the hybrid human–animal forms sometimes seen in biblical visions. Startlingly, the 'foremost' of the bulls had a face 'perfectly like unto Oliver Cromwell's'. The other cattle bowed to him, and he 'leaped up from the earth, with a great kind of joy, that he was their Supreme'. This bull then ran at her, 'and as he was near with his horn to my breast, an arm and a hand clasped me round, a voice said, I will be thy safety.' Suddenly, there was 'a great silence' (recalling the silence in heaven described in the book of Revelation), before 'there broke forth in the earth great fury coming from the clouds', leading to the cattle being 'scattered, and their horns broken, and they tumbled into graves'. Pronouncing God's judgement on Cromwell, Trapnel's vision saturated political developments with apocalyptic significance. It also had the effect of depicting her not only as a persecuted victim but as Cromwell's most significant adversary, the one he ran at first.[19]

If Trapnel saw herself as a prophet, she did not limit this role to being God's messenger but regarded herself as an agent in a cosmic theatre of war, fighting to bring about God's kingdom. 'How has thy servant disputed, declared, remonstrated and appeared in the field against Antichrist,' she declared, 'and how is his language now confounded?' 'Thy servant' ('speaking of herself', the relator clarified) 'must now come forth' and 'thou givest strength unto her . . . to go through with the work'. The prophetic tradition in which she placed herself extended back to the Hebrew prophets. Ezekiel, for instance, was shown a vision of a field of dry bones and was told to prophesy to them. As he did so, the bones came together and were covered in flesh, forming 'an exceeding great army' (Ezekiel 37:2–10), signifying the revival of the 'house of Israel'. Trapnel drew on the language of Ezekiel to articulate her own vision of social and spiritual renewal. 'Oh but can these dry bones live?' she asked, 'Give thy handmaid leave to tell thee that thy children are like dead bones now in the valley, but . . . thou canst make them live, thou canst bring nerves and bones, and knit them together again, let thy servant never be silent till they be brought out of the valley, out of the slimy pit!' Although God would be the one to bring new life, Trapnel regarded herself as playing a vital role in the process: it was her refusal to be silenced, she implied, that would enable God's people to climb 'out of the slimy pit' into which they had fallen.[20]

To Trapnel's mind, then, her prophecies were actively working to establish God's kingdom. God's 'poor and contemptible ones' carry out his 'work . . . in the world', she proclaimed, starting with her songs, which sang a 'passing-bell to those that are in present power'. 'New Jerusalem is coming forth through all this,' she declared, a new world in which social injustice would be righted. Under the 'fifth monarchy', 'the poor beggar that lieth in the street, that knows not where to have a bit of bread, hath nothing but a clothing of tatters, to outward view a very miserable creature', would (as the gospel parable stated) be 'more respected than a rich Dives that goeth in his velvet and diadems of gold every day'. God, after all, preferred 'idiots before the wisdom of the world', and in his kingdom those who were 'counted novices, and shallow fellows, and frantic hand-maids, not fit to stand to speak to the learned' would be God's 'only scribes'. The very existence of her prophecies, published to the nation, indicated that the socially inverted world for which she longed was beginning to be unveiled.[21]

Trapnel therefore saw herself as an agent of revolution. God's voice, she declared,

> speakest with a mighty alarum, and . . . comes forth with much power! Oh, let that voice come forth concerning restoration, and generation-work . . . the prophets of old were willing to look to the Lord, and he sent fiery chariots round about them: Oh, if thine would go forth, who should be able to stand before that wisdom and spirit, by which they speak.

At times, she portrayed herself as a passive vehicle of God's 'mighty' speech: 'Oh, it is for thy sake, and for thy servant's sake, that thy servant is made a voice, a sound, it is a voice within a voice, another's voice, even thy voice through her.' Depicting herself as a 'weak worthless creature, a babe in Christ', she reworked this inferior position into that 'which makes his power the more manifest'. As John Smith noted in his account of prophecy, the genre had always allowed for the possibility of divinely inspired speech, when God's words 'came in abruptly upon' the minds of prophets, captivating them 'by the power of some higher light' and bypassing 'their own understanding'. Trapnel's passive posture during her ecstatic trances suggested this experience, a position that she exploited to stave off gender-based criticisms: 'They will say the spirit of madness and distraction is upon her, and that it is immodesty;

but thou knowest Lord, that it is thy Spirit, for thou hast cast thy servant where she would not, and hast taken her contrary to all her thoughts.'[22] As Smith explained, though, this was not usually the way that prophecy worked. Instead, God generally 'imprinted such a clear copy of his truth upon [prophets] as that it became their own sense, being digested fully into their understandings; so as they were able to deliver and represent it to others as truly as any can paint forth his own thoughts'. In the case of most 'prophetical visions and dreams', 'those words and phrases in which they were audibly expressed to the hearers afterwards or penned down, [were] the prophet's own', as was apparent in the fact that biblical prophets spoke in their own dialects and in a variety of styles.[23] In other words, prophets spoke God's truth but their voices were not bypassed in the process: 'the spirits of the prophets are subject to the prophets' (1 Corinthians 14:32), as Paul had written. Trapnel's prophetic voice, likewise, was not simply 'another's voice', despite what she sometimes claimed. 'I waited for others, and was afraid myself to speak,' she noted, 'until the Spirit came upon me, then I was carried forth to speak beyond my own courage.'[24] If she relied on supernatural sources of courage, she was still the one who was speaking.

Trapnel described herself as a 'poor nothing creature', but she had no hesitation in raising her voice against those in authority: as the literary critic Hilary Hinds observes, beneath Trapnel's 'surface impression of powerlessness' lay 'a strong undercurrent of power'.[25] She compared herself to the biblical prophet Hannah, a woman who continued to speak in public even when she faced slurs on her reputation for doing so. Hannah's message that God 'raiseth the poor out of the dust' (1 Samuel 2:8), as well as her boldness in telling God's enemies that they should 'talk no more so exceeding proudly' (1 Samuel 2:3), chimed strongly with Trapnel. Addressing Cromwell directly in one of her prophecies, she asked 'art thou a rational man, a wise and valiant soldier? How can the commonalty be relieved, and thou hast such great things for thy table? . . . I tell you the Lord God will eclipse your glory, he will put a stammering speech into you, you shall not suck from God's wine-cellars.' For Trapnel, worldly status was irrelevant: 'You will say, do you think to contradict us who are wise, great scholars, and University-men? Yea Lord, thou wilt make a poor silly creature to come out against them, because they have acted so sillily, and thou Lord wilt now take away their glory out of this nation.'[26]

———

ANNA TRAPNEL'S BODY as well as her voice was crucial to her prophetic display.[27] 'Vision! The body crumbles before it, and becomes weak,' she proclaimed. As we saw in relation to Sarah Wight, this stance aligned the seventeenth-century prophet with her biblical forebears: Jeremiah's bones shook, for example, and he was physically 'overcome because of the Lord, and because of the words of his holiness' (Jeremiah 23:9). To the relator of Trapnel's prophecies, the immobility of her body testified to the truth of her inspiration: 'the effects of a spirit caught up in the visions of God did abundantly appear in the fixedness, and immovableness of her speech in prayer, but more especially in her songs . . . [she] seemed to us to be as one whose ears and eyes were locked up, that all was to her as a perfect silence.' People 'say these are convulsion-fits, and sickness, and diseases that make thy handmaid to be in weakness,' acknowledged Trapnel, 'but oh they know not the pouring forth of thy Spirit, for that makes the body to crumble, and weakens nature'. The overcoming of her body, she declared, was a sign of what was to come for society as a whole: 'In these extraordinary workings thou intends to show what is coming forth hereafter; something is a coming forth ... and oh how does thy handmaid bless thee!'[28]

Trapnel fully inhabited the role of a prophet, to the extent that her life as a whole was lived as a prophetic performance. Asked by members of her church to travel to Cornwall to spread her message more widely, for instance, she presented the journey from the moment it was suggested – or instigated by the 'secret whisperings of the Spirit' – until it was completed in prophetically charged terms. Riding along in her coach, 'singing much of the creation excellencies, as trees, grass, and several plants, and corn grew as I went by', she 'rode through towns' while simultaneously being lost in a visionary experience, one that made her oblivious to 'the rattling of the coach' and incapable 'of outward sayings or doings'. Just as her fasting body testified to her prophetic calling through its miraculous strength, her travelling body demonstrated the 'extraordinary' presence of God, who not only preserved her in a dangerous expedition but 'greatly ravished [her] soul' in the process. The journey itself – of which she was given a vision before she set off, complete with the songs that she would sing – functioned as a revelation in which everything carried symbolic meaning: the rattling of the coach (when she was aware of it) spoke of 'the tottering, shaking condition of clergy-function', the judge who sat alongside her represented 'that blessed time that the saints should judge the earth', and the 'dangerous rocky places' over which she journeyed signified 'my rock, Christ'. The thirteen-day trip was presented as one long 'extraordinary' outpouring of the

Spirit, with Trapnel experiencing the 'breakings forth of the light of [God's] countenance and communications' every step of the way.[29]

The triumphant Trapnel who arrived in Cornwall in March 1654 was nevertheless quickly put to the test. Greeted with dark suspicion by some, she found herself among those who 'did not care for [her] company' and spoke disparagingly about 'visions'. For the next two days, regardless, she burned with the 'Spirit's flame', lying in bed and singing. When she later went for dinner in Truro with a Mrs Hill, many flocked to see her, some 'out of goodwill', others 'to gaze' in fascination and to try to catch her out. The authorities moved swiftly. Believing her words to be seditious, they issued a warrant for her arrest. Chanting 'a witch, a witch' as they climbed the stairs to her bedroom, they found Trapnel in a trance, oblivious. Mockingly pinching her nose and pulling the pillow out from under her head, their inability to get a reaction made them threaten to send for the 'witch-tryer of that town . . . with her great pin which she used to thrust into witches'.[30] Walking to the courthouse the next day surrounded by rough crowds who pulled 'wry-faces' at her, Trapnel likened herself to Jesus, who was equally 'derided' on the way to his trial. At the courthouse she was confronted not only by magistrates and clergymen but by the intimidating witch-trying woman, who 'looked steadfastly in [her] face'. Trapnel was nevertheless uncowed, so much so that her enemies later accused her of exhibiting a 'carnal boldness'. Her quick-witted responses electrified the crowded courtroom. Given the widespread rumours that she was a witch, many believed that she would be unable to speak in the presence of magistrates. But Trapnel was not struck dumb. When asked why she had travelled to Cornwall, she replied, 'Why might

Published by J. Caulfield. 1823.

HANNAH TRAPNEL,

a Quaker, and pretended Prophetess.

(From a scarce Print by Gaywood)

For an account of this extraordinary woman, see, Heath's Chronicle, Cromwelliana & the High Court of Justice.

Richard Gaywood, *Hannah Trapnel, a Quaker and Pretended Prophetess*, 1823, engraving.

not I come here? I am a single person, and why may I not be with my friends anywhere?' 'I understand you are not married,' probed a magistrate, making it sound like an accusation, but she turned the tables on him: 'Then having no hinderance,' she replied, 'why may not I go where I please, if the Lord so will?' Quizzed about her 'extraordinary' spiritual impulses, she refused to be drawn: 'when you are capable [of] extraordinary impulses of spirit,' she remarked contemptuously, 'I will tell you.' Such 'bold' speech threw the court into confusion. Everyone began to speak at once, bringing to a chaotic conclusion the proceedings against one said to be a 'frenzy-headed creature', of 'devilish mind, and wicked imaginations'.[31]

Judged to be a threat to national security, Trapnel was sent back to London and thrown into Bridewell prison. Arriving close to midnight, she was greeted by the matron, who quickly categorized her as another one of the 'ranting sluts' under her watch. Trapnel was given a large room, but a sewer ran beneath its small window, making it smell 'grievously'. Highly sensitive to sensory experiences, she found the stench even more unbearable than the rats that ran under her bed as noisily as 'cats and dogs'. Locked in squalor as a shameful 'Bridewell bird', she wondered what her mother would think of her ending up in such a hole. For the first time, she wondered if she could still believe that Christ would be 'king and governor in the earth'. Brought low by a conspiracy of 'rulers and clergy', the stage of prophecy seemed to have been replaced by 'the world's stage of reports and rumours'. Made into 'the world's wonder, and gazing stock', she had to suffer the shame of people assuming she was 'some ill-shaped creature' rather than 'a woman like others that were modest and civil'. She became ill, a sickness she attributed to the 'hard damp bed' and 'cold sheets' in her cell. But she remembered Christ's sufferings and decided that God had not sent her to Bridewell to die but to 'declare the works of the Lord'. She therefore continued to write (or perhaps to dictate her words to another), declaring herself to be a respectable, tax-paying citizen. I am 'Anna Trapnel and no vagabond, nor runagate person', she insisted: 'though I have and may sometimes live in the city, and sometimes in the country, as yourselves do, and why should I be accounted a vagabond more than you?' Nor was she a 'whore', despite what they said about her.[32]

After eight weeks, Trapnel was freed. She continued to travel. Returning to Cornwall the following year, she remained outspoken, refusing to answer the questions posed to her by a trooper because 'thy Lord Protector we own not; thou art of the army of the Beast.' Summoned before the Governor of Pendennis, she refused to attend, falling into a trance.[33] Her lengthy verse prophecies, 'delivered to a gathering of companions in 1657 and 1658', reveal that her animosity to the Lord Protector remained undimmed: the 'voice and Spirit hath made a league/ Against Cromwell and his men,' she sang, 'never to leave its witness till/ It hath broken all of them.'[34]

———

TRAPNEL'S VISIONS COMBINE sharp political commentary with a powerful articulation of the experience of transcendence: 'thou hast taken [thy handmaid] up into thy Mount, who can keep in the rushing wind? Who can bind the influences of the Heavenly Orion, who can stop thy Spirit?' The spiritual and political aspects of her words are not in tension with each other but together stem from her conviction that God's kingdom is in the process of being unveiled on earth. God has provided 'a ladder to the earth', she believes, one capable of gathering up 'our nature to the divine'. If she can ascend to God – 'oh it is good to walk up that ladder, where there is such precious air, and such sparkling stars' – the heavenly can also descend to earth, as she testifies through her descriptions of the world around her, luminous with God. 'O Spirit thou art sweetly seen/ In thy creating hour,' she sings: 'In all things that here come forth/ In every plant and flower;/ O Spirit it sparkles and shines.'[35]

Echoing the sentiments of Andrew Marvell's poem 'The Garden', in which the narrator exults in the experience of having 'a green thought in a green shade', and anticipating both Jane Lead and the English Romantic poets, who would later also praise the inspiration to be found in nature, Trapnel found gardens particularly conducive to spiritual experiences. When she first arrived in Cornwall, she went for a solitary walk only to feel her heart being 'melted' as she came 'under divine speakings in the garden': 'as I thus walked alone in the garden, I had such sweetness from the Lord ... such cordials from the Lord, that I could have walked many hours in that garden.' Drawing on the imagery of the Song of Songs, where the 'spouse', often understood to represent Christ's bride, the Church, is likened to 'a garden enclosed', as well as gospel accounts of Mary's encounter with the risen Jesus in a garden, Trapnel, as always, experienced the events of her life – including garden walks – through the lens of the Bible.[36] Rather than distracting her from the natural world, however, her perception of the spiritual significance of her surroundings generated an ecstatic encounter not just with the Spirit of God but with nature too. Shortly before her journey to Cornwall, she took an evening walk 'in a curious garden, where I saw the pleasant trees, and plants, and walks, and fishponds, and hearing the birds' pleasant notes, all this begat such a harmonious apprehension of God in my heart, that I began to sing forth his praises, and continued [until] it was late in the evening'. Her 'communion' with God not only took place in a garden but was generated by an intense focus on nature, which spoke to her of God.[37]

In her hypnotic hymn-poems, sung in 1657–8, Trapnel again rhapsodizes about gardens, this time focusing on the garden that was 'prepared/ For the sweet crucified Son,/ A place where he delighted in/ Lillies to walk among.' This 'rich garden ... all complete about' was 'well enclosed',

> That no swines might there rent or tear
> Where lay the Sharon rose.
> A garden enclosed for Christ's body
> That no Bulls of Bashan might tear,
> Nor any goring may come in,
> Or rending there appear.
> A garden enclosed for the body
> Of our Saviour dear.
> Whom in gardens so loved to walk
> And always to appear.

While the image of the enclosed garden from the Song of Songs evokes notions of female chastity, Trapnel also associates the walled garden with safety. In one of her earlier visions she had almost been gored by a bull with the face of Cromwell, but here in the fragrant garden where Christ was buried – and where he would subsequently speak to the woman he had chosen to deliver his message – there were no such violent intruders.

This theme of the garden as a haven from the violence of seventeenth-century England – a theme also prominent in Marvell's poetry – appears elsewhere in her prophetic speech. God will hide his people in a nest at the top of a 'high tree', she sings, 'where none shall go and pluck'. They will be 'so closed in',

> That none can scar, nor them afflict;
> No musket shot can come.
> There is not any can draw their spears
> Or at all shoot their cannon.
> Though nests in trees may shaken be
> Yet thine shall e'er remain;
> They rest and nest with Jesus Christ,
> His hand shall them sustain.[38]

As is often the case in Trapnel's multi-layered visions, the biblical, the visionary and the contemporary fuse together in a single image in which the realities of her world are simultaneously brought into focus and transcended. Resting and nesting in a tree with Christ, the saints are removed from the dangerous realm of political and military conflict that at the same time never disappears from view.

Anna Trapnel's Report and Plea (1654), an account of her first visit to Cornwall, culminates in an extraordinary visionary account of the 'lovely land' promised in the new kingdom that Trapnel could glimpse just over the horizon. Her vision of the glorious future awaiting the saints bursts forth in an extended passage hinging on the metaphor of God and his blessings as life-giving water. Taking a biblical image and infusing it with details drawn from seventeenth-century London – a place of dirty swamps as well as the busy river Thames – Trapnel

concludes her work with a sensual stream of consciousness as
fluid and shifting as her central image:

Unto such will the glorious Lord be a place of broad
rivers, not a narrow channel, nor a marshy ditch, where
the flags and rushes cover the water springs, nor a narrow
winding creek, where boats cannot pass along, neither is
it shallow, but deep and broad, a place of broad rivers and
streams, it's indeed an ocean, it comprehends all rivers,
and streams, and this may be said of it, oh the height
and depth, length and breadth, these are rivers that the
waters rise up to the ankles, yea to the knees, and so
to the loins, and at length they become a flowing high
spring, that runs over banks, and fills the meadows, and
Ezekiel gives a report of these high spring waters in his
prophecy, it's good to be dipped or plunged in this Jordan
river which takes away all deformity . . . and it's a com-
forting refreshing river, this is water of life, it recovers
the dying vitals, and fainting spirits, the which none of
men's strong liquors of arts and sciences can do, neither
can any compounded water of human invention be so
effectual, though they [distil] it in the alembic of brain-
study, drawing it through the long pipe of curious witty
phrases, yet such liquors will soon lose their spirits, but
as for the water that the soul draws out of the well of salvation, through faith's bucket which retains the scent and
fragrant smell, and operative nature, and the soul swims
in the broad rivers that are promised Zion, which rivers
will admit no galley with oars to row therein, no troub-
lers shall come there, none of men's gallantry nor ships
of merchandise shall sail there, no Turkish, nor English

galley of power and strength and device managed with
soldier oars shall appear to take the free-born captive,
that river will presently sink such gallies and oars too,
and if so be gallant Council ships, and great numerous
Parliament ships, which are made of wood, and pitch,
and rosin, and tar, and oakum, such stuff will burn to
ashes when the fire comes . . . it's not the clergy nails
that can fasten such ships together and make them sail,
which are heavy lumpish bottoms, that have no nimble
swift motion at all, whereby to do service for King Jesus
. . . But the broad river is preparing, it's making its path
through all opposition, and its ships are all making ready
and preparing to swim: The great Shipwright, I speak
this with reverence and holy awe of God, and say that the
great artificial Shipwright, and carpenter's son . . . which
was the glorious Messiah, this mighty God is fitting his
ships for this time.[39]

Full of yearning for the restorative 'broad rivers' in which the
soul can 'swim', an image of healing and cleansing as well as
freedom and possibility, the passage takes the familiar image
of the water of life and charges it with prophetic and revolutionary power. Characterized by oceanic abundance, the 'broad
rivers' of God's kingdom are a riposte to all that is 'narrow' and
'marshy'. No longer suffering lack and obstruction, the people
of God will burst through into a land of plenty. The 'refreshing' nature of this river, moreover, distinguishes it from the
'compounded' and implicitly polluted 'water of human invention'. Setting the human, the artificial and the cerebral against
the divine, the natural and the sensual, the former is shown
to be a poor substitute for the fragranced waters of God. The

'broad rivers', meanwhile, not only refuse to harbour violence in the forms of galley ships, but exclude 'ships of merchandise'. Gleefully imagining the sinking of such ships and all that they represent, Trapnel also condemns the 'gallant Council ships, and great numerous Parliament ships', equally shown to be unfit for purpose and therefore to be consumed with the fire of God's judgement. As the apocalyptic merges seamlessly with the everyday world of contemporary London, a world in which her father had been a shipwright, Trapnel finally envisages the only vessels left afloat as those crafted by the 'great Shipwright', perfectly suited 'for this time'.

This passage exhibits the imaginative power of Trapnel's prophetic writing, in which the ancient, the biblical, the local and the contemporary fuse to construct a visionary world radiant with alternative possibilities. Deliberately resisting the narrow logic of reason along with what she regarded with contempt as the death-dealing rhetoric of the highly educated, her free-flowing visionary language, piling layer after layer of meaning onto words in sentences that stretch and contort into new forms of expression, begins to bring into being the radically reimagined world for which she yearned.[40] Mocked, feared and imprisoned for the potentially revolutionary consequences of what she had to say – as well as the startling way in which she said it – Anna Trapnel was undaunted. It would take more than 'fierce looks' and 'deep speech gathered up and fetched from both Cambridge and Oxford Universities' to 'affright the Lord's flock', she remarked: 'though they stammer, they shall be understood.' And so 'to those who say it is but pity but I should be hanged, and that would commend a whip to my back, and to all base terms and names, and to Bridewell usage too, I will write defiance.'[41]

Part Three:
'She-Preachers'

6

Elizabeth Attaway

Silly men and women may see more into the mystery of
Christ, than you, for . . . Mary and Susanna (silly women, as
you would be ready to call them, if they were here now) these
knew more of the Messiah, than all the learned priests.
Priscilla Cotton and Mary Cole, 1655

In whomsoever the Spirit stands up and speaks, that person
for that time is a minister, a true minister. The Spirit doth
not regard sexes, the Spirit regards not age, learned or
unlearned. 'Tis not age, nor sex, nor any major part can
minister Spirit, but whom the Spirit pleases.
Christopher Goad, 1653

God hath put no such difference between the male and
female as men would make . . . Those that speak against the
power of the Lord, and the Spirit of the Lord speaking in
a woman, simply by reason of her sex, or because she is a
woman, not regarding the Seed, and Spirit, and power that
speaks in her; such speak against Christ, and his church . . .
Doth the church only consist of men? You that deny
women's speaking, answer; doth it not consist of women
as well as men?
Margaret Fell, 1666

"What, a woman speak!' spluttered the judge when Hester Biddle was brought before him in 1662, having been caught in the act of speaking at an illegal Quaker meeting.[1] Others on the bench shared his incredulity, claiming never to have heard of such a thing before. Almost beyond the limits of credulity, the idea of a woman preaching was such a shocking inversion of the 'natural' order to many in seventeenth-century England that its barest mention demanded the heavy use of exclamation marks. The Presbyterian minister Thomas Hall, for instance, demolished the ridiculous notion that anyone with the necessary skills could preach with the observation that 'if bare gifts were sufficient to make a minister, how many women in this kingdom (who are forbidden preaching yet) would be preachers!' Readily acknowledging that 'gifted women ... have better gifts than many' male preachers, Hall insisted that 'gifts, abilities and endowments both of life and learning' were irrelevant if an individual had not been granted 'power and authority from the church to exercise those gifts'. And given that Eve took it upon herself 'to be a teacher' of Adam before becoming a 'seducer' who 'undid all her posterity', it was not surprising, to his mind, that all women had been 'suspended from public teaching for ever'. No matter how talented a speaker she might be, nothing could make it acceptable for a woman to have 'Peter's keys jingling at her girdle'.

If Hall was scandalized by the very idea of a woman preaching, the insolent intruders against whom he was seeking to 'guard' the pulpit in 1651 were not just female. His immediate targets were some male lay preachers he had discovered in Henley-in-Arden, Warwickshire. Dripping with contempt, he described them as a 'nailer-public-preacher', a 'baker-preacher', a 'plowwright-public-preacher', a 'weaver-preacher' and a 'baker's boy public-preacher', just some of the 'artificers, soldiers, women etc' who 'have turned preachers'. They were members of those 'sects now abroad, Ranters, Seekers, Shakers, Quakers, and now Creepers', because – like rodents – they were apt to 'creep' unwanted into pulpits: "tis for wolves and false prophets to be self-called, and to come of their own accord.' If we allow self-appointed preachers, then 'farewell magistrates, ministers, judges, parliaments etc'. 'Open up one gap in the hedge, and way is made for all the wild beasts to enter,' he added grimly in the margin. All must keep to their appointed place: 'superiors must govern, inferiors obey and be governed: ministers must study and preach, people must hear and obey.'[2]

Hall nevertheless felt himself to be swimming against the tide. Just recently in his own Warwickshire parish of King's Norton, three sermons had been given in a house 'by a long cutler, a nailer and a miller', he lamented, while his own – suitably authorized – sermons were being rudely interrupted on a regular basis, perhaps by the very same people. Even the former chapel of Queen Henrietta Maria in Somerset House – stripped of its altar and other 'idolatrous' trappings by order of the House of Commons – had been overtaken by noisy 'Anabaptists, Quakers, and other sects', many of whom were preaching revolution, according to their opponents.[3] In April 1653 it was reported, for example, that a young glazier preaching there had informed the congregation that they would soon see 'destruction fall on the Parliament'. Attesting to the chaos surrounding such sermons, he had apparently been interrupted by a woman who asked, 'why do you wear cuffs? Neither our Lord nor his disciples ever taught in cuffs.'[4] A few months later, another hostile report claimed that an 'audacious virago, a feminine tub-preacher ... held forth for almost two hours' in the chapel, apparently thumping both a Bible and the pulpit cushions for emphasis.[5] The woman, named in a contemporary newsbook as Anne Pool, was mockingly said to have preached on Isaiah 8:1 – 'thou shalt write with the pen of a man.'[6] If Hall had sought metaphorically to guard the pulpit against unwanted intruders, such guards were also literally put in place: 'it is said there will be a guard the next Lord's day,' noted a report on Pool's sermon, 'and so for time to come to prevent such disturbances.'[7]

The heresy-hunter Thomas Edwards, as we would expect, despaired at these developments. 'What swarms are there of all sorts of illiterate mechanic preachers, yea of women and boy preachers!' he exclaimed in 1646. Appalled by the 'women-preachers in our times, who keep constant lectures, preaching weekly to many men and women', he identified cases in Hertfordshire, where 'some women-preachers . . . expound Scriptures in houses and preach upon texts,' while in Kent there was 'a woman preacher (one at least if not more)' who reportedly also officiated at communion.[8] In the following year, the author of *Tub-preachers Overturn'd . . . shewing the vanity, folly, madness of the . . . lay illiterate men and women, to usurp the ministry and audaciously vent their own hereticall opinions* (1647) demanded that the 'independent illiterate party' explain why they were intruding themselves 'into our pulpits, to infect or touch our congregations with your leprous doctrines'. 'I'll publish to the world your illiterate, mechanic, nonsensical cobbled-fustian-tubbers, men and women,' he declared.[9] Likened to insects, diseases and wild beasts – seen as those who crept, intruded, swarmed and infected – 'illiterate' preachers, both male and female, seemed to these horrified observers to be cropping up everywhere. Where would it all end?

A
SVVARME
OF
SECTARIES, AND
SCHISMATIQVES:

Wherein is difcovered the ftrange prea-
ching(or prating) of fuch as are by their trades
Coblers, Tinkers, Pedlers, Weavers, Sow-
gelders, and Chymney-Sweepers.

By John Taylor.

The Cobler preaches, and his Audience are
As wife as Mofſe was, when he caught his Mare.

Printed luckily, and may be read unhappily, betwixt
hawke and buzzard, 1641.

Title page of John Taylor, *A Swarm of Sectaries, and Schismatiques* (1641).

To William Walwyn, however, defending the gathered churches from Edwards's attacks in 1646,

> a plain discreet man in a private house, or field, in his ordinary apparel, speaking to plain people (like himself) such things as he conceived requisite for their knowledge out of the word of God, doth as much (if not more) resemble the way of Christ and the manner of the apostles, as a learned man in a carved pulpit, in his neat and black formalities, in a stately, high, and stone-built church, speaking to an audience, much more glorious and richly clad than most Christians mentioned in Scripture.

And to the Baptist Thomas Collier – himself maligned by Edwards as 'a mechanical fellow' – attempts by the religious establishment to 'guard' the pulpit from so-called intruders were blatantly self-interested. You speak 'as if it were a reproach and scandal for a nailer, a baker, a plowwright, and a weaver to preach the gospel', he retorted to Hall. Yet if you were to consult the Bible, you would find it hard to discover an example of God choosing those who have been 'bred up idly all the days of their life . . . as the priests of our times have been'. Defenders of the establishment such as Hall would only allow 'idlers' into the pulpit, 'drones that never knew what it was to live lawfully in the world, by a particular calling'. Such ministers were only interested in feeding 'themselves with the fat', he claimed: 'Oh saith the priest, but we will have no prophets nor preachers but ourselves, it's a profitable trade . . . but if you suffer mechanic fellows, men of trades and particular callings to preach, we lose all, they will tell the truth to the people.' The universities who trained ministers were similarly self-interested, argued William

Dell in 1653. 'If the unction of the Spirit alone be sufficient for the ministry', he preached in Cambridge, the universities will say,

> what need is there then of our philosophy, and of our arts and sciences to the ministry of the New Testament? . . . And what need is there of our scarlet and tippets? And what need is there of our hoods and caps? . . . I answer, no need at all, as to Christ's kingdom, and the ministry of that. For it is one of the grossest errors that ever reigned under Antichrist's kingdom, to affirm that universities are the fountain of the ministers of the gospel, which do only proceed out of Christ's stock.[10]

In the war of words over preaching that broke out in mid-seventeenth-century England, then, far more was at stake than the quality of sermons. Some regarded lay preaching as nothing short of a devilish threat to all that was sacred: 'When women preach, and cobblers pray/ The fiends in hell make holiday,' quipped the author of *Lucifer's Lacky* (1641).[11] To radical Protestants, on the other hand, their opponents were the ones mired in error, intent on preserving a corrupt social order that thrived on inequality.

————

WITHIN SUCH DEBATES, women occupied an uneasy position. The anonymous tract *A Discovery of Six Women-Preachers* (1641) indicated that women were preaching in and beyond London by the early 1640s, but the women named and shamed in this pamphlet were apparently preaching only to private female audiences. Even so, the author of the tract found their preaching so discordantly outrageous that he pronounced that

Title page of
*A Discovery of Six
Women-Preachers,
in Middlesex, Kent,
Cambridge, and
Salisbury* (1641).

A
DISCOVERY
OF
Six Women-Preachers, in *Middlesex*,
Kent, *Cambridge*, and Salisbury.
WITH
A Relation of their Names, Manners,
Life, and Doctrine.

Their Names.
{ *Anne Hempstall.* } { *Ioane Banford.* } { *Eliz. Bantroft.* }
{ *Mary Bilbrow.* } { *Susan May.* } { *Arabella Thomas.* }

Printed, 1641.

they must have graduated from the 'university' of 'Bedlam or Bridewell'. Published a few years later, *A Spirit Moving in the Women-Preachers* (1645) identified an even more threatening phenomenon. Not only were women preaching, but 'shallow, weak, ignorant preaching sisters' had 'lately advanced themselves with vain-glorious arrogance to preach' in public to 'mixed congregations of men and women'. These women were unnatural 'sirens' who were 'wearing the breeches', leading 'their husbands by the nose, which way they please'. Operating as 'bold . . . intruders in this sacred work of preaching', they were a 'brazen-faced, strange, new feminine brood', who were 'transgressing the rules of nature, majesty, divinity, discretion, civility'.[12]

The female preacher, a figure who monstrously – even hellishly – refused to keep to her divinely appointed place of subordination, was to some the very embodiment of the world turned upside down.[13] As such, she was a useful symbol of the social as well as the religious threat posed by the radical sects, evidence of their reckless undermining of established order. John Taylor diagnosed 'the dangerous disease of feminine divinity' as one of the 'diseases of the times', complaining in 1642 that it 'is frequently heard in every conventicle', where women 'tattle louder than they used to do at markets'. Sectarians 'would reform the church', he noted, 'and under that pretence deform it', establishing an order in which women 'wear the breeches, and men petticoats'.[14]

Despite their fierce defence of lay preaching, however – and despite widespread perceptions of the emancipated role of women within their meetings – most radical religious sects in seventeenth-century England did not allow women to preach at their meetings. Both the Baptist Thomas Collier and the Independent Thomas Goodwin reiterated the principle that 'women are not permitted to speak in the church,' although Collier qualified this statement elsewhere by declaring that 'women are not altogether forbidden' to speak in meetings but 'may prophesy by permission'.[15] Even in John Rogers's unusually egalitarian Independent congregation in Dublin, where women were vocal in matters of church business, they remained prohibited from preaching. For these groups, Paul's instruction to early Christian communities such as the Corinthians that their women 'must keep silence in the churches, for it is not permitted unto them to speak' (1 Corinthians 14:34) continued to apply.

The Quakers, however, took a very different line. For them, biblical injunctions against women's preaching were not applicable to female Friends who were giving voice to the light within. The Quaker minister Richard Farnworth argued in *A Woman Forbidden to Speak in the Church* (1654) that the 'woman' commanded by Paul to keep silent should be understood allegorically as the 'wisdom of the flesh'. It was the 'carnal part' of both men and women, the 'wisdom . . . gathered out of books and studies', that needed to be quiet so that the voice of the Spirit could speak freely through both men and women. While the 'ignorance' of uneducated women and men was one of the main reasons they were mocked as preachers, Farnworth turned this lack of 'carnal wisdom' into a key justification for the spiritual value of their speech. God 'chooseth the weak things of this world', he reminded his readers: if the 'woman is counted the weaker vessel', then God is more able to fill 'that vessel full of his wisdom'. In a stunning inversion, it was the 'proud priests', those who spoke 'divinations of their own brains, and not from the mouth of the Lord', who were 'not permitted to speak in the church'. Women, on the other hand, were God's ideal mouthpieces.[16]

Quaker women put forward similar arguments, culminating in Margaret Fell's *Women's Speaking Justified, Proved, and Allowed of by the Scriptures* (1666). Writing in 1655 from their cells in Exeter gaol, Priscilla Cotton and Mary Cole echoed Farnworth's allegorical interpretation of the biblical texts that appeared to ban women from speaking in church. In spiritual meetings there was only room for the voice of God, they insisted: the 'woman' told to keep silent by Paul referred to a person of either sex speaking on his or her own terms rather than under the inspiration of the Holy Spirit. To seek to silence women – or men – who spoke in the Spirit, however, was akin to blasphemy.[17]

Katharine Evans's *A Brief Discovery of God's Eternal Truth* (1663), written from her cell in the Inquisitor's Palace in Malta, made a similar case. Those who seek to 'limit the Spirit of God' attempt to 'make the people believe none ought to speak in the name of Christ, but the wise and the learned', she wrote, 'but Christ doth ordain his ministers, and gives them gifts both male and female'. If 'Paul would not permit of a woman to speak in the church', neither do the Quakers, she continued, for they do not listen to either a woman or a 'man that is born of a woman'; that is, to any unspiritual person. But any person who is 'born of God' may 'speak freely', for 'every word that proceeded out of their mouths, is as the words of God's own mouth, which cannot be altered nor changed to all eternity; for such are the vessels that hold the heavenly treasures.'[18]

While these pamphlets maintain an association between the female and the sinful realm of the 'flesh', the Quakers by this means found a way to sidestep the biblical injunction against women preaching, neutralizing its effect on the words and actions of female Friends. The light within, they insisted, operated without regard for the sex, social rank or education of the individual, enabling any who were attuned to this light to speak with the authority of the divine 'seed' that lay within all human beings. The fact that Quaker women were so often writing defences of their right to preach while looking at the walls of prison cells nevertheless speaks for itself in terms of how their radical re-evaluation of supposedly 'natural' hierarchies was viewed by church and state authorities.

When the Quaker George Keith used an exclamation mark in relation to women preaching, though, it was to strike a note of celebration rather than outrage. 'Behold a woman preacher!' he declared in his pamphlet, *The woman preacher of Samaria;*

a better preacher, and more sufficiently qualified to preach than any of the men-preachers of the man-made-ministry in these three nations (1674). Drawing on the biblical account of the woman of Samaria (John 4:7–39), Keith held her up as 'an example unto you all' of 'how to preach'. 'Oh for shame let alone your crying out against women-preachers,' he exclaimed, 'while you are short, exceedingly short of this woman preacher of Samaria.' Ordained ministers speak 'dry, dead, and barren stuff . . . that they have scraped and gathered together out of so many old and worm-eaten authors', he claimed, while she 'spoke what freely rose in her heart, as the Lord taught her'. As a result, he would far 'rather hear this woman of Samaria than hear them'. She did not go to university and was not ordained by a 'company of men' but had the advantage of being 'taught Christ, by Christ himself'. The Samaritans to whom she preached had the good sense not to 'despise her because she was a woman, they did not say unto her (as many now say) thou art a woman, thou should not preach . . . They did not say unto her, go home to your wheel, and your spinning, and such like words, as men commonly now say to women Friends.'[19]

Often – although not always – enjoying the support of their community, Quaker women spoke out boldly, declaring what they believed to be the truth of the light within. While women in other radical religious groups were not so openly encouraged to preach within their communities, however, this did not necessarily prevent them from doing so. And so we turn to the story of perhaps the first and certainly the most notorious public female preacher of the era, Elizabeth Attaway, a London 'lace-woman', sometime Baptist and the so-called 'mistress of all the she-preachers'.[20]

Rembrandt van Rijn, *Christ and the Woman of Samaria among Ruins*, 1634, etching.

IN THE DEEPENING gloom of the late afternoon on Tuesday, 9 December 1645, a sizeable group of people made their way to Bell Alley, Coleman Street, London. Cramming their way into a meeting place, the congregation could barely believe what they were about to witness. Before long, a door to an inner room opened and three women emerged. They were an odd-looking group. One of them – the wife of a major – was dressed elaborately, adorned with a lavish hood, a hanging watch and a pearl necklace. The other two women wore much plainer clothes. All three were clutching Bibles. Making their way across the room to a table, the women took up their positions. But it was not the ornately dressed woman who took the central place. Instead, Elizabeth Attaway, a woman who made a living selling lace in Cheapside, remained on her feet as the other two women sat down. Darting a glance at the smartly dressed woman sitting by her side, Attaway suddenly stepped back, asking her if she would like to say a few words. Blushing, the major's wife shook her head, 'pleading her weakness' and refusing to stand even when Attaway praised 'her gifts and great abilities'. Trying and failing once more to get the other woman to speak, Attaway finally turned back to the congregation. Apologizing that she was 'somewhat indisposed in body, and unfit for this work', she asked if anyone else would like to speak to the meeting. No one responded.

After a short pause, Elizabeth Attaway began to speak. Her supposed incapacity forgotten, she declared that 'those days were come' that had been prophesied in the Bible, when 'God would pour out of his Spirit upon the handmaidens, and they should prophesy.' Abandoning any show of timidity, she prayed for 'almost half an hour' before beginning her sermon, a detailed exposition of John 14:15, 'If ye love me, keep my commandments.' Having preached for 45 minutes, she followed the practice of the General Baptist church of which she had probably been a member by giving the congregation the opportunity to respond. Although 'there was a great company both of men and women' present, no one ventured to speak.

Mustering her courage, the well-dressed woman finally stood up, intending to expand on the 'matter her sister had handled'. But she mumbled her words, causing people in the audience to call for her to 'speak out' until she became so 'disturbed and confounded', 'jumbling' her words in confusion, that she gave up in defeat. Enraged by those who had interrupted her 'sister', Attaway glared at the congregation with 'an angry bold countenance'. 'Setting her face against' the hecklers, she launched into a prayer, calling on God to deal with those 'who despised his ambassadors, and ministers that he had sent into the world to reconcile the world'. As the crowd grumbled their disagreement, she called on God to 'send some visible judgement from heaven upon them'. 'Stop her mouth,' they shouted, forcing Attaway to sit down. 'In brief,' concluded the observer, 'there was such laughing, confusion, and disorder at the meeting that he never saw the like.'[21]

This, then, is the hostile account of a mid-week public sermon by Elizabeth Attaway, perhaps the first female public preacher in seventeenth-century England. Historians have associated Attaway with Thomas Lambe's General Baptist church, a congregation that met in Bell Alley, Coleman Street, leading some to assume that women were free to preach within this congregation.[22] According to Edwards, 'strange things' were done at this church, which attracted a young crowd: 'youths and wenches flock thither', he observed, 'and all of them preach universal redemption'. But Edwards's list of those who spoke at the church, as Jason Kerr points out, identified only men: mainly 'mechanics', they included a twenty-year-old weaver and the soap-boiler Lambe. Noisy and chaotic, the church meetings commonly saw sermons interrupted by members of the congregation, leading to heated disputes on matters of doctrine. 'The members of this church are generally loose,' claimed Edwards, noting that 'many of them turn Seekers.'[23] Thomas Comber in fact later included 'Mrs Attaway the woman-preacher' in the passage on Seekers in his pamphlet.[24] While the lively meetings at which Elizabeth Attaway preached resembled the Baptist meetings described by Edwards, it therefore seems likely, as Kerr argues, that Attaway was 'a pioneering woman preacher' who struck out on her own, taking the initiative to set up breakaway public meetings in which she delivered her unorthodox teachings.[25]

Related with relish by Edwards as evidence of the 'horror and disorder' caused by sectarians, the account of the chaos surrounding Attaway's sermon that day in December must of course be taken with a pinch of salt: Edwards's ever-growing volume of radical religious 'errors' aimed to put his targets in the worst light possible. Yet this biased account perhaps captures something of the awkwardness experienced by the women who were the first of their sex to preach publicly before mixed-sex congregations. Whatever the heartfelt belief of religious radicals in the levelling nature of God's Spirit, they lived in a society in which hierarchies of gender as well as social rank were deeply entrenched, and their awareness of these structures was perhaps evident in the less-than-smooth opening to the meeting, when the women briefly floundered and Attaway apparently struggled to take the floor from the woman sitting by her side.[26]

Writing a few years later in 1651, Mary Cary spoke mov-
ingly of some of the difficulties – internal as well as external
– faced by women in this era. Despite having 'received the
Spirit', she observed, they often remained 'unable to prophesy'. Having 'tasted of the sweetness of the Spirit', they were
'longing for more' but were 'generally very unable to communicate with others, though they would do it many times in their
families, among their children and servants'. In situations where
they felt comfortable taking a lead, they would speak freely.
But when it came to 'communicating to others', 'sometimes
some sprinklings [came] from them, yet at other times they
[found] themselves dry and barren.' Perhaps shedding light
on the experiences of Attaway and her fellow preachers, Cary
highlights the psychological as well as the social and religious
barriers that held women back from speaking freely in public.
Cary's prediction that the 'time is coming' when everyone –
'learned, or unlearned', 'male, or female' – will be 'a publisher
of the gospel' looked forward to an era when women would not
only experience the Spirit being 'poured out upon them' but
would be able to put their spiritual gifts into practice.[27]

It is hard for us to know exactly what happened when
Attaway and the other women stood up to preach that day in
Bell Alley, because the only surviving account was written by
an unsympathetic observer – a common problem when we try
to learn about radical religious women from this era, as Kerr
observes.[28] Despite the fact that we only see her through a distorted lens, though, Elizabeth Attaway was clearly a significant
preacher. Robert Baillie identified her as 'the mistress of all the
she-preachers', drawing on her example to suggest that Baptist
women 'venture[d] to preach' more than did other separatist
women.[29] And while the author of *Tub-preachers Overturn'd*

took aim at multiple male lay preachers, he made Attaway the sole representative of the 'women-Tubbers', mocking her 'tedious, godless, nonsense' sermons as he sneered that she 'could preach nine times a week, morning and night', given that she had so many 'revelations . . . from new light'.[30]

The week after that December meeting, according to Edwards, as many as a thousand people came to hear the women preach, forcing them to move to a larger site 'in the Old Bailey'. After that they preached 'near the French church' in Threadneedle Street, 'at one Mrs Hill's'. On a Thursday afternoon in January 1646, Attaway preached for around an hour to fifty men and women, declaring what to Edwards's mind were 'many dangerous and false doctrines'. Arguing that a new age of the Holy Spirit had dawned, she reportedly rejected the idea of eternal damnation and taught a doctrine of universal salvation, arguing that 'all men shall be reconciled and saved.' But however startlingly heterodox her words, the fact that it was a woman who was speaking them seemed for most observers to overshadow all other considerations.[31] After this sermon, a woman stood up to demand 'what warrant she had to preach in this manner'? Attaway replied that she and her 'sister' had initially preached only to other women, but she had then been asked to open up her meetings to all. Keen not to 'deny to impart those things the Spirit had communicated to her', and aware that 'the glory of God was manifested in babes and sucklings', she had begun to preach in public to both men and women. Unsatisfied, the woman responded that 'she ought not to preach to the world,' causing another woman in the room to interject that 'truth sought no corners.' Seeing that the gathering was in danger of descending into chaos, Attaway resorted once again to an aggressive form of prayer, asking 'God that all those who were present, and did not acknowledge his weak ones that spake for the Spirit of God' would be shown 'the iniquity of their hearts'.

On another occasion, however, Attaway seems to have had the opportunity to speak to members of her audience about something other than the fact that she was a 'she-preacher'. Edwards notes that two 'gentlemen of the Inns of Court' went out of curiosity 'to hear the women preach'. Striking up a conversation with Attaway after she had finished her sermon, they ended up discussing John Milton and his controversial 1643 publication defending the possibility of divorce. Ominously – as it would turn out – she 'asked them what they thought of it, saying, it was a point to be considered of, and that she for her part would look more into it, for she had an unsanctified husband, that did not walk in the way of Sion.'[32]

The scandal of women preaching in general and Elizabeth Attaway's unorthodox preaching in particular was such that in January 1646 the Lord Mayor along with the Common Council of London petitioned the House of Commons, drawing their attention to 'some instances of private meetings of women preachers of new and strange doctrines and blasphemies'. The Committee of Examinations was asked 'speedily to examine the truth of the said informations' and to report 'with all speed to the House'.[33] Before the end of the month 'some women', including Attaway, were hauled before the Committee and threatened with imprisonment.

Not long afterwards, Elizabeth Attaway left the country. As if the scandal of being a 'she-preacher' was not enough, she added to it the infamy of having 'run away with another woman's husband'. The man she went away with was William Jenney, a fellow radical preacher. Unlike her husband in the army who did not share her beliefs, Jenney had attended her sermons. Attaway left behind two children – 'exposed to the world at six and seven', wrote Edwards – while Jenney also abandoned his children along with his pregnant wife, a woman who, according to his letter to her dated 15 February 1646, had been 'a disturber of [his] body and soul'. Noting acerbically in the margin that Jenney's wife 'could not bear nor take well his being night and day with Mrs Attaway but spake against it, and this was the disturbance he complains of', Edwards claims to have seen a letter from Attaway to Jenney in which she expressed sympathy for the 'sufferings' being inflicted on him by his wife. 'The world may see', Edwards concluded, 'what these women preachers are, thus to write to another woman's husband and now to go away together.'[34]

Attaway had been inspired by a prophet in London to go to Jerusalem to meet there with Christ – along with Abraham, Isaac and Jacob – as an aspect of God's plan for the salvation of the whole of mankind, and Jenney had become her appointed companion for this mission. In a letter written later from Holland, William and Elizabeth Jenney encouraged their friends in London to 'cast off' any 'antichristian yokes . . . a chief whereof are unequal marriages': those in the kingdom of God, they believed, should not remain married to unbelieving partners.[35] But whatever the eschatological framing of Attaway's decision to leave her husband and her country, her scandalous departure with another woman's husband played into the hands of those who were only too keen to associate female preachers with the biblical figure of the 'scarlet whore'.[36] 'Your women preach too, and are like to be/ The whores of Babylon, as much as she,' the royalist poet Abraham Cowley penned in 1643, and opponents of female preachers often sought to associate their rebellious speech with a wildly unregulated sexuality.[37] Mocking the 'holy sisters' who met 'in Coleman-street', an anonymous tract published in 1661 had one of them rant that 'if any of those wicked men (which call themselves our husbands) will not give us way to do as we like ... we will forsake and leave their wicked company, and betake us to our brethren's copulation and conjunction with us, where and when and how the spirit shall move us to it.'[38] When Dr Thomas Tully, Principal of St Edmund Hall, Oxford, issued a complaint in August 1672 against 'two women preachers' who were 'disturbing' his Wiltshire parish, he claimed that one of them had 'brought forth two bastards'. 'The business is scandalous,' he intoned, a description that evidently applied both to the unnatural preaching and to the generating of illegitimate offspring, behaviours that to his mind were clearly closely related.[39]

We do not know whether Elizabeth Attaway ever made it to Jerusalem, or what finally became of her. After a few months of visibility in the historical record, she disappeared again without trace. For those crucial months, however, a period spanning 1645–6 when the political and religious temperature of England was at boiling point, she managed amid the cacophonous din of radical dissent in London to stand out from the crowd. While many of the women in this book were supported by the radical religious groups in which they found spiritual homes, Attaway's relationship with the General Baptists was more precarious, their backing of her as a preacher far from clear. Yet with or without their support she was determined to 'speak for the Spirit for God', a resolve that ensured that her voice, however brief and fragmentary its presence in the archive, still echoes down to us today.

7

Hester Biddle

Did not the Lord make all men and women upon the earth
of one mould? Why then should there be so much honour
and respect unto some men and women, and not unto others,
but they are almost naked for want of clothing, and almost
starved for want of bread?
Hester Biddle, 1662

Am I permitted to speak with the king of kings
and may not I speak with man?
Hester Biddle, 1694-5

Hester Biddle (also known as Esther) (*c.* 1629–1697), a well-educated Anglican – raised 'after the best sort of religion and custom of the nation' – did not look in her youth to be likely to end up on the wrong side of the law. But this principled and passionate woman, whose spiritual fervour was inextricable from her commitment to social justice, ended up being imprisoned fourteen times. She spent forty years – more than half of her life – as a Quaker preacher and prophet. Travelling extensively within England and abroad, she followed her conscience even when it meant disregarding the wishes of others, whether priests, magistrates or even her fellow Quakers. Viewed as a troublemaker by authorities in more than one nation – and even by some within her own movement – she raised her voice as loudly and as disruptively as possible to promote her cherished principles of equality, justice and peace.

Biddle's early years were spent in Oxford; she later recalled being alarmed by the 'wild' behaviour of the scholars. Subsequently settling in London, she was initially rigorous in her church attendance, never missing a chance to hear the 'common prayer'. But when 'the King's head was taken off' in January 1649, she was traumatized: her 'heart and soul [were] burdened', making her 'weary of [her] life'. For a year she withdrew into herself, becoming 'deaf to all teachings of men', as the mainstream Protestant faith into which she had been baptised began to lose its lustre. Finding herself tempted by 'vanities, and sinful lusts of the flesh', the 'dead worships, and earthly performances' of the Church of England 'did no good'.[1] Attending meetings did nothing for her soul, which remained 'hungry and was even black with thirst'.

Biddle regarded London as a spiritual wasteland. She almost starved in its 'streets for want of the bread of life', she stated later: 'no peace nor true rest amongst you could I find, neither could any of your chief priests tell me where the Lord was to be found.' Deprived of 'help amongst men' or 'refreshments . . . from their ministry', she felt her soul 'dying and fainting away'. If Biddle metaphorically identified herself with those she saw begging for food on the streets of London, she would later find herself not far from their situation. In her final years she relied on the financial support of others to survive, experiencing at first hand the poverty whose prevalence in the city horrified her throughout her life.

Into the spiritual wilderness of 1650s London stepped Francis Howgill and Edward Burroughs, Quakers from the north of England whose preaching in the capital in 1654 refreshed Biddle's 'weary soul'.² Attending 'a meeting of the people called Quakers', she 'was filled with the dread and power of the Lord' and finally found 'peace of conscience'.³ Relieved to be 'set at liberty', she resolved never again to conform to the established Church, no matter what the consequences. Married before 1655 to the London shoemaker Thomas Biddle, a fellow Quaker, Hester lived with him near St Paul's until the Great Fire of 1666 forced them to move south of the river to Bermondsey. She had four sons, three of whom died during her lifetime. Marriage and children did not hold her back from her mission: from almost the first moment of her 'convincement' as a Quaker she travelled widely, calling wherever she went for a fairer and more godly society.

———

WALKING DOWN THE Strand in London one day in 1659, the Quaker leader George Fox was accosted by a woman with a striking message. Fox's journal does not name the self-proclaimed prophet who spoke to him that day, but a later source identifies her as Hester Biddle. It certainly sounds like her: fiery and bold to the point of recklessness. Stopping Fox in the street, the woman told him that she 'had a prophecy' that Charles, the son of the executed King Charles I, was to return to England, insisting that she 'must go to him to declare it'. Not often known for advocating cautiousness, Fox warned her to keep the prophecy to herself. Such a declaration, he reminded her, was tantamount to treason.⁴ Perhaps on this occasion Biddle held back from delivering what she saw as a divinely inspired message; if so, it must have been one of the only occasions in her life when she did so.

My dearly beloued in that where is immortall and inuisible, doe I
dearly salute thee thou euerlastingly beloued of god and of my soule
who was redeemed out of the body of hell by thy life, and therefore
haue I cause to remember thee whilst I haue breath, and one who
is not yet haue I vnity with his precious life, and I know thou art
satisfied in it, oh my beloued friend, I see thee as a precious pillar
in the temple of the most high god, thy habitation is exceeding beauty-
full, it dazeleth the eyes of the world, the splendour of it is hide from
the vulture eye, there is not many that can behold it, but they are
blessed for euer, oh my beloued father thou hast many valiant ones
in and about this citty, who feareth not thou liues and multitude of
who many are fallen asleepe, and are gathered vp to their fathers,
the generation of the iust, and here are many that are in the way
and are perseuering on, hoping to game the victory, and obtaine the
crowne, of euerlasting life, which is layde vp for the righteous, which
we question not, but we shall inherit, I know and feele thy prayers and
supplications is and cannot chuse but be vnto the Lord for vs, who
were begotten by the life, which proceedeth out of thy bowels, where is
the word of god, which raised our soules out of death, and quickened
our mortall bodyes, and it hath caused vs to stand as liuing witnesses
vpon the earth ouer the beast and the false prophet, we we reigne
yet are our [sufferings] very great, my dear neare Anthony Barnett
and one of our men is kept in for the third time, one hath serui'd
his sentence of banishment the last seuenth day, and the other is
like his next is to haue the same, I haue one child dead at home, my
husband is a prisoner in the fleet, but hath his liberty, and I am in
for the third time taken from the Bull and Mouth where I was vn-
mercifully vsed by Browne, he pinched mee as blacke as a ball, and
kicks mee till I was sore, and strucke mee on the mouth the Lord
forgiue him, he knowes not what he does, my dear friend I know
not whether I may see thee againe or not, but if I desire to be contented
and stand in the will of god, vnto whome I must giue an account
of my stewardship, which if hope I shall giue with ioyfullnesse,
which will add vnto thy comfort, this is a day of hard tryall, and they
will be happy who patiently beareth the indignation of the Lord til
it be ouer past, for it must be poured out vpon the head of the
wicked, this weeke is the sessions, I shall giue thee an account
when it is ouer, and shall lye downe at the present with thee in
the fold of god, whose his armes of power compasseth vs about
who proclaimeth liberty on euery side for our immortall soules
which is dumb in all the fountaine of life continually, oh what shall
I say vnto thee words are too short, and therefore doe I rest in the
bundle of life, which liues for euer, my loue to thy wife and
children and to thy sonne whome I shall be glad to see, to Anthony
Mosse and all friends as thou art deed, all meetings were quiet
the last first day but the Mouth, and there was dear George
who so had taken who had good seruice for god, and for many more
which is aboue 50, thy daughter Esther Biddle farewell.

Hester Biddle's letter to Francis Howgill from Bridewell, 17 October 1664.

BIDDLE WAS FREQUENTLY imprisoned for 'declaring the truth to the people in the public places'. In 1656 she was incarcerated in Banbury, Oxfordshire, for speaking 'against the mayor and magistrates there'. In the same year, she was imprisoned overnight in Cornwall, where a local priest 'threatened to kick her about'.[5] Three years later, she was 'beaten and abused and put into a cage' in Surrey.

After the restoration of the monarchy in 1660, the hostility against nonconformists intensified, until the Quakers were enduring what Joseph Besse later described as a 'fury of persecution'.[6] Identifying the Friends who were particularly resolute in their willingness to hazard 'their estates, liberties and lives . . . by preaching in the assemblies for worship at London', he included Hester Biddle's name.[7] In a letter to the Quaker leader Margaret Fell dated 25 November 1662, Ellis Hookes – the first recording clerk of the Society of Friends – reported that 'last Sunday' the authorities 'took several to prison out of the streets', noting that Hester Biddle had also been 'sent to prison for writing a book'.[8] The letter has survived because it was intercepted by those spying for the authorities, indicating the intensity with which the group was pursued in this era. Writing from within Newgate prison in the same year, Biddle described Quakers being 'cursed, beaten and knocked down' before being thrown into 'nasty prisons until they die'.[9] Writing from Bridewell prison in October 1664, she noted that she was 'in for the third time', having been taken from a meeting at 'the Bull and Mouth where I was unmercifully used by Browne [alderman Sir Richard Browne]', who 'pinched me all black as a hat and kicked me till I was sore and struck me on the mouth'.[10]

———

IN THE SUMMER of 1662, after one of her many arrests, Biddle was put on trial at the Old Bailey in London. Told by the judge – the same Richard Browne who would later assault her – to come up to the bench, 'the power of the Lord rose in her heart as a fire, and a hammer,' and she demanded justice for herself and the three Quaker women alongside her. Their meeting may have been deemed 'unlawful', but such gatherings were not illegal during Cromwell's time, she reminded the judge, asking if he was demanding that their 'consciences . . . change as the laws and governments of the nation change?'

But Biddle had not simply attended a meeting. Much worse, in the eyes of her prosecutors, was the fact that she had been caught preaching. 'We are not like the world, who must have a priest to interpret the scriptures to them,' she writes in one of her tracts. Instead, God speaks to us 'in our own language' and we hear him 'perfectly'. When Biddle spoke in a meeting, she was passing on that 'which cometh immediately from God'. Those on the bench nevertheless found the idea of a woman preaching utterly outlandish. Biddle responded by naming several biblical prophetesses. 'That was a great while ago,' sneered the judge. Yes, she replied, those were the good old days, 'when the church was in her beauty and glory'. The fact that it was now 'a strange thing' to hear of a woman preaching indicated the extent to which 'gross darkness' had fallen on 'the kings and rulers'. Unpersuaded, Browne instructed her that instead of teaching others, a woman 'should ask of her husband at home'. And what if a woman's 'husband should be a drunkard, or a sot', retorted Biddle, should she 'learn of him, to be wicked as he was?' In any case, she continued, 'Christ is my husband, and

I learn of him.' Having failed to silence her, Browne resorted to attacking her reputation, claiming that she had recently left her husband for two years to travel abroad with 'a young man'. Biddle rejected the slur, declaring that she had in fact travelled 'with three women, as she was moved of the Lord'.

Throughout the hearing, Biddle insisted that it was the court and its officers who were the transgressors, not the Quakers. Their meeting was invaded when they were 'quiet and still', she stated, and their attackers were men with swords and canes who acted like madmen. A sword had been thrust in her face and she had been thrown to the ground and trodden upon; she had feared for her life. Replying sarcastically that 'if they had hanged her up, they had served her well enough,' Browne dismissed her claims. 'Thou art a wicked judge,' she exclaimed, with no moral authority; 'why shouldest thou sit there as a judge?'

Biddle was not the only woman to have spoken at the supposedly 'riotous' Quaker meeting. Sarah Cobalt, on trial alongside her, also testified that she had been 'commanded of the Lord to speak', at which point Browne ordered her to 'be silent'. Seeing that there was no prospect of a fair trial, Biddle told the court that 'she had been in many nations, and before judges and benches, but never before such a wicked bench as this.' 'And many nations have been in you,' mocked Browne. Fined 13*s* 4*d* each, the women were taken off to prison until they could make the payment. If this judge had his way he would 'murder us all', shouted Biddle as she was dragged out of the courtroom.[11]

———

HESTER BIDDLE'S CONCERN with injustice was not limited to the fight against the mistreatment of Quakers. She burned with

grief and anger at the inequality of English society and sought
through her preaching and writing to awaken her complacent
neighbours to the cruelties in which they were silently com-
plicit. She tended to look at the bigger picture: rather than
targeting specific individuals, she took aim in her impassioned
pamphlets at entire cities, especially London, but also the
'filthy' cities of Oxford – the city of her youth – and Cambridge.
The cities she described throbbed with all the pleasures that the
seventeenth-century world had to offer. In London there were
taverns, playhouses and numerous places for citizens to feast –
useful, she noted, since their bellies were their gods. Its streets
thronged with prosperous figures who stepped out from their
'goodly houses' adorned in the latest fashions; Biddle was particularly disdainful of the stylish women whose faces were
'decked with black spots'. Piling into alehouses or indulging
in 'ballad singing, cards, and dice', the citizens of London
singlemindedly pursued pleasure. Concerned only with their
own revelry, they were indifferent to those in their midst who
were 'crying for bread'. This 'merciless' city with its vast social
and economic inequalities, she wrote, where 'vulturous' merchants and 'cruel' lawyers pursue their own interests unchecked,
has become spiritually impoverished in inverse relation to its
accumulation of cultural and material wealth.[12]

'Oh London!', she exclaimed,

> thou art grown numerous, and very great, thy beam
> reacheth unto heaven, and thy glory unto the end of
> the earth, and thou hast crowned thy self with dig-
> nity, and hast built thy nest among the stars, and
> sitteth as a Queen, thou hast made thy self strong, and
> hast said in thy heart, thou shalt not see sorrow; thou

seest no scarcity within thy gates, but fulness within thy palaces.

But the poor are 'ready to perish' on the streets: 'both old and young, lame and blind lieth in your streets ... which even melt-eth my heart'. The poor were 'ready to famish', she repeated elsewhere, 'for whose estate and condition my heart is pained within me'. Such inequality was intolerable to Biddle, for whom God made 'all men and women upon the earth of one mould'. 'Why then', she asks,

> should there be so much honour and respect unto some men and women, and not unto others, but they are almost naked for want of clothing, and almost starved for want of bread? And are you not all brethren, and all under the government of one king? Oh repent! . . . be ashamed, and clothe the naked, and feed the hungry, and set the oppressed free.

Imitating the rhetoric of biblical prophets, she warned that if London did not listen, 'know this as from the Lord, thou bloody city, thou shall know his terrible stroke.'[13]

Highlighting the hypocrisy of a self-regarding city that ignored the innocent people who were suffering on its streets 'by reason of oppression', she pointed the finger at the established Church alongside London's legal and political institutions. 'Howl ye lawyers, weep bitterly ye rulers, and judges,' she declared, but also 'lament ye priests, for the day of God's account is coming on.' The priests, like the other 'proud and haughty' people of London, were only interested in amassing wealth: 'thy priests preach for hire, and the people love to have it so.' People were 'crying for bread' at the doors of the churches – the institutions she scathingly labels 'mass-houses' – 'almost naked for want of clothing, and fainting for want of bread'. But the wealthy in their 'gaudy apparel, and outstretched neck[s]' stepped over them, unconcerned. 'O! Feed the hungry, and clothe the naked, and hide not thy self from thy own flesh,' she implored. 'Thy religion is so airy,' she accused her fellow citizens, that

> if any of these that are blind, or lame, or destitute of a being, asketh of thee a penny, or farthing, thou sayest thou hast it not for them. O! Remember the Lord will call thee to an account ... who hath lavishly spent God's creation upon thy lusts, and hath not distributed thy morsel to the poor, and to the needy, the light of Christ in thy conscience condemns thee for thy not so doing, and from that thou cans't not fly.[14]

Biddle had no doubt that God was on the side of the poor against 'kings and princes, dukes and earls, lords and ladies, governors and magistrates, priests and Jesuits', and she aligned the heavily persecuted Quakers with those begging for food. Like those starving on the streets, Quakers to her mind were innocent citizens who were being abused: they were 'sent to prison, or bruised, or knocked down' on a regular basis. Yet God was with them in the 'vast howling wilderness': 'although we are despised in thee, and hated by thee, yet the Lord ... is our Redeemer, who is the portion of our cup and the lot of our inheritance.'[15]

The apocalypse of which Biddle warned in her tracts promised not only to vindicate God's people but to bring about a social revolution. Christ will 'endow' his people 'with all those treasures which this empty world cannot afford', she told her readers: 'bread in your own house and water in your own well, which will satisfy your soul in the time of drought'. Drawing on biblical imagery, she elaborated that at God's table all would eat and be 'satisfied, there is a river as clear as crystal, which runneth softly, of which all drinketh freely'. Christ has 'invited all upon the whole face of the earth . . . to come into his banqueting house', she continued; 'O! Come and drink and eat freely with us, without money and without price'.

The 'high and lofty', by contrast, were about to be reduced to 'dust'. God will 'uncrown you, and bereave you of all your mortal glory', she thundered. He 'will lay your habitations waste, who respects not the person of any, but you shall sit as a widow, that is, rebuked of husband and children, bemoaning herself, even so shall you be'. The new earth, then, was presented in her work in strikingly familiar terms. Those who had 'oppress[ed] the just' would find themselves in the position of those whose needs they had ignored, experiencing the fate of a despised and helpless widow in seventeenth-century London. You may 'build [your] nests in the stars for a short time', she warned, 'yet he . . . who is the king of the saints, and the governor of heaven and earth' will 'pluck [you] from [your] stately thrones and disinherit' you.[16]

As for the 'greedy dumb-dogs' of Oxford and Cambridge, Biddle wrote in 1655, those who 'never have enough, and love greeting in the marketplaces . . . and the upper seats at feasts, and [to] be called of men masters; they are filthy brute-beasts'. In this tract she criticizes the practice of enclosure, describing those who 'join house to house and field to field until there is no place left for the poor'.[17] As Elaine Hobby points out, Biddle is drawing here on the language of Isaiah 5:8, but adapts the verse to emphasize the situation of the poor.[18] 'God exalteth the poor in spirit but the rich he sendeth empty away,' she proclaimed to the university cities, using this biblical sentiment to warn the citizens that their 'pride shall become as filthy rags upon the dunghill'.[19]

———

HESTER BIDDLE TRAVELLED extensively in England, Scotland and Ireland. She also journeyed further afield, often – as she told the judge – in the company of other Quaker women. In 1656 she became one of the first Quakers to travel to Newfoundland, a journey she repeated with Mary Fisher in 1659. John Winthrop, governor of the Massachusetts Bay Colony, was informed in a letter in 1659 that

> Mary Fisher, the Quaker, and another named Esther [Biddle] are arrived at St John's harbour; and there they vent their opinions. I hear 2 or 3 masters of ships are perverted by them ... I hear that some masters of ships forbid their men to hear them. They have both been (as they report) at Constantinople, and in other places among the Turks.[20]

In 1657 Biddle also visited Barbados. And when Katharine Evans and Sarah Cheevers arrived in Leghorn (Livorno, Italy) in 1658, they were told by Mary Fisher that they had just missed Biddle, who was on her way to Alexandria.[21]

Her most famous journey, however, was her last. In 1694–5 she decided to travel to France to confront Louis XIV. So outrageous was this idea that even her fellow Quakers tried to talk her out of it. Writing two decades later, the Quaker historian William Sewel frowned at this example of an 'odd' moment when things occurred that were 'not approved of by those of that Society'. Biddle alone was responsible for the bizarre episode, he emphasized, adding that in his view it would have been better 'left undone'.[22] Too radical for Sewel, Biddle was written out of his history book, just as she has been from most history books since. Having heard Biddle's story from an account she gave of it in Amsterdam, the Dutch minister and historian Gerard Croese nevertheless included it in his *The General History of the Quakers* (1696) (although he added the caveat that 'everyone is at liberty to believe as he pleases').[23] Evidence for the mission has since come to light: state papers record that Biddle was granted a pass for a journey to France in 1694.[24]

According to Croese's account, Biddle approached Queen Mary II for permission to visit Louis XIV, 'because it was a very great grief of heart to her, as she was a woman, and a Christian, that so great and tedious a war was waged between Christians, and such great calamities and slaughters of men, which happened every day, pierced her heart'. Appalled by the Nine Years' War that had been destroying lives in Europe since 1688, Biddle appealed to the queen to allow her to try to bring an end to the conflict, saying 'she would advise and speak to the French king about the same affair.' Warning her that 'such a journey and business would be very difficult and dangerous,' the queen nevertheless granted permission and Biddle set off for Versailles.

Her first stop was with the previous king of England, James II, who had fled to France. Biddle showed him the letter she planned to deliver to Louis XIV, in which she identified herself as an ambassador of 'God, the supreme king of all' and appealed to the French king to make peace 'with the nations he was at war with' and 'put a stop' to the 'overflowing' bloodshed. The letter would be passed on, she was informed. At this, Biddle cried 'am I permitted to speak with the king of kings and may not I speak with man?' The people of England would be scandalized by this response, she added, pointing out that it would confirm their worst suspicions of the king of France, proving that he was 'so high and proud that none [could] speak with him'.

Three days later, she was granted an audience with Louis XIV, whose hatless appearance initially shocked the English Quaker turned peace ambassador. This is 'not the fashion of the kings of England', she exclaimed. Turning to the business of the visit, Louis reassured her that he 'desire[d] peace', asking her to 'tell the Prince of Orange so', refusing to acknowledge William as the king of England.[25] Despite Biddle's efforts, the war continued for several more years.

———

AFTER HER HUSBAND's death in 1682, Biddle found herself living in poverty. Quaker records state that she received weekly financial support as a 'poor Friend', and she was given the accommodation behind the meeting room intended for 'poor widows.' On 5 February 1697, at the age of 67, Biddle suffered a 'stoppage' and died. She was survived by her only living son, Benjamin.[26]

While Elizabeth Attaway's preaching career burned brightly for a few heady months in 1645–6, Hester Biddle preached her Quaker message for many decades, relentlessly maintaining her drive to undermine systems of oppression. Her bold assault on the wealthy and the powerful for their indifference to the poor was often dismissed in her lifetime – as it has been since – as the ravings of an uncomfortably aggressive and radical woman. Yet in her writing we hear a passionately articulated indictment of the growing social and economic inequalities of her era. Biddle depicted London as a stylish and self-indulgent city, a place where cruel self-interest obliterated concern for the vulnerable. Aware of the global context in which London was operating, she also addressed 'all ye that trade by sea', telling them to 'trade no longer with the merchandise of Babylon.' You 'never have enough', she pointed out, and so you 'take people's money for that which is not bread, and their labour for that which satisfies nothing'. But 'a fire goeth forth of [God's] mouth which shall burn up Babylon with all her merchants'.[27] Those in London who were 'cheating and deceiving souls for dishonest gain', she wrote, would themselves be 'dispossessed' when God overturned them 'in flames of fire', leaving their houses 'desolate'. But as well as threatening the greedy and the exploitative with the fires of God's wrath, Biddle confronted the grotesque inequalities of seventeenth-century English society. 'For want of true judgement and equity the just [are] oppressed,' she wrote, 'and the innocent and harmless groaneth for want of righteous rulers and godly judges, and wholesome laws.' But in the kingdom of God that she devoted herself to bringing about on earth, 'equity and justice remaineth world without end.'[28]

Part Four:
'To the ends of the earth'

8

Mary Fisher

From sea to sea, and from island to island; yea verily the
voice is gone forth to the ends of the earth.
Katharine Evans and Sarah Cheevers, 1662

It is hard to imagine a less likely person to have a private
audience with the sultan of the Ottoman Empire in the
mid-seventeenth century than a Yorkshire maidservant. Yet the
incredible adventures of Mary Fisher (*c.* 1623–1698), a woman
who was working in service in Selby when she converted
to Quakerism, illustrate the extent to which Quakers were
inspired to 'walk cheerfully over the world, answering that of
God in everyone', in the words of George Fox.[1] Walk the world
she did, beginning with journeys to Cambridge and elsewhere
in England before voyaging to Barbados and Boston and then,
later, to Turkey to meet the sultan.

Even before she left Yorkshire, Mary Fisher was making
waves. Becoming a Quaker in 1652, when she was approaching thirty years old, she immediately embraced the intense
anti-clericalism of the movement. Going to a church in Selby
one Sunday, she interrupted the minister in the middle of
his sermon, shouting, 'come down, come down, thou painted
beast, come down. Thou art but a hireling, and deludest the
people with thy lies.'[2] Arrested for 'brawling in church', she was

imprisoned in York Castle. But she continued to speak out. If the minister was a 'painted beast', the judge she addressed in her letter from prison was an 'unjust judge', one who needed to amend his ways by learning to treat everyone equally.[3]

———

HILARY HINDS DESCRIBES the 'constitutional restlessness' of the early Quakers, noting that they 'cannot be considered separate from their itinerant constitution ... it made them who they were, and was a major factor in what constituted them as a threat for their opponents'.[4] Mary Fisher's story exemplifies the drive of the Friends to take their testimony of the light within 'to the ends of the earth', and illustrates the antagonism they often provoked on these journeys. While many Christians in England and New England responded to Fisher with hostility, however, those in other national and religious contexts were more welcoming, she claimed. Walking freely 'over the world', she had experiences that challenged dominant English perceptions of which nations and religions were 'civilized' and which were 'barbarous', as Sylvia Brown demonstrates.[5] Believing in the universal principle of the light within, the Quakers had broad horizons. The already-present kingdom of God to which they bore witness was not the possession of any one nation but was a global phenomenon.[6] They travelled, in Fox's words, so that they could answer to 'that of God in everyone': instead of seeing themselves as bringing light to other nations, they sought to demonstrate that this light was already present everywhere on earth.[7]

———

NOT LONG AFTER leaving York Castle, Mary Fisher set off on the first of many journeys. In December 1653, she and her fellow Quaker Elizabeth Williams – who was twenty years her senior – arrived in Cambridge. Once there, they accused some members of Sidney Sussex College of being 'antichrists', informing them that 'their college was a cage of unclean birds and the synagogue of Satan.' Perhaps unsurprisingly, the two women were soon arrested. It was not the content of their speech alone that caused offence, however: the fact that 'two women were preaching' at all was enough to get the mayor's attention. The authorities were appalled that the pair had travelled so far from home and asked them 'whence they came and where they lay last night?' Fisher and Williams assured their accusers that they were not beggars or vagabonds and had 'paid for what they had', but their words did not allay the mayor's suspicions. He asked them to identify themselves. In typical Quaker style, they refused to recognize 'worldly' categories, stating obtusely that 'their names were written in the Book of Life.' Irritated, he demanded to know the names of their husbands. Their reply, that 'they had no husband but Jesus Christ, and he sent them,' was the last straw. The enraged mayor denounced them as 'whores', ordering them to be whipped 'till the blood ran down their bodies'. Charged under an old law against vagrancy, their 'essential crime', as Brown observes, was 'illegitimate travel', having the temerity to transgress 'beyond the patriarchal bounds of their own parishes and families'.[8]

Stripped to the waist in the marketplace, Fisher and Williams were whipped 'in as fierce and cruel a manner as could be, that so their bodies were cut, and slashed, and torn'. They conducted themselves with martyr-like endurance, taking the punishment 'cheerfully' and continuing to exhort the people of Cambridge to 'fear God' right up to the moment they were 'thrust out of town'. The anonymous account of their 'cruel usage' identified the city of Cambridge – where 'no man so much as [offered] them a cup of cold water' – as a place of 'barbarous and unlawful' behaviour, confirming the women's denunciation of the evil lurking behind its civilized front.[9]

———

UNDETERRED, MARY FISHER continued to travel around England, disrupting church services as she went. She was imprisoned at least three times, twice in Yorkshire and once in Buckinghamshire. In 1655 she set her sights further afield. Accompanied by another Friend, Ann Austin, she sailed for Barbados, an island on which there had been English settlers since 1627. Heralded in an English publication in 1676 as 'the finest and worthiest island in the world', Barbados was said to be overflowing with 'muskmelons, grapes, figs, prickly pears, guavas, pomegranates, citrons, soursops and sweet lemons of a vast bigness, and delicate pleasant taste'. Also described as 'the most flourishing colony the English have in the world', over one hundred merchant ships set sail from its shores annually,

Isaac Sailmaker (attrib.), *The Island of Barbados, c.* 1694, oil on canvas.

filled with 'sugar, ginger, cotton, and indigo'.[10] Barbados was the 'sugar centre' of the Caribbean, its production of sugar being made possible by the labour of enslaved people from West Africa. In 1655, when Mary Fisher arrived, there were 20,000 enslaved Africans on the island, a number that had increased to more than 33,000 by 1673.[11]

The first Quakers to arrive in Barbados, Fisher and Austin received a friendly welcome in some quarters, at least, and some sugar planters were soon converted to their cause. Before long there was a thriving Quaker community: by the time George Fox arrived in 1671, there were over a thousand Quakers on the island. Nearly all of them were slave owners. Fox reminded them that Christ died for 'the Tawnies and for the Blacks as well as for you that are called Whites', emphasizing that all are of 'one blood' that 'dwell upon the face of the earth'. Challenging ideas of difference, Fox instructed the Quakers in Barbados to 'consider' how they would feel if they 'were in the same condition as the Blacks are . . . who came as strangers to you and were sold to you as slaves; now, I say, if this should be the condition of you and yours, you would think it hard measure; yea, and very great bondage and cruelty.' He nevertheless claimed that it was a 'slander and lie' to say that Friends were teaching enslaved people to rebel.[12]

When, in 1675, the Barbados authorities uncovered a plot by enslaved Africans to 'fire the sugar-canes', kill their 'masters' and 'choose them a king', they responded brutally. Forty-two enslaved men were executed, some of whom were burned alive, while others were beheaded. The authorities blamed the Quakers, claiming that their practice of including enslaved men and women in their meetings had 'hazarded' the 'safety of this island'.[13] While Fox and other Quakers taught doctrines

Carel Allard, *English Quakers and Tobacco Planters in Barbados*, 1700, engraving.

of spiritual equality and pressed for the better treatment of enslaved people on the island, however, it was not until the late 1670s, when another female Friend from the north of England, Alice Curwen, visited Barbados, that Quakers began to challenge the institution of slavery itself. Berating the widow Martha Tavernor for her refusal to allow her 'servants, whom thou call'st thy slaves', to attend Quaker meetings, Curwen not only told Tavernor that she had 'no right to reign over their conscience in matters of worship', but through her refusal to identify people as slaves called into question the legitimacy of slavery.[14]

───

AFTER VISITING BARBADOS, Mary Fisher and Ann Austin sailed to New England, where in July 1656 they became the first Quakers to land in America. Before they had even disembarked at Boston, the deputy governor of Massachusetts was on their case. Rifling through their possessions, he confiscated one hundred books, which were somewhat theatrically burned in the marketplace by the hangman. The fact that one of the women addressed the deputy governor as 'thee' rather than the polite form 'you' – a characteristic Quaker refusal to show deference – was enough to condemn them as Quakers, and they were immediately imprisoned. Another Quaker observed that the Boston authorities reacted as if a 'formidable army had invaded [their] borders'. Terrified that the women would seek to convert the local population, the authorities nailed up the windows of their jail. Detained and interrogated for five weeks before being sent back to Barbados, the women were accused of being witches and 'stripped stark naked' to be searched for the physical signs or 'witch marks' that would supposedly confirm this claim. 'Searched and mis-used . . . more than modesty can mention', with at least one of those 'searching' them being a man in women's clothing, Fisher and Austin were assaulted 'with such barbarousness' that Austin later claimed that she 'had not suffered so much in the birth' of all five of her children as she did 'under their barbarous and cruel hands'.[15]

———

AFTER ARRIVING BACK in England, Fisher was soon off on her travels again. In 1657 she and some other Friends set off for Jerusalem. Changing direction mid-journey, Fisher ignored the English Consul in Smyrna, Turkey, and everyone else who tried to stop her, as she set off on a long and hazardous trek (possibly accompanied by a fellow Quaker, Beatrice Beckley) to the Turkish city of Adrianople (Edirne). There, she knew, lay the camp of the sultan of the Ottoman Empire, Mehmed IV. A much-feared figure, the sultan – often referred to in England as the 'Great Turk' – was described in Croese's account of Fisher's mission as 'a monster of a man, a deformed sight both in body and mind, as if one strove with the other how to offend, of a black complexion ... cruel, fierce'.[16] Another seventeenth-century publication gave a graphic account of the demise of 'four eminent Quakers of Gloucestershire' at his hands. Having made a 'voyage to Constantinople', they were said to have met with a 'barbarous, cruel and bloody death by the special command of the chief governor the Great Turk, who caused their hands to be chopped off, their tongues to be cut out, and their eyes bored out, and each man to have a sharp wooden stake run in at his fundament quite through his body'.[17]

Mary Fisher nevertheless felt herself 'moved of the Lord to go and deliver his Word to the Great Turk'. Getting close to his encampment, she was warned of the dangers of incurring the sultan's 'displeasure', but she continued undeterred. According to a Quaker report based on her account, the sultan gave her a royal welcome, using interpreters to allow her to convey what she had 'to say to him from the Lord'. Observing the customary Quaker silence before she launched into her message, Fisher was encouraged not to be shy but 'to utter her mind before them all'.[18] In a letter written in 1659, she stated that she sought to bear her 'testimony ... before ye king unto whom I was sent, and he was very noble unto me, and so were all that were about him'. They 'received the words of truth without contradiction', she claimed, demonstrating that 'there is a royal seed amongst them, which in time God will raise.' The sultan and his court were 'more near truth than many nations', she wrote: 'the seed in them is near unto God' and there is 'a love begot in [me] towards them which is endless'.[19]

Rather than seeking to convert the sultan, Fisher seemed intent on demonstrating that the divine light was just as likely to be found in those regarded by the English as 'barbarous' as it was in so-called Christians.[20] The English in Cambridge had whipped her and thrown her out of town without so much as a cup of water, and the Christian authorities in Boston had imprisoned and humiliated her, but the supposedly monstrous 'Great Turk' had welcomed her with kindness and listened to her with respect. Fisher's account of her encounter with Mehmed IV is ultimately less interested in the sultan himself than it is in deploying his apparent kindness as a way of exposing the vice of her enemies closer to home. Her description of her astonishing journey into the heart of what to most of her English contemporaries would have been a place of fearful difference worked to confirm the Quaker principle that God was no 'respecter of persons': his light was to be found in all, often shining the most brightly in the most unexpected of places.

———

IN 1662, AS she was approaching forty years of age, Mary Fisher married a fellow Friend, a shipmaster, and went on to have three children. In November 1662, her husband, along with other Quakers, was arrested in London. Fisher, who was pregnant, tried to stop her husband from being punched in the face but was herself struck on the mouth and thrown to the ground.[21] After her first husband's death at sea (on a return journey from Barbados), she married another Quaker, a shoemaker, in 1678. Fisher and her family ultimately escaped religious persecution in England by emigrating to South Carolina, where after her second husband's death she continued to play a leading role in the local Quaker community. By the time she died in her mid-seventies, she had journeyed far and wide across the globe. In her will she bequeathed to her daughter an 'Indian girl slave named Rayner', revealing that her journey from a life of service in northern England to the position of a well-known Quaker in America did not prevent her from being implicated in the enslavement of others.[22]

———

ENCOUNTERING QUAKERISM AS a young woman in Selby, Mary Fisher could hardly have imagined the horizons, both metaphorical and literal, that would be opened up for her by her new faith. Believing herself to be sent by her 'husband', Christ, to testify to the light within, her disregard for national and religious boundaries was accompanied by a refusal to be constrained by any limits potentially placed on her by gender or social position. The extraordinary range of Fisher's adventures exemplifies the 'tumultuous mobility' of the early Quakers. Possessed of a 'global vision' that set them apart from other radical religious groups in England in this era, theirs was a faith 'born in movement' that 'created a riotous swirl of activity which no-one directed or could even fully track', as the historian Carla Pestana notes.[23] Answerable only to their sense of the light within, early Quaker women travelled fearlessly, convinced that God was with them 'at all times and in all places'.[24] But this attitude could be highly threatening to those into whose territories they strayed, as Katharine Evans and Sarah Cheevers discovered. It is to their story that we now turn.

9

Katharine Evans
and Sarah Cheevers

They said, we were foolish women. We said, we were
the Lord's fools, and the Lord's fools were right dear, and
precious in his sight, and woe to them that do offend them.
Katharine Evans and Sarah Cheevers, 1662

[He] bid me fall down, or bow my body. I told him, my heart
and whole body was bowed under the name of Jesus, but
I should not stoop to his will, nor any man's else.
Katharine Evans, 1662

It is still possible to visit the Inquisitor's Palace in Malta
where the Quakers Katharine Evans (*c.* 1618–1692) and Sarah
Cheevers (*c.* 1608–1664?) were imprisoned for over three years.
With bare stone walls and an arched roof, the cell in which
Sarah Cheevers was incarcerated had a high small window
facing onto the street outside. Down the narrow, dark corridor from her cell was the chamber where the officers of the
Inquisition tortured 'heretics', seeking through physical torment to reform their souls. Waiting 'every hour' for her captors
to 'fetch [her] out' and 'slay' her, Cheevers was also haunted by
the fear that her 'dear yoke-fellow' Katharine Evans was being
taken to that terrible room to be 'pressed . . . with stones'.[1]

Malta was not the first place to which Katharine Evans had travelled. Raised in Somerset within the Church of England, she became a Baptist and then an Independent before joining the Society of Friends in 1654. When Exeter magistrates ordered travelling Quakers to be apprehended as vagrants in 1656, she was one of twenty Friends to be imprisoned. 'Lodged among felons' and lying only on straw, the conditions, according to a Quaker chronicler, were so filthy that 'many of them fell sick and one woman died.' Shortly afterwards, Evans travelled to the Isle of Man, where she reported that 'a soldier came to my bedside with a naked sword, and took me by the arm, and hauled me out of the bed at the tenth hour of the night', ordering her to leave because she was a Quaker. Relentlessly

The Inquisitor's Palace, Birgu, Malta. This small row of cells dates to the time of the women's imprisonment and fits Cheevers's description of the cell in which she was held when separated from Evans.

itinerant, she was whipped in Salisbury marketplace in 1657 and was also imprisoned on the Isle of Wight for several nights. After confronting a priest in Portsmouth, she was locked up with a 'mad woman', while her public preaching also led to her being thrown in 'a blind-house, a filthy nasty place where two madmen had lately died'. Released on this occasion late at night, she 'sat in a field all night' because she 'could not get lodging'. Her confrontation with a priest at Warminster, meanwhile, led to her being 'violently abused', the 'clothes rent off her back'.[2]

Evans was around forty years old and Sarah Cheevers – who was from Wiltshire – was ten years older when they each felt called to leave behind their husbands and children and travel overseas to witness to the light within. The English Consul in Malta reported to the Inquisition that the women claimed God had 'appeared to them in the form of a fire, to undertake this mission'. Cheevers's own account was more measured. God appeared to her 'upon the way', she said, telling her to 'go over the seas to do his will'. Arriving at Malta at the end of 1658, the two women – dressed according to one report in 'Franciscan attire' – distributed books on the streets of the capital, Valletta.[3] They refused to bow to an altar, swiftly identifying themselves as 'heretics and heathens'. They were taken at first to the house of the English Consul – a man by whom they felt betrayed – before being moved in April 1659 to the Inquisitor's Palace in the city of Birgu, the seat of the Roman Inquisition in Malta since 1574.

Initially sharing a cell, the women were confined to a room 'so hot and so close' that they were driven to 'lie down at a chink of the door for air to catch breath'. Fearing that the officers of the Inquisition were trying to smother them, they

Exterior of the Inquisitor's Palace, Birgu, Malta.

Interior of the Inquisitor's Palace, Birgu, Malta.

sat sweating in their tiny cell for weeks on end. Parched and dejected, their skin became 'like sheep's leather' and their hair fell out in clumps. Unable to find comfort – 'when it was day we wished for night, and when it was night we wished for day' – they wrote extensively about their experiences. In what felt like a miraculous turn of events, they were ultimately able to smuggle their writing out of a prison window to a fellow Quaker, who risked his life taking the jointly written account back to England. *This is a Short Relation of some of the Cruel Sufferings . . . of Katharine Evans and Sarah Cheevers* was published in 1662, with an expanded edition – *A True Account of the Great Tryals and Cruel Sufferings undergone by those two faithful servants of God, Katherine Evans and Sarah Cheevers* – appearing the following year.

Providing what the historical archaeologist Russell Palmer describes as a 'unique glimpse' into the experience of being held by the Roman Inquisition in Malta, the women paint a vivid picture of their ordeal.[4] Their faces were so badly 'stung with flies called mosquitoes' that they looked as if they 'had the smallpox'. Disfigured to the point that people 'were afraid' of them, their suffering was used as evidence against them: a friar 'told Sarah he saw an evil spirit in her face'. At times they were deprived of ink and of candles. To make money to buy food, they knitted stockings and mended clothes for other prisoners. Physically and psychologically tormented, they initially 'sought death, but could not find it'. Often refusing the food that they were offered for fear that it was polluted – coming as it did from those who to their mind worshipped idols – when they did eat, they did so 'weeping'.[5]

BEFORE THEY EVEN arrived in Malta, the women had sensed trouble. Having sailed from London to Leghorn (Livorno), the Tuscan port where they briefly encountered Mary Fisher as she undertook her own journey, they were on their way to Alexandria when their ship diverted to Malta, the island – tellingly – 'where Paul suffered shipwreck'. As their ship approached the port, Evans was convinced that the people crowding on the city walls were staring at them. Feeling a chill go down her spine, she wondered 'shall ye destroy us?' 'We have a dreadful cup to drink at that place!' she feared, aligning herself and her companion with Christ as he anticipated his crucifixion.[6]

After their arrest, their captors consulted a cardinal in Rome for advice about how to handle these English prisoners. The response suggests that the Quaker impulse to travel the world was causing considerable irritation, if not outright alarm.[7] Investigate this strange sect, the cardinal instructed the officers of the Inquisition in Malta, and find out the names of its members who are 'scattered all over the world'. Treat the women as though they are mad, he continued, suggesting that this approach would serve as a useful deterrent to those who could well be considering similar journeys to Europe.[8] Evans's jailor later told her that she 'talked like a mad woman', while Cheevers was informed that she 'was a witch' and as such was likely to be burned.[9]

If the Inquisition was hoping to intimidate the women into converting to Roman Catholicism, they soon realized what they were up against. Told that if they would participate in Mass they would be freed, Evans and Cheevers answered that 'the Lord had not committed the charge of our souls to the Pope, nor to them, for he had taken them into his own possession'. They would submit 'to the government of Christ's Spirit' alone. Commanded to kneel to pray, they retorted that they would not pray to order but would only do so if they 'were moved of the Lord'. When Sarah Cheevers was presented with an image of Mary, she stamped her foot and cursed 'all images and image-makers'. She also informed an English friar that his treasured crucifix was an idol. Enraged, he 'called for the irons to chain' her, to which she 'bowed her head and said to him, not only my feet, but my hands and my neck also for the testimony of Jesus'.[10]

In an effort to convince the Quakers of their folly, the friar reminded them that they were 'but a few, and risen up but late', whereas Roman Catholicism consisted of 'many, and had stood fourteen hundred years'. An argument based on institutional tradition was unlikely to be successful, however, given the extent to which Quakers – for whom God was in the process of unveiling new truths – prioritized subjective conviction over external forms of authority. The friar's argument that weight should be given to the numbers of those involved was even more misguided. Seeing themselves as a persecuted minority – as were God's people in the book of Revelation – the Quakers did not need to be in a majority to believe that God was on their side. Cheevers responded that 'if there were no more but she herself, she would not turn, but took her fingers and showed them, if they would tear her jointmeal [joint by joint], she did believe the Lord would enable her to endure it for the truth'. And when Katharine Evans was threatened by a friar with being put 'in a whole pile of chains, where [she] should see neither sun nor moon', she replied that even 'though he had the Inquisition, with all the countries round about, on his side' and she was 'alone by [herself]', she 'did not fear them'.

Setting their sense of conviction against what they regarded to be the 'carnal' external basis of Roman Catholicism, the women pointed to the instruments of torture deployed by the Inquisition as evidence of the failure of their captors to grasp the spiritual nature of God's kingdom. Look at what you use to 'uphold thy kingdom', declared Evans: 'iniquity, double-doors, chains, bolts, iron whips, racks, halters, quarterings, cruelties, bloodthirstiness; what wickedness is there that is not in your kingdom?'[11]

———

KATHARINE EVANS AND Sarah Cheevers may have been at the mercy of the Inquisition, but their account of their imprisonment presents the situation in very different terms. Rather than depicting themselves as victims, they describe themselves as spiritual warriors locked in deadly combat with their opponents. 'Great is their rage, and we have continual war with them, night and day!' they declared. Their captors relied on 'carnal' instruments of 'wickedness', including 'halters and chains', but Evans and Cheevers believed that they had God and the truth on their side, providing them with spiritual weapons whose power far exceeded that of their opponents. Instead of depicting their imprisonment as a defeat, then, they presented it in triumphant terms. Even in the moments of 'deepest affliction, when I looked for every breath to be the last', Evans wrote to her husband, 'I could not wish I had not come overseas ... with my dear and faithful Friend.' For the dark, stifling prison cell was a place of 'ravishments' and 'raptures', within which she felt herself to be invulnerable: no 'swelling seas, nor raging foaming waves, nor stormy winds, though they beat vehemently' will be 'able to remove us'.[12]

At one point, Evans lay ill in bed for twelve days, 'fasting and sweating'. Her suffering enabled her to identify herself with Christ: 'my life was smitten, and I was in very great agony,' she wrote, 'so that sweat was as drops of blood, and the Righteous One was laid into a sepulchre, and a great stone was rolled to the door; but the prophecy was, that he should rise again the third day, which was fulfilled.' Later, she repeated the words that Jesus said he would use to false believers on the Day of Judgement, telling a friar to 'depart from me thou worker of iniquity, I know thee not.'[13] The friar threatened to strike her on the mouth with his crucifix, warning her that she would 'be whipped, and quartered, and burnt that night in Malta, and my mate too: wherefore did we come to teach them?' But her fearlessness ultimately caused her captors to walk away dejected, 'smitten as dead men'. Later that evening, the officers of the Inquisition set up a drum at the prison gate. But Evans simply noted that the 'fire of the Lord consumed it'. Whether or not the drum was literally burned to a crisp is immaterial to Evans's account: her phrasing captures her sense that God was perpetually intervening to protect them from their enemies. Another drum, this time accompanied by guns, returned in the middle of the night. But just as their captors were threatening to 'devour' them, God 'made them to retreat and they fled as dust before the wind'. Ultimately, the women were convinced that their 'souls were out of the Inquisitor's reach'. Spiritually speaking they were unassailable, enabling them to present their experience of persecution in victorious terms. At every turn, they refused to submit to the will of their captors. 'I stood up to [an officer of the Inquisition] and denied him in the name of the Lord ... and said, he had no power over me,' wrote Evans, while Cheevers claimed that God 'bowed them down before us'.[14]

Forced on one occasion to attend Mass, Evans turned her back to the altar. Kneeling, she began to pray loudly. Appalled by their captors' use of 'holy garments (as they call them) of so many colours, that it would make one wonder how the devil did invent it', the women were so 'overcome with their abominations' that they stood for hours 'in great power, trembling and quaking, and bitter mourning', before going 'along the street reeling to and fro, and staggering like drunken men'. Demonstrating the way in which early Quakers, as Hinds observes, 'spoke not only with their voices but with their bodies', the women not only made their objection to Mass visible but also indicated the extent to which they were under the control of God rather than their captors.[15]

When on another occasion they heard a trumpet announcing the presence of the 'Lord Inquisitor', they embarked on an even more scandalous prophetic performance. The 'word of the Lord came unto us', writes Evans,

> saying, we must not eat bread nor drink water in three days, nor I (Katharine) must not speak word in that time, but be silent and sit upon the ground in the Inquisition with very little clothes or nothing upon our heads but ashes, not stoken [stocking] nor shoe on; and the last day Sarah had nothing at all but one petticoat on; and they kept much ado and said, we would mort [die] and go to the Devil, because the wind blew very cold. So in the end the Lord opened Sarah's mouth in prophecy against their superstition, idolatry, and unclean conversation. They came wondering and looked upon us, but could not tell what to say, for we were very dreadful to them. . . . After that they did admire and said, it was the Lord

that did command us and preserve us; if they should have done so, they should have died.

Imitating Hebrew prophets such as Daniel, who prayed to God 'with fasting, and sackcloth, and ashes' (Daniel 9:3), and Ezekiel, who was mute as a sign until God opened his mouth (Ezekiel 3:27), the women made themselves into striking spectacles. Also drawing on the prophetic tradition of Sarah Wight, Anna Trapnel and other female prophets before them – some of whom, ironically, were Roman Catholic – Evans and Cheevers presented their fasting bodies as signs of God's favour, vindicating their message: 'And many a time were we made a dreadful sign and wonder to them,' writes Evans, 'that it can never be forgotten.'[16]

———

IF EVANS AND Cheevers turned the Inquisitor's Palace into a stage on which they could perform as prophets, they were the protagonists of an apocalyptic drama. While imprisoned in Malta, Evans wrote *A Brief Discovery of God's Eternal Truth* (1663), in which she insisted that the 'day of [God's] power ... is come', meaning that 'Antichrist's kingdom' was already being 'destroyed'. Rather than identifying the Antichrist as a specific person, she interpreted this figure as 'that spirit in everyone that doth profess Christ Jesus in words, but doth not profess him in life and power'. This was the spirit that informed her Catholic captors, she said, those who made 'images, and forms, and likenesses without' and said 'it doth represent Christ'. The 'man of sin' alluded to in the book of Revelation, meanwhile, was anyone who focused on 'earthly objects, and visible appearances', while the 'painted harlot' – or the 'whore of

Babylon' – was 'the fallen wisdom' of 'the earthly mind'. Even
the figure of Lucifer should be interpreted metaphorically, she
argued, claiming that he represented that 'spirit which doth
exalt itself over the consciences of any people, to compel them
to a tyrannous law, to worship according to his will, and in his
way, without any commandment or precept from the Lord'.[17]
Understood in such terms, Lucifer was clearly not confined
to Malta but was also rampantly active in England, where
Quakers were being persecuted for their refusal to conform
to the established Church.

Evans therefore establishes an apocalyptic – and a global
– framework for her ordeal in Malta. Believing that she is
living in the end times predicted in the book of Revelation,
she presents her experiences as part of a final cosmic battle
between good and evil. Evans's and Cheevers's account of their
imprisonment similarly describes their experiences through an
apocalyptic lens. In the time of their 'great trial', Evans writes
with words taken from the book of Revelation that the sun was
darkened, the moon was turned to blood, and

> the stars did fall from heaven, and there was great tribu-
> lation ten days, such as never was from the beginning of
> the world, and then I did see the Son of Man coming
> in the clouds with power and great glory . . . the heav-
> ens were on fire, and the elements did melt with fervent
> heat, and the trumpet sounded out of Sion . . . and all
> the enemies of God were called to the great day of the
> battle of the Lord. And I saw a great wonder in heaven,
> the woman clothed with the sun . . . and there was a
> trumpet sounded in heaven, and I heard a voice saying
> to me, the city is divided into three parts . . . and I heard

a voice saying, Babylon is fallen, is fallen, Babylon the
great is fallen.

Although on one level this biblical paraphrasing presents
a metaphorical account of their experiences in the Inquisitor's
Palace, on another level Evans is describing the spiritual battle
in which she believes she and Cheevers are participating. The
moon has not literally turned to blood and nor have the stars
fallen from the sky, but the biblical description of these events,
understood as an allegorical account of the end times, was to
her mind being fulfilled in and through their suffering. 'Dear
Friends and people,' Evans explained, 'whatsoever I have written, it is not because it is recorded in the Scripture, or that
I have heard of such things; but in obedience to the Lord I have
written the things which I did hear, see, taste and handled of
the good word of God.' The Bible, to the Quakers, was less
significant than an authentic – that is, a direct and sensuous
– encounter with the truth (a sentiment complicated by the
fact that the claim to hear, see, and touch 'the Word of life' is
itself biblical (John 1:1)). If Evans wrote that the 'heavens were
on fire', it was not because she had read this in the Bible but
because she was tangibly experiencing in her spirit 'the great
day of the battle of the Lord'.[18]

If for Anne Wentworth, as we will see later, apocalyptic rhetoric provided hope for a Day of Judgement, a future
moment when she would be vindicated and her enemies would
finally be put in their (damned) place, for Evans and Cheevers
the apocalypse was already unfolding before their eyes. Locked
in their humid stone-walled cells, they could hear, see and taste
the elements melting. Identifying themselves – as did many
radical Protestant women in this era – with the woman clothed

with the sun in Revelation 12, they interpreted their moments of triumph – moments that from an outside perspective might seem to suggest their helplessness – as evidence that God was already stirring up the earth to help 'the woman', as he did in the Revelation narrative. The Day of Judgement had already dawned, as the treacherous English Consul – 'consumed as a snail in the shell' – had discovered, to his cost.[19]

Engaged in spiritual warfare against the forces of evil, Evans and Cheevers were not simply battling the Roman Inquisition in Malta but were taking part in a global struggle against Antichrist. Their 'transnational apocalyptic visions', as the literary critic Catharine Gray observes, rendered national identities irrelevant: the only divide that mattered was that between light and darkness.[20] People of 'divers[e] nations' were imprisoned alongside the English Quaker women, who assumed that all their fellow prisoners had the capacity to become attuned to the light within. Other than the Friends who supported them – including the Quaker Daniel Baker, who smuggled their writings back to England – the English both at home and abroad were just as likely to try to stamp out their message as were the Maltese or those in Rome. Cheevers addressed Malachi, the English friar who tormented them in Malta, as 'thou crooked scorpion', informing him that he was an 'Antichrist', 'a bloody persecutor of God and his eternal truth, and the messengers thereof'.[21] On their way back to England after being freed from Malta, they stopped briefly in Tangier only to be confronted by 'the abominations of the wicked in that place; none worse than Englishmen for swearing, lying, pride, drunkenness, whoredoms and such like'. Wherever they were in the world, then, whether home or abroad, Evans and Cheevers saw themselves as engaged in a universal struggle of good against evil, a battle in which they were determined to be 'as bold as lions for God's truth'.[22]

———

HAVING CONVINCED THEIR captors that they would never be converted to Catholicism, Katharine Evans and Sarah Cheevers were finally released. Returning to England in 1663, they launched into further missions together, journeying to Scotland and to Ireland before both being arrested for attending a Quaker meeting in Somerset. Cheevers was told that 'she should not come forth of prison, until she came forth to a stake,' indicating to her supporters that the English authorities had a 'Popish spirit' whose cruelty matched that of the Roman Inquisition.[23] She died not long after being released. Katharine Evans continued to travel, and was imprisoned at least twice more, in Welshpool in 1666 and in Bristol in 1681, before dying in 1692.

Part Five:
Apocalyptical Women

10

Elizabeth Avery

And there appeared a great wonder in heaven; a woman
clothed with the sun, and the moon under her feet,
and upon her head a crown of twelve stars . . . And
she brought forth a man child, who was to rule
all nations.

Revelation 12:1, 5

I found Christ in me, ruling and reigning, and taking all
power to himself, and he hath caught the man-child up
to God, which I brought forth, ie the flesh.

Elizabeth Avery, 1652

Prior to the outbreak of plague in London in 1665, a 'maiden
gentlewoman' lodging in Durham Yard, south of the
Strand, had a vision of a 'lovely virgin' pouring a 'cup of bit-
terness and death on the city' before it burst 'all in flames'.
Later, she saw 'the whore of Babylon, clothed in purple and
scarlet, riding into the city, crying for drink'. The 'whore' went
'into dark places to drink' and returned with 'blood running
out of her mouth', signifying that a massacre was imminent.[1]
Depicting contemporary events through the lens of the book
of Revelation – in which angels pour 'vials of the wrath of God
upon the earth' (Revelation 16:1) – the woman's visions followed

the final book in the Bible in deploying female characters to represent polarized forces of good and evil.

In the book of Revelation, John of Patmos describes a vision of a woman, 'arrayed in purple and scarlet colour, and decked with gold and precious stones', sitting on a seven-headed beast. She held a 'golden cup in her hand full of abominations', and on her 'forehead was a name written, MYSTERY, BABYLON THE GREAT, THE MOTHER OF HARLOTS AND ABOMINATIONS OF THE EARTH' (Revelation 17:3–5). Representing the Roman empire, within which the early Christian communities were being persecuted at the time of the book's writing, this 'whore' was drunk 'with the blood of the saints' (Revelation 17:6). The 1599 Geneva Bible translation wasted no time identifying the 'whore of Babylon' with the Roman Catholic Church. Her red and purple clothes, it noted, evoked the garments of the 'Romish clergy', putting it beyond doubt that this biblical 'harlot' signified Roman Catholicism.

A figure symbolizing evil, the 'great whore' in Revelation is set against other female figures who represent salvation. 'Babylon' – or Rome – is contrasted with the 'holy city', the 'new Jerusalem', said to come 'out of heaven, prepared as a bride adorned for her husband' (Revelation 21:2). As well as the 'whore' and the 'bride', though, there is another female figure in Revelation, one who is not quite so easy to categorize. She is the 'woman clothed with the sun', a 'great wonder' who has 'the moon under her feet, and upon her head a crown of twelve stars' (Revelation 12:1). This cosmic woman, said in the notes of the Geneva Bible to represent the true Church, is heavily pregnant. She gives birth to a messianic 'man child', one who it is said will 'rule all nations' (Revelation 12:5). The birth of this child – who is swiftly taken up to heaven – leads to a war between the angels and a devilish dragon and his armies, forcing the woman to flee to the wilderness. Once there, the earth is said to have 'helped the woman', swallowing up the flood with which the dragon tried to drown her.

Associated with both the heavens and the earth, at once transcendent and vulnerable as she flees for her life after giving birth to a fragile promise of redemption, the woman clothed with the sun resonated powerfully with radical religious women in seventeenth-century England.[2] Evoking maternal forces of renewal, she modelled courage under persecution. Her triumphs, such as they were, did not come easily. She nevertheless represented hope, including the hope of living in harmony with a world that could be a place of shelter as well as destruction. The 'apocalyptic woman', as she was sometimes termed, did not evoke the annihilation that we tend to associate with the term 'apocalypse' today. Her role in giving birth to a potential source of redemption together with her ability to unite the heavens and the earth told a different story, one that anticipated the utopian 'new earth' (Revelation 21:1) with which the book of Revelation concluded. A place where 'a pure river of water of life' flowed and a 'tree of life' bore fruit and grew leaves 'for the healing of the nations' (Revelation 22:1–2), the new earth evoked the possibility of renewal. If the book of Revelation presented its readers with vivid images of destruction as well as feminized symbols of goodness and evil (potentially reducing women to the polarized roles of virgin or 'whore'), it also therefore furnished them with an alternative narrative in which a woman could play an active, positive role in the redemptive drama of the end times.

When radical Protestant women including Elizabeth Avery, Anne Wentworth and Jane Lead read the book of Revelation,

William Blake, *The Great Red Dragon and the Woman Clothed with the Sun*, c. 1805,
pen and grey ink over graphite.

'Revelation of St John: The Woman Clothed with the Sun', woodcut
by Albrecht Dürer from *Apocalipsis cu[m] figuris* (1498).

then, they found a repertoire of apocalyptic images that could be used to speak not only of judgement but of the renewal of the world. For these women, crucially, the triumph of good over evil promised in the final book of the Bible did not have to be postponed until the end of time. The 'new Jerusalem', they believed, was already in the process of descending from heaven to earth. Identifying with biblical accounts of the end times which they – along with many in their era – related to their own historical moment, they saw themselves as key players in this cosmic drama.

———

THE BOOK OF Revelation spoke of a conflict between good and evil that many in the seventeenth century believed would reach a climax in their lifetime. Many believed, moreover, that the imminent defeat of Antichrist would inaugurate a new era – a millennium – in which the saints would reign either with or on behalf of Christ on earth, entailing a radical transformation of the social and political order. Mary Cary's *A New and More Exact Mappe* (1651) gave a detailed account of the new world that was about to be unveiled. 'In 1646 the Beast ceased to prevail against the saints,' she declared, and by 1701 there would be 'complete deliverance'. Very soon, then, 'the confusions, and combustions, and oppressions and troubles that were in the old frame of the world' would be 'forgotten'. The Bible promised the meek that they would inherit the earth, but so far 'for the most part, wicked men have possessed the earth' and the saints have 'never had any inheritance in it'. But everything was about to change: 'meek and sweet spirits' would be made 'princes in all the earth'. 'What a wide difference will there be between their condition now, and their estates then!' she exclaimed: 'How comfortably and . . . how happily the saints shall live in this new world.'

The Hebrew prophet Isaiah outlined a vision of a 'new earth' in which no one would die before the age of one hundred and the people of God would be able to 'build houses, and inhabit them' and 'plant vineyards, and eat the fruit of them', no longer having to 'labour in vain' to benefit another (Isaiah 65:20–23). Cary's 'map' of the new world applied these words to mid-seventeenth-century England: 'no infant of days shall die; none shall die while they are young; all shall come to a good old age,' she promised. Isaiah's prophecy was on the point of being fulfilled: the people of God 'shall not be afflicted for the loss of their children; for they shall live till they be a hundred years old; and not an old man shall die that hath not filled his days'. They will

> enjoy their houses and gardens which they shall build and plant for themselves, living comfortably and peaceably in them . . . by the work of their hands, they shall purchase estates, and they shall be long enjoyed by them and their children; no strangers shall deprive them of them . . . strangers shall not drink the wine, nor eat the food, nor inhabit the houses, nor wear the apparel, for which they have laboured, but they and their children shall comfortably enjoy the work of their hands.

The biblical vision imported into Cary's 'map' illustrates the fact that eschatological transformation was not envisaged in exclusively spiritual terms. The changes for which both Isaiah and Mary Cary longed included an end to infant mortality and to economic exploitation: seen in these terms, the kingdom of

God involved ordinary people being able to enjoy a 'comfortable subsistence' without 'grief and vexation'.

Cary was undoubtedly calling for a revolution. If the saints were to be 'redeemed from the servitude and slavery in which they have been subjected to men' and were not always to be 'sufferers', they might well have to resort to violence, she stated: the 'saints' must 'fight against such as would murder and destroy them (as the associates of the Beast would)'. If they went into battle against 'the wicked cruelties of evil doers', binding 'their kings in chains, and their nobles with fetters of iron', they would see their former oppressors 'come bending unto them', bowing 'down at the soles of their feet' and bringing them 'their wealth, their riches, their treasures, their silver and their gold'.[3] If Cary's vision of the new earth was ultimately one of harmony and peace, she believed that such a world would not come into being without the overthrow of the existing order.

FOR THE WOMEN we will meet in the final part of this book, as for Mary Cary, the time was short, but this brought with it the hope that not only England but the world as a whole was on the brink of social and political as well as religious transformation. The three women whose voices we will hear in these next chapters were writing at very different moments in the seventeenth century: Elizabeth Avery published her daring work of theology during the political upheavals of the 1640s, Anne Wentworth wrote her angry accounts of her abusive husband in the 1670s, and Jane Lead began to publish her visionary works in the final decades of the century. Despite all longing for the radical transformation of society, the three women had very different styles and approaches. Jane Lead in fact objected to the prophecies of Anne Wentworth, noting in her journal that Wentworth yearned for 'plagues and vials of wrath to come immediately upon the formal churches', whereas Lead preferred to focus on the 'kingdom of love'.[4]

Despite their differences, though, all three of the women published innovative interpretations of the book of Revelation. Elizabeth Avery's theological treatise presented an allegorical rather than a literal reading of the apocalypse, one that challenged established narratives of imminent global destruction. Anne Wentworth, meanwhile, interpreted the final book of the Bible in highly personal terms, using its narrative of justice for the marginalized and persecuted to frame her own story of surviving spousal abuse. In doing so, she altered the gender dynamics of the biblical book, setting female virtue against male malice. If Wentworth's publications celebrated women as the speakers of truth, Jane Lead's visionary works went even further, presenting not only the saints but the divine in feminized terms. Working creatively with the genre of apocalyptic writing, these radical women published some of the boldest theological and autobiographical works of the century, works that in their different ways challenged the religious and gendered orthodoxies of their times.

———

UNITED IN THEIR outrage, a group of ministers decided in 1648 that they could no longer tolerate the publication of what they saw as 'heresy'. Naming and shaming those guilty of propagating 'the errors of our times', their publication, *A Glass for the Times*, pointed the finger at many men but only one woman: Elizabeth Avery (*fl.* 1614–53).[5] Her book, *Scripture-Prophecies Opened* (1647), was peppered with 'errors', they claimed, questioning as it did the resurrection of the body and suggesting that the 'soul is God'.[6] Such notions associated Avery with the doctrines of the notorious Family of Love. A pamphlet published earlier in the century had mocked Familists for reading the Bible allegorically, accusing them of saying that 'Christ and Antichrist were no real persons, but fashions of mind.'[7] Whatever the inaccuracies of this caricatured account, those influenced by Familist ideas – which continued to circulate in England into the seventeenth century – tended to interpret the Bible in relation to the inward experience of believers, for example reconfiguring heaven and hell as internal spiritual states.[8] As well as echoing these forms of radical religious belief, Avery's writing intimated that she adhered to doctrines of 'heavenly flesh' associated with the radical Reformation, including the idea that God could be 'manifested in the flesh of his saints, as in the humanity of Christ'.[9]

Such notions appalled Avery's brother, the minister Thomas Parker, who was living in New England. Perhaps fearing that he would be shamed by association, he published an open letter to his sister in 1650 in which he publicly repudiated her 'heretical opinions'.[10] Parker was not only disturbed by the content of Avery's book but by the very fact of its existence. 'What will you make yourself to be, a goddess?' he sneered: your 'horrid' book is an 'attempt above your gifts and sex'; 'your printing of a book, beyond the custom of your sex, doth rankly smell.' To Parker, it was unacceptable that 'a weak woman' – 'ignorant of the wiles of Satan' – had taken it upon herself to throw off the combined 'reason' and 'rule' provided by her father and brother, both of whom were well-known dissenting ministers. Their opinions, he knew, had become irrelevant to his sister now that she believed herself to be 'taught immediately by the

Spirit'. Driven by 'fancy and not reason' and therefore 'a lost woman, a lost sister, and lost eternally', Avery, in her brother's eyes, illustrated the terrible consequences of a woman not only coming up with her own reading of the Bible but daring to circulate her 'opinions' in print. An 'ignorant' woman, he raged, was making 'a chaos and confusion' not only 'of the Scriptures' but of the entire hierarchical social order.[11]

————

SIX YEARS AFTER the publication of *Scripture-Prophecies Opened*, Elizabeth Avery's words appeared in print again, this time as one of the testimonies published by John Rogers in *Ohel, or Beth-Shemesh* (1653). Her conversion narrative, delivered to the Independent congregation in Dublin, began with her account of the loss of three of her children (her fourth child also died later), a tragedy that left her inconsolable, 'in a horror, as if I were in hell'. A letter from a minister offered only momentary relief. One morning, however, 'God wonderfully appeared.' Falling into 'a trance for a while', she was left 'full of joy'.

During the civil war years, Avery resembled a Seeker, turning away from religious communities to God's 'teachings within me . . . for I had his Spirit, his voice speaking within me, and God alone was with me'. Capturing both the intensity and the isolation of her spiritual experience, she described leaving her husband behind to travel to Oxford in the hope of meeting like-minded believers. Once there, however, she continued to feel alienated. Huddled in a garden one day bemoaning her 'tormented' condition, she began to map her experiences onto those described in Revelation. Her suffering, she believed, resulted from a battle between the flesh and the spirit, a struggle that was resolved when God reassured her that she was saved. She had powerful subjective experiences of God, who drew her 'on, higher and higher in himself', leaving her resolved to 'write down what God had done' for her soul.

Elizabeth Avery and her husband subsequently moved to Dublin, where in 1651 she joined the Independent church fellowship meeting at Christ Church Cathedral. Women played an unusually active role in this congregation, since John Rogers, to the despair of his critics, went further than most ministers in 'giving power to women'.[12] God bestowed 'his Spirit much upon' women, Rogers insisted, arguing that they must be free to declare 'their visions of truth' through 'speaking, pleading, prophesying, or the like'.[13] In his marginal notes to Avery's testimony, Rogers drew attention to the status of her father (Robert Parker was a dissenting minister who had been forced into exile in Amsterdam), affirming the spiritual status of a woman who had been publicly denounced as an 'infamous apostate'. When she described her ongoing sense of alienation in Oxford, he noted that she did not care 'for self, but for God and his people'. While others had sought to silence her, Rogers and the Dublin community provided Avery with a platform from which to speak.

———

THERE IS ONLY one further mention of Elizabeth Avery's name in the historical record. A contemporary diary records that her child was christened on 14 June 1653, suggesting, as Crawford Gribben notes, that her rejection of church rituals had weakened by this point.[14] Beyond this intriguing mention, we do not know what became of Avery. Alongside her testimony, however, we have the daring theological publication that got her into so much trouble. Presented in the form of three letters,

Scripture-Prophecies Opened boldly challenges mainstream beliefs about the apocalypse. Almost all aspects of Christian apocalyptic belief are 'to be understood otherwise than hath been formerly', she argues. Proposing a radically interiorized interpretation of the book of Revelation, Avery celebrates the fact that the renewal promised by the Bible is already beginning to take place in the hearts of believers. She introduces her book by noting her own 'weakness and contemptibleness', claiming that she is merely the 'instrument' God has employed to topple 'the wisdom of the wise'. Later, however, she asserts that her prophetic revelations eclipse those found in the Bible, demonstrating that her 'weakness' does not, to her mind, undermine the value of her words. 'I fear not reproach,' she states: 'though I may be counted mad to the world, I shall speak the words of soberness.'[15]

Her first letter explores the significance of 'Babylon', the city associated with the 'great whore' in the book of Revelation. Protestants usually took Babylon to represent the Roman Catholic Church, but Avery argues that Babylon should be understood more broadly as a principle of 'confusion and error'. The fall of Babylon refers not to a specific historical event but to each person's experience of salvation, she argues. Babylon, then, is already falling, person by person, even though she admits that the process is somewhat slow going: 'Babylon and Antichrist is fallen in a very inconsiderable number of saints,' she notes. Babylon ultimately operates as a malleable principle of evil in her writing, one that she associates with both the 'arbitrary power' of the Church of England and 'the foregoing Parliament of England'.

In her second letter, Avery reconsiders biblical narratives of the destruction of the heavens and the earth. Several biblical texts have been taken to predict the 'utter dissolution of this visible heaven and earth', she notes. But while many believe that the heavens and the earth will be destroyed by fire, she disagrees, insisting that the 'visible heavens' will not be 'dissolved'. When the Bible describes 'heaven' passing away, this is simply a metaphor for the scrapping of religious rituals. The 'earth' that will go up in flames, moreover, is not the earth as such but 'the best part of man, as his natural wisdom, and human learning, and gifts'. A new heaven and a new earth will be formed, but it will be 'a heaven within us'. This process has already begun: 'for now heaven is passing away with a great noise, and the elements are melting with fervent heat, and the earth and the works thereof are burning up, which is all accomplishing in the saints.'

For Avery, those who believe that the earth will be destroyed are working from the assumption that the material world is evil. But the earth is 'harmless in itself', she insists. By 'the blessing of God it doth much good . . . and accordingly it shall not be burnt up, for the curse is taken from the earth, in that redemption that was in Christ'. Far from heading for an apocalyptic conflagration, the earth will exist indefinitely: 'we cannot find in Scripture that the visible heaven and earth are to have an end; for we find to the contrary, that they are to continue.'

Avery's third and final letter addresses the issue of the resurrection of the dead. If we are to understand resurrection, she suggests, we first need to know what we mean by death. Contrary to common-sense notions, death, for Avery, does not primarily refer to the mortality of the body. True death, she states, is spiritual death, or separation from God. The passing away of the body is merely the casting aside of an outer garment, the throwing away of that which is no longer required by the spirit. The material dimension of our humanity goes back to the earth while 'the spirit returns to God that gave it', suggesting that the 'soul which is in all mankind, is God himself'. Once again, Avery is proposing doctrines associated with the Family of Love, who were said to describe the body as 'nothing but the beetle's skin which is in the end to turn back into the mother-earth, the spirit being then clothed with a garment that is from heaven, all beautified with the lovely-being'.[16]

Despite the radical religious heritage of some of her key concepts, Avery claims to be presenting brand new revelations. 'We must look for new discoveries, such as have not been yet,' she writes. The overthrowing of established interpretations was a vital dimension of eschatological transformation. Believing herself to be living in the last days of history, she cites the biblical prediction that the end times will be characterized by an unprecedented outpouring of God's Spirit. Everything that has gone before, including the Bible, was based on incomplete revelation. Focused on 'the letter only', its truth-value is limited. It is only now, in the 'time of the glorious appearing of the second coming of Christ', that 'more glorious manifestations' will appear: God is finally bringing 'to light those things which have been a long time hidden in darkness'. Elizabeth Avery's writings did not so much re-interpret the apocalypse, then, as participate in its manifestation. Her declaration of new truths demonstrated that she was living in the end times, an era characterized by the sweeping away – or the burning up – not of the material earth but of established forms of knowledge, as the Spirit finally made known through daughters as well as sons 'that which hath been kept secret from the beginning of the world'.

———

ELIZABETH AVERY RETURNED more than once to the figure of the woman clothed with the sun, reworking the Revelation account of this character for her own purposes.[17] In *Scripture-Prophecies Opened*, the apocalyptic woman of Revelation 12 represents every believer, each one of whom has 'brought forth a man-child', representing 'the glorious manifestations of God in the flesh' of the saints. In her testimony, published some years later, the woman clothed with the sun makes another appearance. On this occasion, Avery identifies herself with the figure. She says that she 'found Christ in me, ruling and reigning, and taking all power to himself, and he hath caught the man-child up to God, which I brought forth, ie the flesh (by his incarnation)'. In both allusions, then, the apocalyptic woman who delivers a messianic 'man-child' signifies the redemption not only of the spirit but of the 'flesh'.

When Avery speaks of 'heaven within us' in *Scripture-Prophecies Opened*, she describes it as 'God manifested in the flesh of his saints, as in the humanity of Christ', indicating her embrace of the radical doctrine of 'heavenly flesh'.[18] An unorthodox teaching that flourished among some radically Reformed thinkers in Europe in the sixteenth century, the doctrine of 'heavenly flesh' – in which Christian theology fused with alchemical concepts – taught that Christ's body was formed of a celestial substance wholly distinct from the corrupt materiality of fallen bodies. God's people were able to participate in this heavenly flesh, transcending their fallen materiality as they progressively became more spiritually refined and able to share in Christ's celestial body. Later in the century, Jane Lead, as we will see, joyfully embraced the doctrine, celebrating her ability to escape the limitations of her mortal body as she apprehended a 'sparkling' celestiality encompassing body, mind and spirit. Decades earlier, Elizabeth Avery was also writing that the 'manifestation of Christ' in the 'flesh . . . doth begin to appear in some, and we do likewise expect it in general unto all the Saints, when God shall bring them out of darkness into his marvellous light; which is begun, and shall increase until it be perfect day'. This process would culminate in the experience of resurrection, when saints would be transformed into a 'body mystical' comprised of 'spiritual bodies' not 'distinct one from another' or from the divine but integrated into 'the fullness of God'.[19]

Drawing on distinctive doctrines within radical Protestant theology and applying them to her own life as well as to her wider account of humanity and the earth, Avery illustrates the extent to which radical Protestant women in this era worked with apocalyptic concepts and images to articulate alternative understandings of themselves and their world. In the next chapter, we will see how another woman – Anne Wentworth – also drew on apocalyptic language for her own purposes, in her case to help her to speak out about decades of abuse.

II

Anne Wentworth

... they would not have me the Lord to choose a weak
woman yet can they not at all hinder me; for I have chosen
thee, to be my battle-axe, to cut all formality down ... Thy
hard-hearted husband and these cruel people ... shall not
be lords and kings no more over thy conscience, to make thy
body and soul to bow to them ... for I King Jesus come to
give my children rest, and thou art a free woman.

Anne Wentworth, c. 1679

Anne Wentworth (1630–*c.* 1693) survived decades of abuse.[1]
Originally from Lincolnshire, she married William
Wentworth, perhaps a glove dealer, in about 1652, and they lived
together in London. In the eyes of the world, her husband, a
well-regarded member of a Baptist congregation, was as 'moral,
honest, just-dealing [a] man as any of them', a man with 'the
gift of his tongue ... very fit for business and employment in
this world'. But behind closed doors it was a different matter.
Wentworth was 'grossly abused' by her husband. He was such
a 'scourge and lash' to her that her neighbours knew she 'lived
in misery'. His 'barbarous actions' and 'unspeakable tyrannies'
so assaulted her 'mind and body' that she feared for her life.
For eighteen long years, he walked all over her: using the words
of Isaiah 51:23 she writes that she had to lay her 'body as the

ground, and as the street for him to go over'. By the beginning of 1671, when she was forty years old, she was physically spent: 'consumed to skin and bone, a forlorn sad spectacle to be seen, unlike a woman; for my days had been spent with sighing, and my years with crying'. She was taken ill with a 'hectic fever', one caused, she believed, by the 'great oppression, and sorrow of heart' that she had been forced to smother for 'so long in [her] own breast'. Miraculously brought back from the 'point of death' in 'the nick of time', she believed herself required by God to declare the 'testimony, given her by the Lord Jesus, to ... the world'. Unfortunately for her husband, this testimony consisted of a searingly honest description of how William Wentworth had 'led [her] in a wilderness of affliction'. Fearing to 'enrage [her] husband and all his brethren' with her account of his 'cruelty', Anne Wentworth initially hesitated to tell her story. But God commanded her to do so, to the extent that he sent an angel, she claimed, who threatened to kill her if she remained silent. And so she 'fell to writing', finding that once she put pen to paper she could not stop. Finally summoning the courage to leave her husband, she argued that she was merely follow-ing the 'great law of self-preservation'. Not only was her life in danger, but 'it was necessary to the peace of my soul, to absent myself from my earthly husband.' She would never return, she maintained, unless he became 'a new man, a changed man, a man sensible of the wrong he has done me with his fierce looks, bitter words, sharp tongue and cruel usage'.[2]

Anne Wentworth's revelations were greeted by her com-munity with hostility, as she knew they would be. She and her husband were members of a Particular – or Calvinist – Baptist church, many of the members of which were unable to 'bear the truth to be spoke of their brother'. But Wentworth felt compelled to 'speak truth'. 'The more they dashed at it, and beat the poor weak instrument for it', the more God reassured her that 'he would have this work done, and [had chosen] such a weak, foolish, despised woman as I.' To bear witness against William Wentworth, she insisted, was to do the work of God: her husband was not only a violent bully but a hypocritical Christian, and to expose him as such uncovered the false religiosity he embodied. Wentworth was not simply fighting for herself, then, but was God's 'battle-axe, to cut all formality down'. In the eyes of the Baptists, she was a 'proud, passionate, revengeful, discontented, and mad woman', one who had 'unduly published things to the prejudice and scandal of [her] husband' and 'wickedly left him'. But such slander and persecution, to her mind, aligned her with Christ. If they had been true Christians, she remarked, they would not have 'pierced and wounded me so deep, when I had been for 18 years such a woman of sorrow, and acquainted with grief'.[3] It was Anne Wentworth's ability to place her experience of spousal abuse in the context of a wider spiritual battle that enabled her to speak out about her suffering. Believing herself to be the persecuted victim not just of one malicious man or even of the Baptist community but of the forces of Antichrist, her crusade to expose the truth about her husband became nothing short of an apocalyptic struggle.

Intent on revealing the full horror of what she had suffered, Wentworth wrote a detailed account of her experiences. Her husband was enraged. On 13 February 1674, he brought three men to 'fright, and amaze, and astonish' her. So upsetting was this encounter that it caused her to have a miscarriage. This shedding of 'innocent blood' cried 'aloud for vengeance', she insisted. Filling her 'full of sorrow for no other thing but writing', her husband and his allies had tried to 'make a rape of [her] soul, to have it bow down to [them]'. Yet it was Anne Wentworth rather than her husband who was hauled before the leaders of their Baptist church. They charged her with 'rejecting and neglecting their church' (including refusing to dress as they instructed), and with 'dissatisfying' her husband (she was accused of saying that 'his tongue should cleave to the roof of his mouth' and of staying away for one night 'without his leave'). But God told her that they were wrong to 'say I the Lord would not command thee, to do anything against thy earthly husband's will'. The Baptists were mistakenly equating a husband's authority with that of God, she pointed out. But it was God, not William Wentworth, who was her 'soul's husband' and the one to whom she would remain loyal.[4]

Alienated from her family and church community, her name dragged through the mud, Anne had more struggles to come. In the summer of 1677 her husband abruptly sublet their home, removing all the furniture so that she had 'neither bed, nor anything to sit on', as well as 'no meat, drink or money'. She tried to stand her ground, refusing to leave, but after a few days he sent some family members to remove her by force. Taking her against her will to a house in Hoxton, her husband believed that he had finally bullied her into silence. But Wentworth continued to write her 'book of experience'. Her husband then committed what to her mind was his most despicable act to date. Having failed to prevent her from writing, he resorted to stealing her work. Making off with her manuscripts, including a book she had written for her daughter, William was pursued by his distraught wife all the way to Glovers' Hall. When Anne came 'to the chamber-door, where he and his company were locked up, they would not open, but spoke hard words'. And so on 25 September 1677 Anne Wentworth lost six years' worth of writing. My 'persecuting lying enemies' names shall all rot and stink upon the earth for what they have done', she cried. Suspecting that they had 'consumed' her books 'in the flames', she called for God's 'fierce wrath' to fall on them. This 'one thing, in taking the book away from [her] like a most wicked man', was enough to shut William Wentworth 'out of heaven': 'if he do not repent, and deliver it to thee again, he shall never enter into my rest,' God tells her.[5]

By the following month, Anne Wentworth and her daughter were in hiding. The 'cruel unchristian actings' of her husband had become so terrifying that she had been forced to 'fly for [her] life'. Her only so-called crime, she insisted, was her 'writing . . . oh, injustice!'[6] But she was more determined than ever to expose the crimes committed not only by her husband but by the Baptist community that was protecting him. In 1676 she published *A True Account of Anne Wentworth's being cruelly, unjustly, and unchristianly dealt with by some of those people called Anabaptists*, followed in 1677 by *A Vindication of Anne Wentworth*. Later, she published two further works, *The Revelation of Jesus Christ, just as he spake it . . . unto his faithful servant Anne Wentworth* (1679), and *Englands Spiritual Pill . . . which the Almighty hath revealed unto Anne Wentworth* (*c.* 1679). In all her writing, the prophetic interweaves with the autobiographical as she presents her struggle with her husband and the Baptist community as an aspect of the wider apocalyptic battle of good against evil.

Wentworth's story ends on a note of triumph. After her husband had locked her out of her home, God promised her that by the following summer she would be able to return. She was told to take courage and send to have the bill pulled off the door, which thy earthly husband hath set on, to let the house, for to keep thee out: but he shall not. For I the Lord will return thee in, and ask no leave of him for it is thy home: bid the man deliver up the keys to thee . . . I the Lord will put thee in possession.[7]

Months later, she received a mysterious message telling her that the door to her home was open. Wentworth and her daughter immediately returned home, changing the locks so that her husband had 'not power to come and put her out'. Supported by her friends, who provided her with furniture and helped with her expenses, Wentworth was jubilant. Back in the house where she had first begun to speak the unvarnished truth about her life, she continued to write and to battle for her story to be heard and believed.

———

ANNE WENTWORTH'S WRITING is infused with the language of the Bible. In Genesis 3:15, God cursed the serpent – usually taken to represent Satan – saying that he would 'put enmity between thee and the woman, and between thy seed and her seed; it shall bruise thy head, and thou shalt bruise his heel'. This verse was often interpreted as referring to Jesus, the 'seed' or descendant of Eve, whose death would conquer evil. Wentworth wove the language of this passage into her story, writing that God hated to 'see men trample upon truth, and wound and bruise my heel, and now he will raise truth up more bright to break their head'. Her opponents, including her husband, were therefore identified as devils who were wounding a figure of truth in the form of Anne Wentworth herself. If the 'truth' would 'break' their 'head', this consequence would be via her words.

The book of Revelation, promising as it did that malevolent authorities would be overthrown and a persecuted minority vindicated, was a particularly useful resource for Wentworth as she presented her story. In common with the women in this book, Wentworth believed herself to be living in the final days of history. For her, however, the imminent Day of Judgement primarily represented the moment when she would be vindicated. 'As near as New-Year's day is,' she warned in 1677, 'before that day the Lord will begin to cast a cloud of his anger upon all them that have done me so great wrong, and persecuted me without a cause, and stroke after stroke will follow, until all hypocrisy be discovered and formality thrown down, and whole Babylon sink like a stone never to rise up any more.'[8] 'As they have abused thee, so shall they have of me,' God tells her:

> Shall not I the Lord judge this people, when vengeance belongeth unto me? I will recompense them . . . as they have been cruel, so will I be cruel, as they have oppressed, so will I the Lord oppress, as they have wounded and had no pity, so will I the Lord wound and have no pity, as they have shed blood, so will I the Lord shed blood.

In this passage, typical of her writing, Wentworth paraphrases Hebrews 10:30 ('vengeance belongeth unto me, I will recompense'), before imitating the language of Hebrew prophets such as Jeremiah. Speaking in the voice of God, Jeremiah promised the people of Israel that 'all they that devour thee shall be devoured and all thine adversaries, every one of them, shall go into captivity; and they that spoil thee shall be a spoil, and all that prey upon thee will I give for a prey' (Jeremiah 30:16). Echoing the rhetorical structure of this and similar passages, Wentworth applies prophetic messages of judgement to her own situation. God's words, delivered through her pen, swerve startlingly from a global to a domestic frame of reference: 'I the Lord will be with thee, and take care of thee, and I will pay the rent for thee, trust thou in my word. For I am Lord of all the earth, and all the earth is mine ... I see how thou went'st out of that house by force in a storm, but I the Lord will send thee in again in a calm.'

The author of the preface to *Spiritual Pill* was acutely aware of how Wentworth might come across to her readers. Do not 'stumble' over the fact that 'she speaks for herself', he or she warned. Implicitly acknowledging that Wentworth appeared to be more than a little self-obsessed, the preface conceded that it might seem odd that God 'makes so much ado with Anne Wentworth's personal condition, suffering, vindication and with putting her in her former state and house'. These matters, however, had 'mystical tense or meaning': for God to return Wentworth to her former home was a sign that he would 'bring his exiled church ... to her primitive state again'. Wentworth's life therefore carried symbolic significance, illuminating God's dealings with his people more generally. Depicting Wentworth as a representative of the true Church, this preface identifies her with the woman clothed with the sun: both Wentworth and the woman described in Revelation 12, it notes, were 'mean' – ordinary – women who were 'in a desperate condition' and 'forced to fly'.[9] According to this preface, then, to read Wentworth's story is akin to reading the book of Revelation. In both texts, the reader must look beyond the surface of the story to uncover its deeper spiritual meanings. 'My oppressions and deliverance', agreed Wentworth, 'had a public ministry and meaning wrapped up in them.' 'A great wonder from heaven will be wrought,/ And no creature upon earth hath me taught,' she stated, further identifying herself with the woman clothed with the sun. On 9 May 1678, moreover, she received a revelation showing God's 'loving kindness towards his church, under the . . . figure of Anne Wentworth'.[10] Both Wentworth and her supporters therefore understood her experiences in symbolic and apocalyptic terms. For her to overcome her husband was a sign that the end was nigh: Satan, she wrote, was 'upon his last legs'.[11]

———

IN ANNE WENTWORTH's writing, as in apocalyptic writing generally, situations tend to be depicted in polarized terms: everything is seen through the lens of a contest between good and evil. This binary approach is evident in her tendency to set up a stark contrast between female innocence and male malevolence. Her enemies, she notes, are 'dying, angry men'. Baptist leaders cannot bear to think that God will 'look upon a poor weak despised woman that is trampled under the feet of men', she observes. It is beyond their comprehension that God could 'own a woman and disgrace a man'. But God 'pleaded the cause of a poor, desolate, despised woman against men and devils'.[12]

Wentworth repeatedly identifies herself as the 'Zion' to her husband's 'Babylon'. Mount Zion in the book of Revelation was the place where the saints stood with the Lamb of God, a holy place that was set against the evil associated with Babylon. God makes it plain that she and her husband are representatives of 'Zion and Babylon, of the true and false church . . . he is the oppressing, and thou the oppressed . . . thy husband is justified of men, and thou art condemned of them: But I the Lord will justify thee, and condemn both him and them . . .

thou shalt have a crown of life, when they have shame.' Making
the conflict between her and William into a microcosm of the
apocalyptic struggle between good and evil, Wentworth therefore aligns her husband with the false church. She has been
stigmatized by her community but it is her husband who is
the 'great whore' of Babylon. 'The Lord shewed me why the
people did not understand me, nor my work,' she writes. It is
because they 'blind themselves with pouring so much upon a
man and his wife, and will look no further'. Patriarchal thinking has distorted their outlook so that they write 'all faults in
[her] forehead', accusing her of 'delusions and disobeying of
[her] husband'. Yet if they were not 'stark blind', they would
see 'what I the Lord am doing . . . how I have placed the two
spirits in a man and his wife, to figure out Zion and Babylon,
which I purposed before the beginning of the world'.[13]

While English Protestants in this era often identified
the 'whore of Babylon' with the Roman Catholic Church,
Wentworth argues that the Babylon represented by her husband is 'spread over the whole face of the Christian world, and
everywhere found among the literal and outward churches', that
is, in all forms of empty religious practice. Nowhere is Babylon
more present, in fact, than among the Particular Baptists, her
former community, who 'exceed the Papists in sinning'. Their
religion 'stinks': they have the 'same oppressing spirit that the
Pope of Rome doth'. For Wentworth to expose the truth about
her abusive husband and the community that is shielding him
is for her to have 'a hand in Babylon's ashes'.[14] Interpreting her
experiences through an apocalyptic lens, Wentworth therefore
reworks apocalyptic discourse on her own terms. Aligning herself with both the 'great wonder' – the woman clothed with the
sun – and with Zion, she demonizes her husband and his allies

– among them some key Baptist leaders – as the embodiment of Babylon and its 'whore'. The threat to the true Church, in her accounts, comes from powerful male figures who victimize female speakers of the truth.

Wentworth's husband and his allies deployed the usual repertoire of misogynistic abuse. 'I am reproached as a proud, wicked, deceived, deluded, lying woman,' she notes, 'a mad, melancholy, crack-brained, self-willed, conceited fool, and black sinner, led by whimsies, notions, and kniff-knaffs [jests] of my own head: one that speaks blasphemy, not fit to take the name of God in her mouth; an heathen and publican, a fortune-teller, an enthusiast.' She tackles the accusation of madness head on: it is in the 'rotten interest of my adversaries ... to believe me a person beside myself', she points out, 'for if I be found in a right mind, how mad must they be discovered to have been, in their blind rage and fury against me and my testimony?' She is also labelled a 'whore', her reputation tarnished by malicious rumours that she keeps 'men company' and lives 'a scandalous life in an alms house'. Yet her predictions of the Day of Judgement turn the table on her accusers. My 'persecutors ... must stand without with the dogs and sorcerers, and whoremongers, and murderers, and idolaters', she declares: and in 'that day shall my mouth be opened ... and I shall speak, and be no more reviled, nor more abused, no more persecuted'.[15]

———

IN JULY 1677, Wentworth wrote to the king that she had heard a 'dreadful terrible voice' announcing that 'here is the severest judgements that ever was, now a coming on the land, such as never was before nor never will be again.' Confident in her prophetic calling ('I am no lying prophet'), she nevertheless asked the king to 'pass by the bad English in this, being it is a woman who hath no help of man'.[16] Is it possible to detect a hint of pride in this apparent apology? After being downtrodden for decades, Wentworth had finally achieved a measure of independence. Having accepted for years her designated role as the 'ground' for her husband to step on, her discovery of her voice through her writing had marked the end of her subservience. She had been 'contented to yield up [her] life' to her husband, but he had wanted her to 'bow down' her soul, too. This was a step too far; her soul was a 'precious jewel' that belonged to God alone. She writes that God has promised that her 'hard-hearted husband and these cruel people', who have 'ruled over thee in great rigour and great severity', will not 'be lords and kings [any] more over thy conscience, to make thy body and soul to bow to them. This shall not be when I the Lord come to sit upon my throne, to rule all nations . . . for I King Jesus come to give my children rest, and thou art a free woman, to worship me in spirit and truth, and no man shall make thee afraid for thy following of me.' As a 'free woman', she could exercise her 'just and necessary liberty . . . to publish the things which concern the peace of [her] own soul, and of the whole nation'. She was also determined to be economically independent, administering 'to [her] own necessity' and not being 'burdensome to any'.[17]

In October 1677, state documents record that 'the predictions of Mrs A. Wentworth are to be heard next week by some in town . . . There is much talk of it.' Yet just a month later, it is noted that 'our friend Mrs. A[nne] W[entworth]'s friends begin to decline her predictions, and her too.' Some notable people had initially been 'much affected' by her claims, but 'she cannot or will not be positive when and what the great things she wrote about to the king will be.'[18] In making specific predictions about judgments that had failed to materialize, Wentworth had damaged her reputation as a prophet.

The context in which Wentworth was prophesying was very different to that in which earlier figures such as Sarah Wight and Anna Trapnel had made their declarations. Following the Restoration, as Rachel Adcock notes, 'prophetic discourse, the predominant literary mode used by Dissenting women pre-Restoration, became a reminder of the disordered Commonwealth period and was discredited as dangerous, seditious, and a sign of madness.' In the face of intense persecution, the sects of the civil war era that had survived into this later period were concerned to create for themselves a more acceptable public image, one no longer defined by the 'enthusiasm' that was a dirty word. Their female members were not able to speak as openly as they had done previously: for women, 'the authoritative position of public preacher or prophet was for the most part left behind,' notes Adcock.[19]

Wentworth's publications nevertheless testify to the fact that some women did continue to speak and to write as prophets in England in the 1670s and beyond. The only surviving copy of Wentworth's *Englands Spiritual Pill* was bound together with two of Anna Trapnel's works in a Scottish volume in 1689, implicitly recognizing Wentworth as the heir of the earlier radical prophet.[20] As Sarah Apetrei and Hannah Smith observe, while 'public displays of piety' by women may have been discredited following the Restoration, this did not mean that space was not 'created for female voices'.[21] It was in the last decades of the seventeenth century, in fact, that one of the most prolific female visionaries of the century began to publish her works, as we will see in the next chapter.

12

Jane Lead

Great heroes, ye must now give way,
And learn a female general to obey.
Jane Lead, 1696

Dive into your own celestiality and see with what manner of
spirits you are endued: for in them the powers do entirely lie
for transformation.
Jane Lead, 1697

L ooking back over her life at the age of 77, Jane Lead (1624–
1704) conceded that her experiences had been 'exceeding
strange'. For over sixty years she had been overwhelmed by
'constant visitations of the Spirit of wisdom and revelation'.
How could 'the world' either know or 'judge of' such a life?
Even the seventeenth century did not quite know what to do
with someone this otherworldly. A Protestant mystic, Lead
called herself a 'heavenly spy', one 'sent before-hand to be a
speculator, to behold the pattern of those heavenly things,
which are to be replanted, in like manner and order here in
this world'.[1] Her language, to one exasperated contemporary,
was 'quite out of the way of the education, or conversation, or
even reading of women'. To her admirers, though, the fact that
her writing was 'utterly strange' – 'not suitable to the genius of

this polite age, and especially of this nation' – only confirmed her divine inspiration.[2]

Notable for her innovative reworking of the teachings of the German mystic Jacob Boehme (*c.* 1575–1624), whose female figure of divinity, Sophia – or Wisdom – she developed on her own terms, Lead had a significant impact on radical religious circles across Europe.[3] Writing vivid, sensual prose (and sometimes poetry), she emphasized the power of the visionary imagination, anticipating the work of English Romantic writers, including William Blake.[4] Taking the concept of Sophia in a new direction – as Sarah Apetrei notes, the 'radical implications' of the Sophia doctrine for women 'remained unrealized until Jane Lead' – and placing the experiences of women at the centre of her visions, Lead, as Nigel Smith observes, constructed a 'feminized religion', one that challenged 'nearly all the prevalent sexual ideologies of the time'.[5] Although she did not agitate for social and political reforms in the same way as earlier prophets such as Mary Cary or Anna Trapnel, Lead proposed a radically altered version of Christianity. Placing a female figure within the godhead, her visionary writing jettisoned catastrophic and vengeful forms of apocalypticism in the name of a distinctive millennialism characterized by gradual and peaceful processes of transformation through which, in the end, all would be saved.[6]

Fascinating in her own right, Lead is also interesting because of what she reveals about the persistence of mysticism in England at the end of the seventeenth century. Mysticism emphasizes direct experiences of God, potentially including a sense of union with the divine.[7] For Protestants in the seventeenth century, as we have seen, personal experiences of God were synonymous with authentic faith. In the Restoration era, however, there was widespread hostility to the 'enthusi-asm' – or emphasis on divine inspiration – often associated with mysticism, which was assumed by many to be the enemy of rationality and civil order. Lead and the circle around her nevertheless demonstrate that mystical beliefs – along with fervent apocalypticism – were still being articulated in radical terms in late seventeenth-century England.[8]

———

BORN IN 1624 into a wealthy Norfolk merchant family, Jane Lead was sixteen years old when she first heard the voice of God. Her family, who were Anglicans, were celebrating on Christmas Day with music and dancing when 'very suddenly and surprisingly ... a sudden grievous sorrow was darted as fire into her bowels'. God spoke to her in a 'soft whisper', telling her to 'cease from this' because he had 'another dance to lead [her] in'. Jane escaped from the party into her father's study, where she described her experience to a local preacher and friend of the family. He encouraged her to believe that she had been chosen by God for 'something good and great'. In common with many Protestants of her era, she subsequently became preoccupied with 'the consideration of her interior state'. For the next three years, she suffered 'great anguish', worrying for example that she had 'persisted in a falsehood' about something trivial. Going to live with her brother in London when she was eighteen, Jane had the opportunity to hear the antinomian preacher Tobias Crisp teach that we are 'discharged from the fault and guilt' of sin. Comforted with this 'sweet message' of love and grace, and after having a vision of a sealed pardon, she finally gained assurance of her salvation.[9]

After returning to Norfolk in 1643, Jane married the merchant William Lead, and they lived together in King's Lynn and later in London. The couple had four daughters, two of whom died in childhood. Despite being described by his wife as a 'magnificent husband', William's financial mismanagement meant that when he died in 1670 Jane was left 'mired in manifold, deep and most desperate poverty'. At this traumatic time, she was 'visited once again with a vision from God', in which she was reassured that the 'loss of outward things . . . served only to prepare the path by which the heavenly powers and gifts could descend into souls unhindered'.[10]

Such proved to be the case, as Lead soon began to experience powerful visions. In April 1670 she was in the country visiting a friend, taking 'lonely walks in a grove or wood; contemplating the happy state of the angelical world'.[11] Suddenly,

> there came upon me an overshadowing bright cloud, and in the midst of it the figure of a woman, most richly adorned with transparent gold, her hair hanging down, and her face as the terrible crystal for brightness.

This was Sophia, whom Lead – unlike Boehme – imagined in highly personal terms.[12] Sophia told her that she would be reborn, 'for out of my womb thou shalt be brought forth after the manner of a spirit'. For the next three days, Lead walked 'in the silent woods', stunned. Then, while she was sitting under a tree, 'the same figure in greater glory' appeared to her again, 'saying, behold me as thy mother'. Soon afterwards, Lead returned to London, where on arrival she found herself 'encompass'd about with [a] heavenly host, and made a spirit of light'.[13]

Sophia, illustration from *Gemma Sapientiae et Prudentiae*, c. 1735.

Lead aligned herself with another visionary, John Pordage, the leading English proponent of Boehme's teachings.[14] Decades earlier, Pordage and his wife had established a mystical community in Berkshire, where they spoke with angels.[15] Pordage's wife died in 1668, and from 1674 until his death in 1681, Lead lived in a household with him, 'in great spiritual happiness'. Her economic 'straits and cares' during this period were severe enough for her brother to offer to take her in, and one of her daughters was keen for her to accept this offer. Yet Lead was determined to 'hazard the loss of all' to remain with her 'appointed mate' in her spiritual mission.[16]

Lead's first work, *The Heavenly Cloud Now Breaking*, was published in 1681, followed by *The Revelation of Revelations* in 1683. In 1692 she went to live in an alms house for poor widows, from where she continued to publish accounts of her visions. By the 1690s, Lead's works were circulating across Europe. Francis Lee, a physician, came across her writing in Leiden in the mid-1690s, prompting him to visit her in London. He soon became a devoted supporter, eventually marrying her daughter. Together with Richard Roach, rector of St Augustine in Hackney, Lead and Lee became the leaders of the Philadelphian Society, a millenarian group emphasizing divine revelation and spiritual regeneration.[17] According to Lead, a 'new and glorious church' was beginning to arise, as faultless as the church of Philadelphia described in the book of Revelation. There was no need to wait until the end of time to experience heavenly perfection: 'there are some at present living', she claimed, who were in the process of being 'fully and totally redeemed'. This chosen few had already experienced 'the revelation of the kingdom and glory of God within the soul', allowing them to taste 'the powers of the world to come, or of the future blessed age'.[18] The kingdom of God, in other words, was already advancing on earth, even if most people did not realize it yet.

The Philadelphians were a small group, perhaps consisting of around one hundred people. The Toleration Act of 1689 theoretically permitted them to hold meetings, but public hostility forced them to petition a London magistrate for protection, only to be told to 'purge themselves of those evil reports that were generally dispers'd ... concerning them'.[19] Among the rumours was the false allegation that Lead claimed to be the grandmother of a new messiah. This 'sect', wrote an accuser, are 'under the direction of Jane Lead', believing not only that she is 'the apocalyptical woman' described in Revelation but that 'from out of the daughter of Lead shall be brought forth a new Christus, who is to be partaker both of the celestial and terrestrial nature.' The Philadelphian Society withdrew from public view in 1703, and in the following year, Jane Lead, eighty years old and by now blind, died. She had published seventeen visionary works, making her, as Paula McDowell points out, one of the most prolific female authors of the seventeenth century.[20]

———

JANE LEAD'S WRITING focuses on her own experiences. She can 'give no other direction', she says, than what she has herself 'been taught in, and in some degree ... put into practice'. Her most significant work is her spiritual journal *A Fountain of Gardens* (4 vols), the title of which is taken from Song of Songs 4:15. In it, she writes that when she withdrew into herself she found 'a more pure air, than I could meet without me'. When you are 'introverted' into the 'inward deep', she observes, 'God's immediate teaching [opens] in the centre of your own soul.'[21]

For Lead, it is thrilling to consider 'what we mortals are, from whom our descent is, and what manner of spirit we consist of, and exist by':

> For until we understand our own eternal being, we cannot know God, the Being of all Being. For as we are the inbreathed soul from God, we live in his essence . . . we consist of the higher principles, and worlds above, as likewise of those below . . . O how great is the mysterious greatness of the soul, that liveth vailed, covered, and unknown to itself?[22]

While many seventeenth-century Protestants emphasize the moral corruption of humanity, Lead celebrates the divine potential of both men and women. Given that our inner being is 'an essence derived from God', we should wake up to our 'own spirit's sovereignty'.[23] Salvation, she claims, comes from within. Redemption in her work is frequently represented by images of birth, but it is we who must give birth to ourselves: the godly have 'no dependency upon what is without themselves, each one having the deified seed, [is able] to procreate these angelical births from themselves'. Salvation, she teaches, is ours for the taking. 'Bring your Christ forth,' she instructs her readers, 'thus shall each one become a Christ (or an anointed) from this deified root opening within their own soul.'[24]

Lead's belief that we have a divine principle within echoes the teachings of Plotinus (204/5–270), the father of Neoplatonism. In his only piece of autobiographical writing, Plotinus describes his experience of 're-awakening':

I come to be outside other things, and inside myself.
What an extraordinarily wonderful beauty I then see! . . .
I then realise the best form of life: I become at one with
the divine, and I establish myself in it.

Plotinus taught that something of our soul had always
remained connected to the immaterial realm of the divine.[25]
To reconnect with this aspect of our being was to come back
to our essential nature: becoming 'one with the divine' did not
involve a loss of the self but enabled it to 'establish' itself in
more authentic terms.

Like Plotinus, Lead is unafraid of celebrating the beauty
of her inner being, an entity that merges with God. Blending
Neoplatonism with Christian theology, she writes of the regenerated soul being 'taken with its own beauty and comeliness'.
Having put on the 'fine robe of the resurrection', it is free to
'admire' itself: 'whereas self-love was in the old body to be abro-
gated and denied; here is all lawful to be owned, for now it loves
the Holy Trinity in itself.' There is a 'God like Almightiness
within our selves', if we would only open our eyes to see it.
'There was somewhat in me of infinite Being that was too great
to be kept under the tuition and law of that which was earthly
and terrestrial,' she claims. To access this 'infinite Being', we
must undergo a process of purification, one that she describes
in alchemical terms: once the 'dross and tin' of the 'earthly and
terrestial' is burned away, we will uncover the 'golden matter'
of our divine essence.[26]

———

BY THE END of the seventeenth century, Jane Lead was proposing a doctrine of universal salvation, a highly unusual teaching

in this era.[27] There will be a 'restitution of the whole lapsed creation, whether human or angelical', declares the title page of *A Revelation of the Everlasting Gospel Message* (1697). We are 'flourishing towards . . . translated life', she writes two years later, insisting that nothing is excluded from this transformative process. Even 'corrupt and putrifactious matter' will 'receive clarifying and healing'. 'What more joyful tidings can come to our ears', she exclaims, 'than this one everlasting age, that shall swallow up all those ages wherein sin and death hath reigned; with all those miserable effects that have been ever since the creation of this world?' The swallowing up of 'sin and death' entails redemption for all: not only all human beings but even Satan and the fallen angels will in the end be saved. Christ will 'reconcile all to himself which was at odds with him', she insists: 'the plaster provided is much broader than what the wound of sin hath made.'[28]

For Lead, then, neither humanity nor the planet is doomed. The end times will be characterized not by violent conflagration but by gradual regeneration, as everything slowly reintegrates into 'the divine Being, from which [we] did proceed at first, pure as God is pure'. This process requires us to have an inner experience of death, resurrection, ascension and glorification: Lead has already passed through all four of these stages, she claims. In the end, 'nothing of Adam's weak or impotent nakedness' will remain: all 'sin, wrath, and misery' will be swallowed up and all that has 'been impaired, desolated, and made miserable by transgression' will 'be repaired and redeemed'.[29]

———

AS WE SAW in Anne Wentworth's works, apocalyptic writing tends to present the world in polarized terms, depicting a clear-cut battle between forces of good and evil. For Lead, however, binary thinking results from the Fall: redemption means that all 'contrarities' will 'cease'. Drawing on Neoplatonic thought, she describes salvation in terms of everything returning to its point of origin in 'one pure element'. Evil, within this philosophical model, is a 'non-entity', a principle of division overcome by the unity of Being. For Lead, 'divine harmony' is already beginning to be achieved on earth, and her visions are playing an active role in its manifestation.

One of the 'contrarities' that Lead seeks to overcome in and through her writing is the division between the body and the spirit. She often speaks negatively about the body, referring to it at one point as the 'vile tent of humanity'. But her vision of the 'new heavens and earth' is not purely spiritual: the perfect world includes redeemed bodies as well as spirits.[30] In order to attain the perfection of divine being, the division between bodies and spirits must be transcended. In her visions, the bodies of those who have been regenerated are indistinguishable from their spirits.[31] On 7 November 1674, for example, she describes a vision of those who have been 'divinely modified in their bodies ... appearing in a golden lustre of brightness'. Drawing on alchemical imagery, she witnesses the redeemed – including herself – beginning to 'ascend out of bodies terrestrial' as they 'put on figurative bodies bright and ethereal, corresponding to the nature of the star-like sparkling spirits'.[32]

If the division between body and spirit is overcome by the redemptive process, so is the destructive division between male and female. Jacob Boehme taught that redemption involved transcending 'the divided sex of male and female': before the Fall, he stated, the 'angelical Adam' was both 'male and female'.[33] Drawing on Boehme alongside Galatians 3:28 ('there is neither male nor female, for ye are all one in Christ Jesus'), Lead in one of her first publications declares that in the New Jerusalem sexual difference will be obliterated:

> As to the outward sex, there shall be no distinction, though the typical priesthood admitted none but males in its day: All of that is done away, for signs and figures in this ministration do fly away like a cloud: male and female are alike here, therefore the Holy Ghost doth include both in one, swallowing up all in the newness, strength, power and glory of his own springing new birth ... *Where there is neither Male nor Female but Christ is all, and in all.*

Sophia, she elaborates, is 'not limited to male or female, for she may assume either according to her good pleasure, for she is both male and female for angelical generation'.[34]

In one striking vision, Lead sees Christ, 'all bright, as the body of heaven for clearness'. Exhaling white mist, his body pours forth not only blood but milk. He has pipes fixed on his 'breasts, [which] sprouted milk', enabling Lead to be breast-fed, 'sucking down the spiritual sweets'.[35] The 'spiritual body', this vision suggests, not only encompasses both male and female characteristics but fuses together the human and the non-human: Christ's body also sprouts with the branches of an olive tree. In Lead's early visions, then, perfection is represented by the overcoming of binaries. Bodies are reconciled with spirits, humans with the divine, male with female. In her later work, however, she moves away from Boehme's emphasis on androgyny, preferring instead to describe both God and the redemptive process in distinctively female terms.

———

LEAD FREQUENTLY RETURNS to images of pregnancy and childbirth in her writing.[36] In the days of the apostles the Holy Spirit came 'down as a shower', she notes, but God's blessing now appears 'by way of a birth'. The New Jerusalem, moreover, is the 'mother city ... who [is] to bring forth her first and freeborn to replenish the new earth and heavens'. But it is Sophia, the 'Eternal Virgin-Wisdom', who is the ultimate mother figure. 'She was before all, as being the co-essential creating power in the deity,' and to experience resurrection life is to be 'born again out of her virgin womb'.[37] Women were often assumed to play a passive part in reproduction in this era, and both Boehme's and Pordage's accounts of Sophia emphasize her passivity.[38] Lead, on the other hand, depicts Sophia in far more active terms. Throughout Lead's writing, childbirth is depicted as a cosmically powerful act.[39] She describes 'the mighty birth-working power', and 'the womb which conceiveth and brought forth numberless birth-powers into a manifest existence', emphasizing the creative power of a female generative force that she associates with redemption itself.[40]

Strikingly, Lead's visions sometimes describe reproduction occurring without any male involvement at all. In one dream, for example, she sees a nest of eagles. This reveals that Sophia, or the 'eternal virgin wisdom of God', will sow 'her virgin seed, into [Eve's] womb, and she shall be made fruitful, and shall bear twins ... and they shall make a perfect church on earth'. The regenerated Eve will join in 'union with her true guide and mate, the virgin wisdom of God' to 'bring forth a royal offspring': once Sophia 'espouses herself' to her mate, Eve will become 'the mother of celestial and heavenly children'. If Lead celebrates female fertility, however, it is only of the spiritual kind. The productive spiritual union of Sophia and the 'eternal Eve' will displace the destructive fertility of the 'earthly Eve', whose 'multitude of children' are 'the brats of Babylon'.[41]

Lead's depiction of redemption in terms of childbirth generates some truly startling images. In one vision, she identifies herself with Christ on the cross. 'Everyone's hand was against me,' she writes,

> adding weight and pressures to her, that was bleeding upon the cross already, crying *crucifie, crucifie in dying, let her die.* Now I seeing that I was to tread the wine-press alone and to encounter the potent spirits, the throne-princes of darkness, I cried and was in strong travail.

The agonies of the cross in this vision fuse with a description of labour, as 'every pang and throw did open the birth of life.'[42] Reimagining Jesus's crucifixion in terms of the agony of childbirth, Lead identifies Christ's anguish with female forms of suffering. In doing so, she reformulates his work of redemption as a specifically female act of generating life.

———

JANE LEAD'S WRITING is suffused with the imagery of the book of Revelation, and the woman clothed with the sun plays a pivotal role in her visionary world.[43] The trials of the apocalyptic woman in the wilderness after giving birth were often taken to refer to the persecution of God's people before the Reformation. For Lead, however, the 'mystical' birth alluded to in the Revelation narrative had not yet taken place.[44] In December 1676, she was told that the 'man-child' born to the woman clothed with the sun represented the Holy Spirit. This 'birth' was 'yet to come', after the 'most holy seed of God' was planted into those of 'perfect heart' who were prepared for 'high and heavenly converse'.

Lead envisaged herself and her fellow Philadelphians playing a key role in the delivery of this 'child'. They already carried the 'living birth-stone within'. If they retreated from the 'solaces of this world' – imitating the apocalyptic woman's flight to the wilderness – the 'high extracted matter' that had been 'sown within' would be delivered, enabling them to 'bring in another kingdom'. Their collective labour was already underway:

> for a true travail has gone forth, not by one only in singularity, but by many, who have been carried into the spiritual wilderness, in abstraction and separation from all worldly conversation, ascending upon the eagle-wing so high, as to acquaint themselves with the high throne dominions in the heavenly places.

Once the 'saints' had delivered the 'man-child', they would gain 'dominion and power over the earth'. Mary was not transformed by the birth of Jesus, Lead notes, but to give birth to the Holy Spirit was a far more momentous undertaking. Those chosen for this role would be 'more dignified and honoured' than Mary herself, as was signified by the apocalyptic woman's 'bright flaming garment' and crown, declaring 'that to her was given the command and power to bear sway within the celestial region'.[45]

Lead's revelations, to her mind, are synonymous with this 'holy birth'. She is delivering new forms of spiritual life, enabling 'both males and females' to 'bear rule' and to have 'all sublunary things ... under their feet'. She nevertheless wonders why the birthing process is taking such a long time: why is 'this birth of almighty strength [sticking] in the place of breaking forth'? The reason, she is told, is that 'bodily vehicles' must be 'fitted and sanctified, by the residing of the Holy Ghost' before they are able to deliver spiritual life, and for most this is still to take place.[46]

Lead therefore sees herself as a prophetic figure who is in the vanguard of millennial processes of renewal. In another of her dreams – identified in the contents of *A Fountain of Gardens* volume II as 'The Wonder-Woman' – she sees a small woman wearing a crown. Reminiscent of the woman clothed with the sun – described in the Bible as 'a great wonder' – her face is 'bright as the sun, and clear as the moon'. The 'wonder-woman' challenges Lead to 'see what ye may arrive to be in me', before handing over a child, 'all lovely and fair'. Unexpectedly heavy, the baby slips through Lead's arms, causing her to give a 'great screek' before she realizes that the child is unharmed. Lead interprets this dream to mean that 'a virgin woman' is yet 'to be revealed out from the heavens', of whom Mary the mother of Jesus was a mere forerunner. At first, she thinks that this figure is of a purely spiritual nature: she is 'all arrayed in a body sapphire-like and not in the garb of the mortal creature'. She then realizes that the 'wonder-woman' is human: her 'pure heavenly glory' coexists with a 'creaturely being'. It is then revealed to Lead that she herself is this 'wonder-woman'. 'There is somewhat of grace to you peculiarly by this prophecy,' she is told, meaning that she is to be 'trusted with more considerable dignities and powers, tending to wisdom's star sparkling crown'.

A few days later, Lead remembers that she had once longed for a son. But although she has not given birth to a 'son by

The Contents of this Second Volume.

Detail from the contents page of Jane Lead, *A Fountain of Gardens*, vol. II (1697).

earthly generation' she will give birth to 'a pure Nazarite, given unto [her] from the Lord'. It is not surprising, then, that rumours flew that Lead saw herself as either the mother or the grandmother of the Messiah.[47] But Lead envisages her maternal role in purely spiritual terms: echoing the language used in the Bible to describe Mary, she describes herself as 'happy' and 'blessed' that 'a spoiless Nazarite lily' will be born from her 'spiritual womb'.[48]

———

AS DID ELIZABETH AVERY before her, Lead interpreted the book of Revelation in metaphorical terms, reading its account of violent conflict as a representation of struggles within the individual. The book of Revelation's predictions 'are first to be accomplished in your own heavens and earth', she states. She has personally encountered the 'fury, hellish force and wrath of the dragon', for example, which have been overcome by God's 'powerful might within me'. If we want to see the 'passing away of the old heavens and earth', she continues, we must look for this 'in our selves'. Lead therefore offers what she terms a 'mystical' interpretation of Revelation, claiming that its predictions are 'to be fulfilled in holy and heaven-born saints'.

Lead's internalized reading of the events described in Revelation raises the question of what material difference the arrival of the New Jerusalem will make to the world. She confronts this issue directly in *The Revelation of Revelations*. It is true, she admits, that there is 'little appearance' of the New Jerusalem yet 'upon the visible stage of the world': 'the elect stones' – or people of God – are 'at present lying amongst the rubbish of confusion'. The heavenly city will ultimately 'descend and cover the whole earth', but this will only occur once the people of God have 'finished their inward transformation'. In the meantime, the eschatological processes that are underway within individuals remain largely hidden. Christ's 'glorious reign' will not 'break out all at once', she warns. Her readers must instead look for its gradual unveiling 'in the unsealed book of life within'.[49]

This was a far cry from the social and political revolution associated with the imminent reign of the saints by the Fifth Monarchists. As Phyllis Mack observes, Lead was 'silent on the political and social issues that had engaged the prophets of the Civil War period'.[50] Yet if Lead remained vague on the details of how the resurrection life that she and others were experiencing would change the world, her feminized account of regeneration was nevertheless radical in different terms, questioning as it did established notions of gender as well as dominant interpretations of the apocalypse. Rather than propagating images of violent judgement, her visions reimagine the world in alternative – 'sparkling' – terms. 'There is a vein of gold in eternal nature's garden, that has not yet been pierced into,' she declares, 'which, when the divine artists shall be sent forth, shall be broken up and run most free, as the true elixir appropriated and reserved for this age.' It was her role, via her visions, to give expression to this 'vein of gold', conjuring up a world ruled by Sophia – a 'springing paradise' – where all was 'obedient to the law of love'. Imagining this 'everlasting gospel of love, goodwill, and peace' in her publications was a way of bringing into being a more peaceful form of existence, opening 'a torrent of boundless blessings upon the world'.[51]

WHILE JANE LEAD and Anne Wentworth both aligned them-selves with the Revelation figure of the woman clothed with the sun, their interpretations of what it meant to be an 'apoca-lyptical woman' could not have been more different. Wentworth longed for the imminent Day of Judgement as the moment when she would triumph over her enemies, whereas Lead's visions anticipated the arrival of a 'New Jerusalem' characterized by peace and unity. Lead objected to Wentworth's prophecies, noting in her journal on 29 December 1677 that she wanted 'no part' in Wentworth's vengeful version of 'divine justice', one that desired 'plagues and vials of wrath to come immediately upon the formal churches'. Wentworth, she writes, is mistaken not only in relation to the timing of Christ's return, but in her beliefs about the nature of his kingdom. 'The Lord restore her, and give her a more distinct discerning of Spirits,' she con-tinues, because 'the kingdom of love . . . is that which will open, and be strong to prevail.'[52] For Wentworth, the book of Revelation promised that God would one day take vengeance on her male oppressors. But Lead did not believe that God's kingdom had to be awaited. We are already able to generate 'new births, altogether supernatural', she asserts: 'whatever thy

Jesus acted here and did, thou mayest not fear to imitate: that which is formed in thee, will certainly drive thee to this.' Our salvation, she claims, is ours for the taking. Instead of waiting for Christ to return in the skies, we should 'take present care of the heavens of [our] mind'. 'Dive into your own celestiality and see with what manner of spirits you are endued,' she exclaims, 'for in them the powers do entirely lie for transformation.'[53]

Afterword

This book is entitled *Voices of Thunder*, but whose voices have we have been hearing speak? As we saw in Chapter Two, the women telling the stories of their lives insisted on the spiritual significance of their experiences. Neither their sex nor their social status had any bearing on their importance in God's eyes, leading them to believe that their stories deserved to be heard. At the same time, however, they denounced what they saw as their corrupt and sinful selves so that they could embrace alternative spiritual identities, ones often constructed through the language of the Bible. For the women in this book, to be locked within the confines of one's own being – or to speak with one's 'own' voice – was quite literally a hellish fate, one from which they were desperate to escape. It was their sense of God's voice – filtered through the language of the Bible but experienced as speaking within them – that propelled them to speak and to write. They saw themselves as God's instruments, his agents on earth. Anne Wentworth, for instance, referred to herself as God's 'battleaxe', the weapon he would use to bring down his enemies, a role that empowered her to speak about the abuse she had endured at the hands of her husband. Her story, to her mind, was not simply her own: instead, her struggle with her husband played a crucial part in the unfolding apocalypse. For Wentworth, as for all the women in this book, this sense that they were caught up in a wider spiritual battle – a battle that was ultimately God's – did not minimize the importance of their personal experiences but infused them with nothing short of eternal significance.

Part of the thrill of encountering these women lies in allowing ourselves to hear the complexity of these voices from the past, voices that – like Elizabeth Barton's uncanny prophetic speech – stem not simply from their own mouths but from multiple points of origin: personal, spiritual, biblical, communal. Hearing their stories, we are confronted with accounts of radical women whose actions and words defied patriarchal forms of authority, indicating the extent to which 'religious radicalism could challenge the institutions and values articulated at the heart of early modern society,' as Naomi Pullin observes.[1] The principles of spiritual equality that these women along with their male counterparts proposed struck at the heart of the ideologies of supposedly 'natural' and God-given hierarchical order that underpinned seventeenth-century English society. The response of conservative figures such as Thomas Edwards to the sectarians may seem comically excessive, but the alarm felt by Edwards and others points to the fact that the radicals – with their insistence that God was 'no respecter of persons' – were calling into question some of the most cherished principles governing the ordering of society.

Among these principles, of course, was the belief in male superiority, a principle challenged so profoundly within radical religious circles that one theologian pronounced that 'the history of enthusiasm [or the belief in direct divine inspiration] is largely a history of female emancipation.'[2] To describe the women in this book as 'emancipated' would be to sweep over the inequalities that they continued to experience. As we have seen, for example, most radical religious groups in seventeenth-century England and Ireland did not permit women to preach in a formal capacity in their meetings. Despite the remaining constraints, however, sectarian women were able for a time at least to embrace undeniably radical forms of behaviour and expression. They preached, they travelled independently of men and they published theological treatises, offering their own – often highly unorthodox – readings of the Bible. More than one woman in this book adhered to the radical doctrine of 'heavenly flesh', arguing that humans could participate in Christ's 'celestial flesh', while women, according to Sarah Apetrei, were 'disproportionately represented among those defending the doctrine of universal salvation in seventeenth-century England'.[3] These are women who made their own interpretations of the Bible known, even when their views diverged drastically from mainstream Protestant theological positions.

What, then, is the legacy of these women? Accounts of radical religion in seventeenth-century England often conclude on a downbeat note, emphasizing the transitory nature of the revolutionary upheavals of the civil war years. With the Restoration, runs the familiar narrative, came a return to the rule of reason and civic order, with the visionary hopes of the radicals relegated to the status of dangerous delusions, the 'idle fancies of lunatic brains', in the mocking words of one Restoration play.[4] The most radical group in terms of female 'emancipation' – the Quakers – were heavily persecuted after the Restoration, and their earlier 'enthusiastic' expressions of faith, including the shockingly confrontational behaviour of female Friends, were to some extent curtailed within the movement so that it could acquire a more respectable image. Other radical religious groups, including the Fifth Monarchists, vanished altogether.

As we have seen, however, neither radical Protestantism nor its female proponents disappeared after the Restoration. Anne Wentworth might have faced a more sceptical audience than did Sarah Wight or Anna Trapnel when she published her apocalyptic pamphlets, but publish them she did. The mystic Jane Lead's prolific visionary output, meanwhile, was only just getting going in the 1680s. The Quakers, too, may have adopted a more sedate public image after the Restoration, but the organization of women's meetings from the 1670s onwards continued to give women a prominent position in the movement, even when such a move generated 'serious opposition', as Keith Thomas points out.[5]

However fervently the authorities hoped that the civil war sects and their unruly female members could be wiped from the collective memory, the women who had preached, published, travelled and newly interpreted the Bible left their mark. Holding fiercely to principles of spiritual equality and the supremacy of the individual conscience and living out the implications of these principles in courageous fashion, the women in this book – along with many other women and men like them – shook the very foundations of society. While the context in which they operated means that they cannot be identified in straightforward terms as the mothers of feminism, the radically levelling ideas that they promoted continued to haunt English society, contributing to later emancipatory movements that called into question oppressive and hierarchical social orders. It is impossible, as Apetrei notes, 'to isolate suffrage, socialist or democratic movements in the English-speaking world from the activism of nonconformists'.[6]

The literary legacy of the works we have encountered in this book is also significant. Rose Thurgood composed one of the earliest-known English conversion narratives, identifying her as an important figure in the history of autobiographical writing in English. The vivid, sensuous language of Anna Trapnel, meanwhile, strikingly unusual both in its time and since, produced visionary works whose literary descendants include the mystical writings of Jane Lead as well as the poetry of the English Romantics, including William Blake. Often unschooled and yet seeking to articulate in authentic terms their intense experiences of God, the women in this book created new forms of spoken and written expression that are hauntingly beautiful in their emotional and spiritual directness. Their voices may at times have thundered, striking terror into the heart of some of their contemporaries, but at other moments they whispered, mused and sang, creating a rich archive whose full literary as well as historical significance is only just beginning to be uncovered.

References

INTRODUCTION

1 Thomas Edwards, *The Third Part of Gangraena* (1646), p. 170.
2 Katherine Chidley, *The Justification of the Independent Churches of Christ* (1641), pp. 22–3.
3 Thomas Edwards, *Reasons against the Independent Government of Particular Congregations* (1641), p. 26.
4 Chidley, *Justification*, pp. 26, 29.
5 See Sara Mendelson and Patricia Crawford, *Women in Early Modern England, 1550–1720* (Oxford, 1998), pp. 405–9.
6 Sarah Apetrei, *Reformation of the Heart: Gender and Radical Theology in the English Revolution* (Oxford, 2024), p. 3.
7 On personal experience as the 'primary authority' within puritanism, see Geoffrey F. Nuttall, *The Holy Spirit in Puritan Faith and Experience* (Oxford, 1946), p. 7.
8 Martin Luther, *Secular Authority: To what extent it should be obeyed* (1523), trans. C. M. Jacobs, in *The Works of Martin Luther*, vol. III (Philadelphia, PA, 1930), pp. 252–3.
9 Quoted in *Quaker Faith and Practice*, 5th edn (London, 2013), 19.07.
10 John Bunyan, *Grace Abounding to the Chief of Sinners* (1666), p. 79.
11 Meric Casaubon, *A Treatise Concerning Enthusiasme* (1655), p. 3.
12 Anne Wentworth, *A Vindication of Anne Wentworth* (1677), p. 15.
13 On radical Protestantism and mysticism, see Nigel Smith, *Perfection Proclaimed: Language and Literature in English Radical Religion, 1640–1660* (Oxford, 1989), p. 17.
14 Thomas Stapleton, *A Fortresse of the Faith* (1565), f.134v.
15 On the 'fractured landscape' of Puritanism before the 1640s, see David R. Como, *Blown by the Spirit: Puritanism and the Emergence of an Antinomian Underground in Pre-Civil-War England* (Stanford, CA, 2004).

16 Henoch Clapham, *Error on the Right Hand, through a Preposterous Zeal* (1608), ff. A2–A4.

17 Thomas Edwards, *Gangraena, or a catalogue and discovery of many of the errors, heresies, blasphemies and pernicious practices of the sectaries* (1646), Part 1, p. 89.

18 See Nigel Smith, *A Collection of Ranter Writings: Spiritual Liberty and Sexual Freedom in the English Revolution* (London, 2014).

19 Edwards, *Gangraena*, Part 1, 'The Epistle Dedicatory', pp. 16–17.

20 Augustine, Sermon 12, *The Works of Saint Augustine: Sermons*, vol. 1, trans. Edmund Hill, ed. John E. Rotelle (New York, 1990), p. 300.

21 John Calvin, *The Institution of Christian Religion* (1561), trans. Thomas Norton, 1.3.1, 3.2.22.

22 John Sheffeild, *A Good Conscience the Strongest Hold* (1650), 'To the Conscientious Reader'.

23 Henry Walker, *The Heavenly Guide to the True Peace of Conscience* (1641), pp. 2, 5.

24 Sheffeild, *A Good Conscience*, p. 25.

25 T. Goodwin, P. Nye, S. Simpson, J. Burroughs and W. Bridge, *An Apologeticall Narration* (1643), p. 25.

26 Luther, *Secular Authority*, pp. 251, 253.

27 Calvin, *Institution*, 3.19.14; 3.19.15; 4.20.31.

28 Katharine Evans, *A Brief Discovery of God's Eternal Truth* (1663), p. 33.

29 Edwards, *Gangraena*, Part 1, 30, 34.

30 Keith Thomas, 'Women and the Civil War Sects', *Past and Present*, 13 (1958), p. 44.

31 Martin Marprelate (pseud.), *Oh Read Over D. John Bridges* (1588), p. 5. The 'Marprelate' tracts were primarily written by Job Throckmorton MP.

32 Richard Bancroft, *A Sermon Preached at Pauls Crosse 9 February 1588* (1588), pp. 2, 5, 15, 16, 22, 25, 26, 82, 84, 87, 58.

33 Robert Baillie, *Anabaptism, the True Fountaine of Independency* (1647), pp. 55–65.

34 George Gillespie, *Wholesome Severity Reconciled with Christian Liberty* (1645), 'To the Christian and Courteous Reader'.

35 Thomas Hall, *The Pulpit Guarded* (1651), p. 13. See also Anon., *A Discourse Concerning Puritans* (1641), p. 57, and Edward Reynell, *An Advice against Libertinism* (1659), p. 21.

36 Thomas Taylor, *Baxter's Book . . . Confuted* (1671), p. 223.

37 Henry Church, *Divine and Christian Letters to Relieve the Oppressed* (1636), pp. 27–8.

38 On the question of whether women outnumbered men in seventeenth-century sects, see Bernard Capp, *The Fifth Monarchy Men: A Study in Seventeenth-Century English Millenarianism* (London, 1972), p. 82; J. F. McGregor, 'The Baptists: Fount of all Heresy', in *Radical Religion in the English Revolution*, ed. J. F. McGregor and B. Reay (Oxford, 1984), p. 47; Rachel Adcock, *Baptist Women's Writings in Revolutionary Culture, 1640–1680* (London, 2015), pp. 1–3; Como, *Blown by the Spirit*, pp. 51–2.

39 Phyllis Mack, *Visionary Women: Ecstatic Prophecy in Seventeenth-Century England* (Berkeley, CA, 1992), p. 1.

40 Edward Burrough, *A Brief Relation of the Persecutions and Cruelties that have been acted upon the people called Quakers* (1662), p. 5.

41 On 'going naked as a sign', see Hilary Hinds, *George Fox and Early Quaker Culture* (Manchester, 2011), pp. 50–51.

42 Elaine Hobby, *Virtue of Necessity: English Women's Writing, 1646–88* (Ann Arbor, MI, 1988), p. 26.

43 Patricia Crawford, 'Women's Published Writings 1600–1700', in *Women in English Society, 1500–1800*, ed. Mary Prior (London, 1985), p. 159; see also Catie Gill, *Women in the Seventeenth-Century Quaker Community: A Literary Study of Political Identities, 1650–1700* (London, 2005), pp. 1–5.

44 John Rogers, *Ohel; or, Beth-shemesh* (1653), pp. 472, 475.

45 Zachary Crofton, *Bethshemesh Clouded* (1653), pp. 187–9.

46 John Bastwick, *Independency not Gods Ordinance* (1645), pp. 45, 93, 110–13; Katherine Chidley, *A New Yeares Gift* (1645), p. 13.

47 George Fox, *Concerning Sons and Daughters, and Prophetesses Speaking and Prophesying* (1661), pp. 5–6, 9.

48 On Dorothy Hazzard, see Adcock, *Baptist Women's Writings*, pp. 74–8.

49 David R. Como, *Radical Parliamentarians and the English Civil War* (Oxford, 2018), p. 42.

50 Edward Terrill, *The Records of a Church of Christ, Meeting in Broadmead, Bristol, 1640–87*, ed. Edward Bean Underhill (London, 1847), pp. 5–36.

51 Nigel Smith and Laurent Curelly discuss the importance of hearing the 'idiosyncratic voices' of individuals if we are to understand radicalism in this era: Smith and Curelly, eds, *Radical Voices, Radical Ways: Articulating and Disseminating Radicalism in Seventeenth- and Eighteenth-Century Britain* (Manchester, 2016), pp. 1–10.

52 Evans, *A Brief Discovery*, pp. 26–7.

53 Mary Cary, *A Newe and More Exact Mappe* (1651), p. 238.

54 See Apetrei, *Reformation of the Heart*, p. 165.

55 Andrew P. Vella, *The Tribunal of the Inquisition in Malta* (Msida, 1964), pp. 31–7; see Mack, *Visionary Women*, p. 147.

56 Edwards, *Gangraena*, Part 1, p. 14.

57 *Apologeticall Narration*, pp. 23–4.

58 British Library Add. MSS 29546, f. 117, transcribed in Albert Peel and Leland H. Carlson, eds, *Cartwrightiana* (London, 1951), pp. 60–63.

59 Hendrik Niclaes, *Comoedia: A Work in Rhyme* (English trans. 1574), p. 6.

60 Hendrik Niclaes, *Exhortatio. 1. The First Exhortation* (English trans. 1574), no page numbers.

61 Anon., *A Discovery of the Abominable Delusions of those who call themselves the Family of Love* (1622), Preface, p. 54.

62 See Christopher Carter, 'The Family of Love and Its Enemies', *Sixteenth Century Journal*, XXXVII/3 (2006), p. 654.

63 Christopher Marsh, '"Godlie matrons" and "Loose-bodied dames"': Heresy and Gender in the Family of Love', in *Heresy, Literature and Politics in Early Modern English Culture*, ed. D. Loewenstein and J. Marshall (Cambridge, 2006), p. 60.

64 Clapham, *Error on the Right Hand*, pp. 47, 55.

65 See Como, *Blown by the Spirit*, pp. 34–6.

66 William Walwyn, *The Power of Love* (1643), pp. 8, 31. See Como, *Radical Parliamentarians*, pp. 192–3.

67 Alec Ryrie, 'Seeking the Seekers', *Studies in Church History*, LVII (2021), pp. 185–209, 194.

68 *George Fox: The Journal*, ed. Nigel Smith (London, 1998), pp. 12–13.

69 Testimony of Elizabeth Avery in Rogers, *Ohel; or, Beth-shemesh*, p. 404.

70 See McGregor, 'The Baptists', p. 25.

71 Brad S. Gregory, 'Anabaptist Martyrdom: Imperatives, Experience, and Memorialization', in *A Companion to Anabaptism and Spiritualism, 1521–1700*, ed. John D. Roth and James M. Stayer (Leiden, 2007), p. 478.

72 John Stow, *The Abridgement or Summarie of the English Chronicle* (1607), pp. 393–4, 397. See Carter, 'The Family of Love', p. 655.

73 Baillie, *Anabaptism*, p. 7.

74 Anon., *Bloody Newes from Dover: Being a True Relation of the Great and Bloudy Murder, Committed by Mary Champion (an Anabaptist)* (1647). See Adcock, *Baptist Women's Writings*, p. 37.

75 See Andrew Bradstock, *Radical Religion in Cromwell's England: A Concise History from the English Civil War to the End of the Commonwealth* (London, 2011), p. 4.

76 Thomas Helwys, *A Shorte Declaration of the Mistery of Iniquity* (1612), p. 46.
77 Edwards, *Gangraena*, Part 1, pp. 92–5.
78 Baillie, *Anabaptism*, p. 53; McGregor, 'The Baptists', p. 47.
79 Smith, 'Introduction', *Ranter Writings*, p. 8.
80 Cited in Andrew Sharp, ed., *The English Levellers* (Cambridge, 1998), p. 103.
81 *A Manifestation from Lieutenant-Colonel John Lilburne, Mr William Walwyn, Mr Thomas Prince, and Mr Richard Overton . . . commonly (though unjustly) styled Levellers* (1649), cited in Sharp, *The English Levellers*, p. 161.
82 Anon., *The Faithfull Narrative of the Late Testimony and Demand made to Oliver Cromwell* (1655), pp. 6–7, 22, 36.
83 See Capp, *Fifth Monarchy Men*, pp. 20, 131.
84 Cary, *A Newe and More Exact Mappe*, pp. 122–30.
85 Capp, *Fifth Monarchy Men*, pp. 84, 14, 134.
86 Mary Cary, *Twelve Humble Proposals* (1653), pp. 3–12.
87 Mack, *Visionary Women*, p. 1.
88 Fox, *Journal*, pp. 13, 39–40.
89 See Rosemary Moore, *The Light in Their Consciences: Early Quakers in Britain, 1646–1666* (University Park, PA, 2021 edn), pp. 11–19.
90 See Mack, *Visionary Women*, pp. 1, 247.
91 See Catharine Gray, *Women Writers and Public Debate in Seventeenth-Century Britain* (Basingstoke, 2008), p. 185.
92 See Bradstock, *Radical Religion*, p. 104.
93 See Hinds, *George Fox and Early Quaker Culture*, pp. 50–51.
94 Fox, *A Journal* (1694), p. 213; Gray, *Women Writers*, p. 185.

ONE: ROSE THURGOOD

1 The narratives were discovered by Jeremy Maule, who generously told me about his find.
2 All references to Rose Thurgood's narrative are taken from my critical edition of the two conversion narratives, *Scripture Women: Rose Thurgood, 'A Lecture of Repentance' and Cicely Johnson, 'Fanatical Reveries'* (Nottingham, 2005), pp. 1–27. The manuscript records that Thurgood wrote her account in March 1636, and it was transcribed into the volume on 3 March 1637. These dates could refer to the new-style dates March 1637 and March 1638. Given the ambiguity, I refer to the date of composition for Thurgood's narrative as 1636–7.

3 David R. Como discusses the circulation of antinomian ideas in manuscripts in *Blown by the Spirit: Puritanism and the Emergence of an Antinomian Underground in Pre-Civil-War England* (Stanford, CA, 2004), pp. 54–7.

4 On antinomianism, see Como, *Blown by the Spirit*.

5 William Walwyn declared that he 'had long been established in that part of doctrine (called then, Antinomian) of free justification by Christ alone; and so my heart was at much more ease and freedom, than others', *Walwyns Just Defence* (1649), p. 8. See Nicholas McDowell, *The English Radical Imagination: Culture, Religion, and Revolution, 1630–1660* (Oxford, 2003), pp. 75–6.

6 William Walwyn, *The Power of Love* (1643), 'To Every Reader'.

7 See Anon., *False Prophets Discovered. Being a true story of the Lives and Deaths of two Weavers (late of Colchester) viz. Richard Farnham and John Bull; who affirmed themselves the two great Prophets which should come in the end of the world* (1642), no page numbers.

8 *CSPD* 1637–8, pp. 188–9. John Bull's petition to Archbishop Laud details his 'many months' labour of beating hemp' in Bridewell, having been accused, without trial, of being a false prophet, *CSPD* 1637–8, p. 66. Farnham was also sentenced to 'hard labour' in Bridewell, p. 606.

9 State papers record that Elizabeth Addington was 'seduced' into a 'felonious' marriage, 'her former husband being alive', by Farnham's 'fanatical persuasions that her husband was dead', *CSPD* 1636–7, p. 606.

10 On the antinomian emphasis on the passivity of the believer, see Como, *Blown by the Sprit*, p. 35.

11 Thomas Heywood, *A True Discourse of the Two Infamous Upstart Prophets* (1636), 'To the Reader'.

12 *CSPD* 1636–7, pp. 459–60.

13 See Como, *Blown by the Spirit*, p. 36.

TWO: TESTIMONIES

1 *Spirituall Experiences, of Sundry Beleevers* (1653), pp. 40, 5, 57, 26–7, 43.

2 Kathleen Lynch, *Protestant Autobiography in the Seventeenth-Century Anglophone World* (Oxford, 2012), p. 125.

3 See for example the testimony of 'I. I.', *Spirituall Experiences*, p. 21. Nigel Smith identifies 'H. W.' as Henry Walker, *Perfection Proclaimed: Language and Literature in English Radical Religion, 1640–1660* (Oxford, 1989), p. 43. See also Lynch, *Protestant Autobiography*, pp. 136–40.

4 *Spirituall Experiences*, 'The Practise of the Gathered Churches'.

5 *Spirituall Experiences*, p. 42.

6 Powell, 'The Epistle', *Spirituall Experiences*.

7 *Spirituall Experiences*, p. 120; William Perkins, *A Case of Conscience* (1592), 'To the godly reader', pp. 40–45, 54–5.

8 William Perkins, *The Whole Treatise of the Cases of Conscience* (1606), p. 116.

9 John Rogers, *Ohel; or, Beth-shemesh* (1653), p. 360.

10 Rogers, *Ohel*, pp. 354, 361, 291–2, 449–50.

11 John Milton, *Areopagitica*, 2nd edn (1644), pp. 31–2; this passage is cited in Owen C. Watkins, *The Puritan Experience* (London, 1972), p. 28.

12 *Spirituall Experiences*, pp. 11–13.

13 *Spirituall Experiences*, pp. 357–68.

14 *Spirituall Experiences*, p. 359.

15 Richard Rogers and Samuel Ward, *Two Elizabethan Puritan Diaries*, ed. M. M. Knappen (Chicago, IL, 1933), p. 63.

16 See Jason Yiannikkou, 'John Rogers', ODNB.

17 On the influence of the ministers on these collections, see Smith, *Perfection Proclaimed*, pp. 38–42. See also Donatella Pallotti, '"Out of their owne mouths"? Conversion Narratives and English Radical Religious Practice in the Seventeenth Century', *Journal of Early Modern Studies*, 1/1 (2012), pp. 73–95.

18 Rogers, *Ohel*, pp. 354, 361–2.

19 *Spirituall Experiences*, pp. 33–6.

20 Isaac Ambrose, *Media* (1649), pp. 69–96.

21 Rogers, *Ohel*, p. 423; *Spiritual Experiences*, pp. 17, 111, 116–17, 125, 132.

22 Samuel Petto, 'The Epistle to the Reader', *Roses from Sharon* (1654), printed alongside his *The Voice of the Spirit* (1654).

23 *Spirituall Experiences*, pp. 160–91. On the dramatic nature of 'M. K.'s account, see Smith, *Perfection Proclaimed*, p. 54, Lynch, *Protestant Autobiography*, pp. 134–5, and Abigail Shinn, *Conversion Narratives in Early Modern England: Tales of Turning* (London, 2018), pp. 200–201.

24 Rogers, *Ohel*, p. 418.

25 *Spirituall Experiences*, pp. 68–76.

26 Rogers, *Ohel*, p. 417.

THREE: ELIZABETH POOLE

1 On female prophets and illness, see Phyllis Mack, *Visionary Women: Ecstatic Prophecy in Seventeenth-Century England* (Berkeley, CA, 1992), p. 34.

2 William Lambarde, *A Perambulation of Kent* (1576), pp. 149–52; *Miscellaneous Writings and Letters of Thomas Cranmer*, ed. John Cox (Cambridge, 1846), pp. 272–3.

3 Lambarde, *Perambulation*, p. 152.

4 *Miscellaneous Writings and Letters of Thomas Cranmer*, pp. 272–3.

5 Gilbert Burnet, *The Abridgement of the History of the Reformation* (1682), p. 116.

6 Lambarde, *Perambulation*, p. 152.

7 L. E. Whatmore, 'The Sermon against the Holy Maid of Kent and Her Adherents Delivered at Paul's Cross, November the 23rd, 1533, and at Canterbury, December the 7th', *English Historical Review*, LVIII/232 (1943), pp. 463–75, 469; James Gairdner, ed., *Letters and Papers, Foreign and Domestic, of the reign of Henry VIII*, vol. VII, 1534 (London, 1883), p. 29; vol. VI, 1533 (London, 1882), p. 590.

8 Lambarde describes a book entitled *A marveilous woorke of late done at Court of Streete in Kent*, consisting of 24 leaves and printed by Robert Redman, *Perambulation*, p. 149.

9 Gairdner, *Letters and Papers*, vol. VI, pp. 369, 589; vol. XIII, 1538 (London, 1893), p. 314.

10 Lambarde, *Perambulation*, p. 152.

11 Thomas Cranmer, *A Confutation of Unwritten Verities* (1556), no page numbers.

12 John Foxe, *Actes and Monuments* (1583), p. 1054.

13 Cranmer, *Confutation*, no page numbers.

14 Thomas More, *A Dialogue Concerning Heresies* (1529), *The Complete Works of St. Thomas More* (New Haven, CT, 1981), ed. Thomas M. C. Lawler et al., vol. VI, pp. 92–3. See also Cranmer, *Confutation*, and Richard Rex, 'Jane Wentworth', *ODNB*.

15 Cranmer, *Confutation*, no page numbers.

16 Thomas Norton, *A warning against the dangerous practises of the papists* (1569), no page numbers.

17 Cuthbert Tunstall and John Stokesley, *A New Yeares Gift Dedicated to the Popes Holiness* (1579), no page numbers.

18 Gairdner, *Letters and Papers*, vol. VI, pp. 585–8.

19 *Miscellaneous Writings and Letters of Thomas Cranmer*, p. 273.

20 Gairdner, *Letters and Papers*, vol. VI, pp. 588–9.

21 Tunstall and Stokesley, *New Yeares Gift*, no page numbers.
   On the tradition of political prophecy, see Bernard Capp, *The
   Fifth Monarchy Men: A Study in Seventeenth-Century English
   Millenarianism* (London, 1972), p. 17.

22 Burnet, *Abridgement*, pp. 119–20.

23 'An Act Concerning the Attainder of Elizabeth Barton and Others',
   The Statutes of the Realm, ed. John Raithby, vol. III (London,
   1810–28), pp. 446–8.

24 Gairdner, *Letters and Papers*, vol. XIII, p. 314. See Diane Watt,
   'Reconstructing the Word: The Political Prophecies of Elizabeth
   Barton (1506–34)', *Renaissance Quarterly*, L/1 (1997), p. 159.

25 Watt explores Barton's connections with St Bridget of Sweden
   and St Catherine of Siena in 'Reconstructing the Word',
   pp. 138–9.

26 *Mercurius Politicus*, 201, 13–20 April 1654, p. 3430.

27 Diane Purkiss, 'Producing the Voice, Consuming the Body: Women
   Prophets of the Seventeenth Century', in *Women, Writing, History,
   1640–1740*, ed. Isobel Grundy and Susan Wiseman (Athens, GA,
   1992), pp. 139–58, 158.

28 Purkiss notes that radical Protestantism saturated 'the believer's
   body with iconic or semiotic significance' but argues that prophecy
   involved 'a radical dislocation of the voice from the body', ibid.,
   pp. 140–41. On the bodily nature of the 'state of grace' for Anna
   Trapnel, see Hilary Hinds, 'Soul-Ravishing and Sin-Subduing:
   Anna Trapnel and the Gendered Politics of Free Grace', *Renaissance
   and Reformation*, XXV/4 (2001), pp. 117–37. On prophecy and women's
   bodies, see also Elizabeth Bouldin, *Women Prophets and Radical
   Protestantism in the British Atlantic World, 1640–1730* (Cambridge,
   2015), p. 8, and Mack, *Visionary Women*, p. 34.

29 See Nigel Smith, *Perfection Proclaimed: Language and Literature
   in English Radical Religion, 1640–1660* (Oxford, 1989), pp. 18, 31.
   Bouldin notes the 'inherent theatricality' of prophetic acts, *Women
   Prophets*, p. 8.

30 See Smith, *Perfection Proclaimed*, p. 26.

31 William Greenhill, *An Exposition of the five first chapters of the
   prophet Ezekiel* (1650), pp. 10–11.

32 See Smith, *Perfection Proclaimed*, p. 31.

33 John Smith, *Select Discourses* (1660), pp. 277, 175, 171–2, 182, 222, 226.

34 On prophecy and non-verbal performance, see Elizabeth Stell,
   'Beyond Oral and Written Prophecy: Prophetic Performance and
   Performativity', *Dead Sea Discoveries*, XXIX/3 (2022), pp. 410–37.

On Ezekiel's theatricality, see Shimon Levy, *The Bible as Theatre* (Eastbourne, 2022), pp. 178–9, and Kelvin G. Friebel, *Jeremiah and Ezekiel's Sign-Acts: Rhetorical Nonverbal Communication* (London, 1999).

35 Greenhill, *Exposition*, pp. 373–4, 414.

36 Smith, *Select Discourses*, pp. 191, 244, 197, 273.

37 John Gadbury, *Natura prodigorum; or, a discourse touching the nature of prodigies* (1660), pp. 190–91.

38 William Greenhill, *An Exposition Continued* (1649), pp. 554–60.

39 George Fox, *Concerning Sons and Daughters, and Prophetesses Speaking and Prophesying* (1661), pp. 5–6, 9–11.

40 See Thomas Camm, *A Testimony to the fulfilling the promise of God, relating to such women who through the pouring out of God's spirit upon them, are become prophetesses, daughters and handmaidens* (1689), pp. 8–9.

41 Anna Trapnel, *The Cry of a Stone* (1654), 'To all the wise virgins in Sion', no page numbers.

42 Smith, *Select Discourses*, p. 271.

43 Eleanor Davies, *Ezekiel the Prophet Explained as Follows* (1647), p. 4; Eleanor Davies, *The Lady Eleanor Her Appeal* (1646), p. 39.

44 Mary Cary, *The Resurrection of the Witnesses* (1648), p. 19.

45 Watt, 'Reconstructing the Word', p. 144.

46 Smith, *Select Discourses*, pp. 200, 208.

47 Cary, *Resurrection*, p. 24, 'To the reader', p. 38. On Cary's understanding of prophecy and her presentation of herself as a minister, see Mack, *Visionary Women*, pp. 90–91, and Bouldin, *Women Prophets*, pp. 42–3. On prophecy as interpretation of the Bible, see Smith, *Perfection Proclaimed*, p. 26, and G. Sujin Pak, *The Reformation of Prophecy: Early Modern Interpretations of the Prophet and Old Testament Prophecy* (Oxford, 2018), p. 18.

48 Cary, *Resurrection*, 'The Epistle Dedicatory', 'To the reader', pp. 65–7, 124, 128. On the overlap between personal experience and prophecy, see Smith, *Perfection Proclaimed*, pp. 24–32.

49 Martin Luther, *A Sermon on the New Testament, that is on the Holy Mass* (1520), cited in Pak, *The Reformation of Prophecy*, p. 53.

50 Cary, *Resurrection*, p. 67.

51 Elaine Hobby, 'Prophecy', in *A Companion to Early Modern Women's Writing*, ed. Anita Pacheco (Malden, MA, 2002), p. 279.

52 William Kiffin, *A Briefe Remonstrance* (1645), pp. 2–3.

53 Elizabeth Poole, *An Alarum of War, Given to the Army* (1649), pp. 8–9.

54 See Manfred Brod, 'Elizabeth Poole', odnb, and Susan Wiseman, *Conspiracy and Virtue: Women, Writing, and Politics in Seventeenth-Century England* (Oxford, 2006), pp. 163–6.

55 C. H. Firth, ed., *The Clarke Papers*, 4 vols (London, 1894), vol. ii, pp. 150–54.

56 Elizabeth Poole, *A Vision: Wherein is manifested the disease and cure of the kingdom* (1649), pp. 1–6.

57 Firth, ed., *Clarke Papers*, vol. ii, pp. 163–9.

58 Marcus Nevitt, 'Elizabeth Poole Writes the Regicide', *Women's Writing*, ix/2 (2002), p. 238.

59 On the representation of Abigail in early modern conduct books and the ambiguous nature of the biblical narrative, see Victoria Brownlee and Laura Gallagher, 'Overview: Reading Old Testament Women in Early Modern England, 1550–1700', in *Biblical Women in Early Modern Literary Culture, 1550–1700*, ed. Victoria Brownlee and Laura Gallagher (Manchester, 2015), pp. 31–2.

60 Poole, *An Alarum of War*, p. 13. On Poole and Abigail, see Nevitt, 'Elizabeth Poole', p. 244.

61 Anon., *To Xeiphos ton martyron, or, A brief narration of the mysteries of state* (1651), pp. 69–70. These passages were later reprinted as *The English Devil, or, Cromwel and His Monstrous Witch Discover'd at White-Hall* (1660).

62 *Mercurius Pragmaticus*, 26 December 1648–9 January 1649.

63 On the link between the prophetic and the political in relation to Poole, see Wiseman, *Conspiracy and Virtue*, pp. 143–75.

64 Manfred Brod, 'Politics and Prophecy in Seventeenth-Century England: The Case of Elizabeth Poole', *Albion*, xxxi/3 (1999), p. 411.

65 Elizabeth Poole, *An[other] Alarum of War* (1649), pp. 1–7.

66 cspd 1667–8, p. 369.

67 See Nancy Bradley Warren, *The Embodied Word: Female Spiritualities, Contested Orthodoxies and English Religious Cultures, 1350–1700* (Notre Dame, in, 2010).

FOUR: SARAH WIGHT

1 John Gerard and Thomas Johnson describe the frogbit (a floating plant similar to water lily) found 'swimming or floating in every ditch' on Lambeth Marsh, *The Herbal or Generic History of Plants* (1633), p. 818.

2 Wight's words throughout this chapter are taken from Sarah Wight and Henry Jessey, *The Exceeding Riches of Grace Advanced*

by the Spirit of Grace, in an Empty Nothing Creature, 2nd edn (1647).

3 Kate Chedgzoy, 'Other Maids: Religion, Race, and Relationships Between Girls in Early Modern London', in *Literary Cultures and Medieval and Early Modern Childhoods*, ed. N. J. Miller and D. Purkiss (London, 2019), p. 188.

4 See Susan Wiseman, *Conspiracy and Virtue: Women, Writing, and Politics in Seventeenth-Century England* (Oxford, 2006), pp. 97–9.

5 See Catharine Gray, *Women Writers and Public Debate in Seventeenth-Century Britain* (Basingstoke, 2008), p. 76.

6 Wiseman, *Conspiracy and Virtue*, p. 140.

7 See Gray, *Women Writers*, pp. 81–90.

8 Isaac Ambrose notes that he 'read the story of Mistress Sarah Wight, I found many a sweet passage in it, that exceeding affected me, and melted my heart', *Media* (1649), p. 79. She is also cited in William Lyford, *The Plain Man's Senses Exercised* (1655), p. 179, and *Three Sermons Preached at Sherborne* (1654), p. 11.

9 See Timothy Rogers, *A Discourse concerning Trouble of Mind and the Disease of Melancholy* (1691), p. 428.

10 See Barbara Ritter Dailey, 'The Visitation of Sarah Wight: Holy Carnival and the Revolution of the Saints in Civil War London', *Church History*, LV/4 (1986), p. 450.

11 John Smith, *Select Discourses* (1660), p. 266.

12 Anon., *The Protestants and Jesuits up in Arms . . . Also, a true and wonderful relation of a Dutch Maiden* (1611), pp. 2–4. See Teresa Feroli, *Political Speaking Justified: Women Prophets and the English Revolution* (Newark, NJ, 2006), p. 108.

13 John Fletcher and Philip Massinger, *Love's Cure, or The Martial Maid* (1615), 2.1.23–7. As Matt Williamson points out, this allusion conflates Fliegen with Jane Balan, another 'miraculous maid', *Hunger, Appetite, and the Politics of the Renaissance Stage* (Cambridge, 2021), p. 128.

14 Nathaniel Wanley, *The Wonders of the Little World* (1678), pp. 589–91.

15 Williamson, *Hunger*, p. 130. On the 'manifestation of the prophet as a passive and entirely purified receptacle of divine energy . . . the maiden who preached prone, holding forth from a sickbed', see Phyllis Mack, *Visionary Women: Ecstatic Prophecy in Seventeenth-Century England* (Berkeley, CA, 1992), p. 34.

16 Williamson discusses Fliegen and others like her in the context of interest in wonders and prodigies in this era, *Hunger*, p. 128.

17 Gray describes Wight's 'spectacular prophetic performance', *Women Writers*, p. 79.

18 See Kathleen Lynch, 'Whatever Happened to Dinah the Black? And Other Questions About Gender, Race, and the Visibility of Protestant Saints', in *Conversions: Gender and Religious Change in Early Modern Europe*, ed. Simon Ditchfield and Helen Smith (Manchester, 2017), p. 263.

19 Imtiaz Habib, *Black Lives in the English Archives, 1500–1677* (London, 2008), pp. 209–12. See also Lynch, 'Whatever Happened to Dinah the Black?'

20 Chedgzoy, 'Other Maids', pp. 197–9.

21 John Latimer, *Annals of Bristol in the Seventeenth Century* (Bristol, 1900), p. 344.

22 See Carola Scott-Luckens, 'Propaganda, or Marks of Grace? The Impact of the Reported Ordeals of Sarah Wight in Revolutionary London, 1647–52', *Women's Writing*, IX/2 (2002), p. 222.

FIVE: ANNA TRAPNEL

1 Anna Trapnel, *A Legacy for Saints* (1654), pp. 8–10, 13; Anna Trapnel, *Anna Trapnel's Report and Plea* (1654), p. 8; Anna Trapnel, *The Cry of a Stone* (1654), pp. 18, 74, 67.

2 Trapnel, *Legacy*, pp. 9, 38. Hilary Hinds discusses Trapnel's 'blissfully corporeal vision of the state of grace' in 'Soul-Ravishing and Sin-Subduing: Anna Trapnel and the Gendered Politics of Free Grace', *Renaissance and Reformation*, XXV/4 (2001), p. 127.

3 *A Lively Voice for the King of Saints and Nations* (1657) and a thousand-page folio without a title page held in the Bodleian Library, Oxford, dated 1659 in the library catalogue.

4 Trapnel, *Legacy*, pp. 2–6.

5 Ibid., pp. 9–14; *Cry*, p. 3.

6 Trapnel, *Legacy*, pp. 26–41; *Cry*, p. 3.

7 Trapnel, *Cry*, pp. 4–5.

8 Hilary Hinds, 'Introduction', *Anna Trapnel's Report and Plea* (Tempe, AZ, 2016), p. 2.

9 See Habakkuk 2:11–12: 'the stone shall cry out of the wall … woe to him that buildeth a town with blood!'

10 'Marchamont Nedham to the Protector', *CSPD* 1654, p. 393; Trapnel, *Cry*, pp. 8–9; Trapnel, *Legacy*, p. 37; Trapnel, *Report and Plea*, p. 52.

11 Trapnel, *Cry*, p. 10; Anon., *The Faithfull Narrative of the Late Testimony and Demand made to Oliver Cromwell* (1655), pp. 19, 33, 35–6.

12 *CSPD* 1653–54, p. 306.

13 Anna Trapnel, *Strange and Wonderful Newes from White-Hall* (1654), p. 3.

14 *Severall Proceedings of State Affaires*, no. 225, 12–19 January 1654, pp. 3562–3.

15 Letter dated 21 December 1654, signed 'B. T.', Bodleian Library Rawlinson MS A21, f.. 325, quoted in Champlin Burrage, 'Anna Trapnel's Prophecies', *English Historical Review*, XXVI/103 (1911), p. 532.

16 Trapnel, *Cry*, p. 50; 'Marchamont Nedham to the Protector', *CSPD* 1654, p. 393.

17 *Mercurius Politicus*, 201, 13–20 April 1654, p. 3430.

18 See Nigel Smith, *Perfection Proclaimed: Language and Literature in English Radical Religion, 1640–1660* (Oxford, 1989), pp. 86–90, 94–5.

19 Trapnel, *Cry*, pp. 6, 13.

20 Ibid., pp. 41, 24.

21 Ibid., pp. 63, 11; *Legacy*, pp. 15–16; *Report and Plea*, p. 54.

22 Trapnel, *Cry*, pp. 42, 63, 67; John Smith, *Select Discourses* (1660), p. 232.

23 Smith, *Select Discourses*, p. 273.

24 Trapnel, *Cry*, p. 66.

25 Hilary Hinds, *God's Englishwomen: Seventeenth-Century Radical Sectarian Writing and Feminist Criticism* (Manchester, 1996), p. 96.

26 Trapnel, *Report and Plea*, p. 35; *Cry*, pp. 68–9.

27 On Trapnel as an imitator of Wight, see Smith, *Perfection Proclaimed*, p. 49. On the role of the body in Trapnel's prophecies, see Hinds, *God's Englishwomen*, p. 122, and Hinds, 'Soul-Ravishing and Sin-Subduing', pp. 117–37.

28 Trapnel, *Cry*, pp. 70, 74, 14, 29.

29 Trapnel, *Report and Plea*, pp. 8–11.

30 Ibid., pp. 21–2.

31 Ibid., pp. 23–5, 37, 52.

32 Ibid., pp. 40, 45–50.

33 *The Public Intelligencer*, 13, 24–31 December 1655, pp. 193–4.

34 Quoted in Burrage, 'Anna Trapnel's Prophecies', pp. 526–35, 528.

35 Trapnel, *Cry*, pp. 17, 48; *Lively Voice for the King of Saints*, p. 46.

36 See Song of Songs 4:12–16. See Matthew Prineas, 'The Discourse of Love and the Rhetoric of Apocalypse in Anna Trapnel's Folio Songs', *Comitatus*, XXVIII/1 (1997), pp. 90–110.

37 Trapnel, *Report and Plea*, pp. 11–13, 5.

38 Trapnel, *Lively Voice for the King of Saints*, pp. 80, 48; *Cry*, p. 49.

39 Trapnel, *Report and Plea*, pp. 57–8.
40 On Trapnel's use of language, see Hinds, *God's Englishwomen*, pp. 122–8. On her resistance to rationality, see Kevin Killeen, '"People of a deeper speech": Anna Trapnel, Enthusiasm, and the Aesthetics of Incoherence', in *The Oxford Handbook of Early Modern Women's Writing in English, 1540–1700*, ed. Elizabeth Scott-Baumann, Danielle Clarke and Sarah C. E. Ross (Oxford, 2023), pp. 203–15.
41 Trapnel, *Report and Plea*, pp. 55, 58.

SIX: ELIZABETH ATTAWAY

1 Anon., *The Third Part of the Cry of the Innocent for Justice* (1662), pp. 35–8.
2 Thomas Hall, *The Pulpit Guarded* (1651), pp. 2, 11, 60–62, 15–17, 13, 22–3.
3 Jean d'Espagne, *The Harmony of the Old and New Testament* (1682), Preface.
4 Clarendon Papers, newsletter 15 April 1653, cited in C. H. Firth, 'Cromwell and the Expulsion of the Long Parliament in 1653', *English Historical Review*, VIII/31 (1893), p. 529.
5 R. Barclay, *The Inner Life of the Religious Societies of the Commonwealth* (London, 1876), p. 157n.
6 *Kingdoms Weekly Intelligencer* 129, 19–29 July 1653, p. 930.
7 *Severall Proceedings of State Affaires*, Issue 199, July 1653, p. 3149.
8 Thomas Edwards, *Gangraena, or a catalogue and discovery of many of the errors, heresies, blasphemies and pernicious practices of the sectaries* (1646), Part 1, 'The Epistle Dedicatory', pp. 84, 89.
9 Anon., *Tub-preachers Overturn'd* (1647), pp. 10–11, 14–15.
10 William Walwyn, *A Prediction of Mr Edwards his conversion, and recantation* (1646), p. 14; Thomas Collier, *The Pulpit Guard Routed* (1651), p. 4; William Dell, *The Stumbling-Stone* (1653), p. 27.
11 John Taylor, *Lucifer's Lacky* (1641), no page numbers.
12 Anon., *A Discovery of Six Women-Preachers* (1641), p. 5; Anon., *A Spirit Moving in the Women-Preachers* (1645), pp. 2–5.
13 See Sarah Apetrei, *Reformation of the Heart: Gender and Radical Theology in the English Revolution* (Oxford, 2024), p. 8.
14 John Taylor, *The Diseases of the Times* (1642), no page numbers.
15 Thomas Collier, *The Right Constitution and True Subjects of the Visible Church of Christ* (1654), p. 26; Thomas Goodwin, *Of the Constitution, Right, Order, and Government of the Churches of Christ* (1696), p. 8; Collier, *Pulpit Guard Routed*, p. 79. See Curtis W. Freeman,

A Company of Women Preachers: Baptist Prophetesses in Seventeenth-Century England (Waco, TX, 2011), pp. 14–16, and Ian Birch, 'The Ministry of Women among Early Calvinistic Baptists', *Scottish Journal of Theology*, LXIX/4 (2016), pp. 402–16.

16 Richard Farnworth, *A Woman Forbidden to Speak in the Church* (1654), pp. 2–6.

17 Priscilla Cotton and Mary Cole, *To the Priests and People of England* (1655), pp. 6–7.

18 Katharine Evans, *A Brief Discovery of God's Eternal Truth* (1663), pp. 35, 47.

19 George Keith, *The Woman Preacher of Samaria* (1674), pp. 1–15.

20 For examples of women preachers being ostracized by fellow Quakers, see Catie Gill, '"Ministering Confusion": Rebellious Quaker Women (1650–1660)', *Quaker Studies*, IX/1 (2005), pp. 17–30; Robert Baillie, *Anabaptism, the True Fountaine of Independency* (1647), p. 53.

21 Edwards, *Gangraena*, Part 1, pp. 84–6.

22 See Jason A. Kerr, 'Elizabeth Attaway, London Preacher and Theologian, 1645–46', *Seventeenth Century*, XXXVI/5 (2021), p. 749.

23 Edwards, *Gangraena*, Part 1, pp. 92–4.

24 Thomas Comber, *Christianity no Enthusiasm* (1678), p. 89.

25 See Kerr, 'Elizabeth Attaway', p. 734.

26 See ibid., p. 744, and Stevie Davies, *Unbridled Spirits: Women of the English Revolution, 1640–1660* (London, 1998), p. 104.

27 Mary Cary, *A Newe and More Exact Mappe* (1651), pp. 237–9.

28 See Kerr, 'Elizabeth Attaway', pp. 748–9.

29 Baillie, *Anabaptism*, p. 53.

30 *Tub-preachers Overturn'd*, pp. 15–16.

31 See Davies, *Unbridled Spirits*, p. 107.

32 Edwards, *Gangraena*, Part 1, pp. 87–8; Part 2, pp. 10–11.

33 '15 January 1646', *Journal of House of Commons*, vol. IV: *1644–46* (London, 1802), pp. 407–8.

34 Edwards, *Gangraena*, Part 1, appendix pp. 121–3.

35 Ibid., Part 2, p. 117. See Kerr, who identifies Elizabeth Jenney as the former Mrs Attaway, 'Elizabeth Attaway', p. 739.

36 Attaway is compared to the 'scarlet whore' of Revelation 12 in *Tub-preachers Overturn'd*, p. 15.

37 Abraham Cowley, *The Puritan and the Papist* (1643), p. 6.

38 Anon., *The holy sisters conspiracy against their husbands . . . designed at their last farewell of their meeting-houses in Coleman-street* (1661), p. 6.

39 *CSPD* 1672, p. 457.

SEVEN: HESTER BIDDLE

1 Hester Biddle, *The Trumpet of the Lord Sounded Forth unto these Three Nations* (1662), pp. 14–15.

2 Hester Biddle, *A Warning from the Lord God of Life and Power, unto thee O city of London, and to the suburbs round about thee* (1660), p. 7.

3 Biddle, *Trumpet*, p. 15.

4 *George Fox: The Journal*, ed. Nigel Smith (London, 1998), p. 269.

5 Anon., *The West Answering to the North* (1657), pp. 85–7.

6 Joseph Besse, *A Collection of the Sufferings of the People Called Quakers*, vol. 1 (1753), pp. 365, 564, 689, 484.

7 Ibid., p. 484.

8 Norman Penney, ed., *Extracts from the State Papers Relating to Friends, 1659–64* (London, 1911), p. 154.

9 Biddle, *Trumpet*, p. 5.

10 *CSPD* 1664–5, pp. 35–6.

11 Biddle, *Trumpet*, p. 11; Anon., *The Third Part of the Cry of the Innocent for Justice* (1662), pp. 35–8.

12 Biddle, *Warning*, pp. 11, 3, 5; *Trumpet*, pp. 5–6.

13 Biddle, *Trumpet*, pp. 6, 12; *Warning*, p. 11.

14 Biddle, *Trumpet*, p. 5; *Warning*, pp. 5–6, 10–11.

15 Biddle, *Trumpet*, p. 6; *Warning*, pp. 17–18, 10.

16 Biddle, *Trumpet*, p. 12; *Warning*, pp. 12–17, 6.

17 Hester Biddle, *Wo to thee city of Oxford* (1655), no page numbers.

18 Elaine Hobby, '"Oh Oxford Thou Art Full of Filth": The Prophetical Writings of Hester Biddle, 1629(?)–1696', in *Feminist Criticism: Theory and Practice*, ed. Susan Sellers (Hemel Hempstead, 1991), pp. 159–64.

19 Biddle, *Wo to thee city of Oxford*, no page numbers.

20 Letter from Richard Blinman to John Winthrop, *Winthrop Papers*, vol. V (Boston, MA, 1943), transcribed in Hans Rollman, 'Anglicans, Puritans, and Quakers, in Seventeenth-Century Newfoundland', unpublished paper presented to the Atlantic Canada Studies Conference, St John's, May 1992.

21 Henry J. Cadbury, 'Friends and the Inquisition at Malta', *Journal of the Friends' Historical Society*, LIII/3 (1974), p. 224.

22 William Sewel, *The History of the Rise, Increase, and Progress of the Christian People Called Quakers*, vol. 1 (1722), Preface.

23 Gerard Croese, *The General History of the Quakers* (1696), p. 267.

24 *CSPD* 1694–5, p. 295. The pass was issued on 5 September 1694. See Lydia L. Rickman, 'Esther Biddle and Her Mission to Louis XIV', *Journal of the Friends' Historical Society*, LIII (1972–5), pp. 38–45.

25 Croese, *History of the Quakers*, pp. 267–8.

26 See Elaine Hobby and Catie Gill, 'Hester Biddle', *ODNB*.

27 Hester Biddle, 'Something in short unto the sons and daughters of men as I was moved by the Spirit of God', in Thomas Woodrove, *A Brief Relation of the State of Man before Transgression* (1659), pp. 25–37.

28 Biddle, *Warning*, pp. 4, 20, 19; 'Something in short', p. 31.

EIGHT: MARY FISHER

1 The phrase is from a letter written by Fox in 1656, George Fox, *A Journal* (1694), p. 213.

2 See James Raine, ed., *Depositions from the Castle of York* (1861), p. 54, quoted in Sylvia Brown, 'The Radical Travels of Mary Fisher: Walking and Writing in the Universal Light', in *Women, Gender, and Radical Religion*, ed. Sylvia Brown (Leiden, 2007), p. 41.

3 'From Mary Fisher presiner at Yarke', undated, A. R. Barclay MSS, vol. CCCXXIV, f. 173, Library of the Religious Society of Friends, London, quoted in Brown, 'The Radical Travels', p. 39.

4 Hilary Hinds, *George Fox and Early Quaker Culture* (Manchester, 2011), pp. 101, 107.

5 On Fisher and challenges to ideas of difference, see Brown, 'The Radical Travels', pp. 39–64.

6 See Carla Gardina Pestana, 'Atlantic Mobilities and the Defiance of the Early Quakers', *Journal of Early Modern History*, XXVIII (2023), pp. 187–208.

7 See Brown, 'The Radical Travels', p. 48. On the nature of Quaker preaching, see Hinds, *George Fox and Early Quaker Culture*, pp. 38–40.

8 Brown, 'The Radical Travels', p. 43.

9 Anon., *The First New Persecution, or a true narrative of the cruel usage of two Christians by the present mayor of Cambridge, as it was certified from thence by an eminent hand* (1654), pp. 1–7. See also the letter describing these events appended to James Nayler, *Churches Gathered Against Christ* (1654), pp. 20–21.

10 Anon., *Great Newes from the Barbadoes* (1676), pp. 3–14.

11 See Hilary Beckles, 'The "Hub of Empire": The Caribbean and Britain in the Seventeenth Century', in *The Oxford History of the British Empire*, vol. I: *The Origins of Empire*, ed. Nicholas Canny, Alaine Low and Wm Roger Louis (Oxford, 1998), pp. 224–7.

12 George Fox, *Gospel Family-Order, Being a Short Discourse Concerning the Ordering of Families, Both of Whites, Blacks and Indians* (1676),

pp. 13–14, 16–18; George Fox, *To the Ministers, Teachers and Priests (so called, and so stiling your selves) in Barbadoes* (1672), pp. 5, 69. On the early Quaker stance on slavery, see Hinds, *George Fox and Early Quaker Culture*, pp. 128–45; Brycchan Carey, *From Peace to Freedom: Quaker Rhetoric and the Birth of American Antislavery, 1657–1761* (New Haven, CT, 2012), pp. 49, 58; Katherine Freedman, 'Sustaining Faith: Quakers and Slavery in the Early Anglo-Atlantic, 1655–1679', *Journal of Global Slavery*, III/3 (2018), pp. 211–33, and Stephen W. Angell, 'Early Quaker Women and the Testimony of the Family, 1652–1767', *New Critical Studies on Early Quaker Women, 1650–1800*, ed. Michele Lise Tarter and Catie Gill (Oxford, 2018), pp. 50–68.

13 *Great Newes from the Barbadoes*, pp. 9–12; *The Laws of Barbados* (1699), p. 121.

14 Anne Martindell, *A Relation of the Labour, Travail and Suffering of that faithful servant of the Lord Alice Curwen* (1680), p. 18. See Carey, *From Peace to Freedom*, pp. 67–9.

15 George Bishop, *New England Judged* (1661), pp. 5–12; Anon., *New-England's Ensigne* (1659), p. 7.

16 Gerard Croese, *The General History of the Quakers* (1696), p. 276.

17 John Elias, *A True and Strange Relation of the travels, adventures, and great persecution of four eminent Quakers of Gloucestershire* (1674), title page.

18 Bishop, *New England Judged*, pp. 19–20.

19 The letter is printed in Brown, 'The Radical Travels', p. 53.

20 See ibid., pp. 46–60.

21 Joseph Besse, *A Collection of the Sufferings of the People Called Quakers*, vol. 1 (1753), p. 388.

22 See A. S. Salley, 'Abstracts from the Records of the Court of Ordinary of the Province of South Carolina', *South Carolina Historical and Genealogical Magazine*, 12 (1911), pp. 70–71, quoted in Angell, 'Early Quaker Women', pp. 50–68.

23 Pestana, 'Atlantic Mobilities', pp. 1–22.

24 Martindell, *A Relation*, f. A1.

NINE: KATHARINE EVANS AND SARAH CHEEVERS

1 Katharine Evans and Sarah Cheevers, *A True Account of the Great Tryals and Cruel Sufferings undergone by those two faithful servants of God, Katharine Evans and Sarah Cheevers* (1663), p. 74. On Cheevers's descriptions of her incarceration, see Russell Palmer, 'Contextualizing the *Cruel Sufferings (For the Truths Sake) of*

Katharine Evans and Sarah Cheevers: A Historical Materialist Perspective', *ANQ: A Quarterly Journal of Short Articles, Notes and Reviews*, XXXI/1 (2017), pp. 12–13.

2   Andrew P. Vella, *The Tribunal of the Inquisition in Malta* (Msida, 1964), pp. 31–7; Phyllis Mack, *Visionary Women: Ecstatic Prophecy in Seventeenth-Century England* (Berkeley, CA, 1992), p. 147; Joseph Besse, *A Collection of the Sufferings of the People called Quakers*, vol. 1 (1753), p. 149; John Whiting, *Persecution Exposed*, 2nd edn (1791), pp. 468–70; Evans and Cheevers, *True Account*, pp. 156–7.

3   See Vella, *The Tribunal*, pp. 31–7.

4   Palmer, 'Contextualizing the *Cruel Sufferings*, pp. 11–17.

5   Evans and Cheevers, *True Account*, pp. 14, 142, 26.

6   Ibid., pp. 8, 6, 2–3.

7   See Vella, *The Tribunal*, pp. 31–7. On the 'fright' generated by the 'intensity of [Quaker] itinerancy', see Carla Gardina Pestana, 'Atlantic Mobilities and the Defiance of the Early Quakers', *Journal of Early Modern History*, XXVIII (2023), pp. 187–208.

8   Vella, *The Tribunal*, pp. 31–7.

9   Evans and Cheevers, *True Account*, pp. 37, 49, 143.

10 Ibid., pp. 15, 78, 29.

11 Ibid., pp. 33–5, 268–9.

12 Ibid., pp. 148, 108–9.

13 In Matthew 7:23 Jesus says 'I never knew you: depart from me, ye that work iniquity.'

14 Evans and Cheevers, *True Account*, pp. 19, 17, 20–21, 36, 77.

15 Hilary Hinds, *George Fox and Early Quaker Culture* (Manchester, 2011), p. 50.

16 Evans and Cheevers, *True Account*, pp. 229–30.

17 Katharine Evans, *A Brief Discovery of God's Eternal Truth* (1663), pp. 28–33.

18 Evans and Cheevers, *True Account*, pp. 23–5.

19 Ibid., pp. 160, 52.

20 See Catharine Gray, *Women Writers and Public Debate in Seventeenth-Century Britain* (Basingstoke, 2008), pp. 188–90.

21 Evans and Cheevers, *True Account*, p. 266.

22 Ibid., pp. 257, 259.

23 Whiting, *Persecution*, p. 475.

TEN: ELIZABETH AVERY

1 *CSPD* 1677–8, pp. 412–13.
2 See Elizabeth Bouldin, *Women Prophets and Radical Protestantism in the British Atlantic World, 1640–1730* (Cambridge, 2015), pp. 89–118.
3 Mary Cary, *A Newe and More Exact Mappe* (1651), pp. 202, 209, 71, 263, 266, 274, 286, 289, 300, 309–10, 83, 125–6, 62, 66.
4 Jane Lead, *A Fountain of Gardens*, vol. II (1697), pp. 520–21.
5 See Crawford Gribben, *God's Irishmen: Theological Debates in Cromwellian Ireland* (Oxford, 2007), p. 166.
6 T. C., *A glasse for the times by which according to the Scriptures, you may clearly behold the true ministers of Christ, how farre differing from false teachers* (1648), p. 5.
7 Henoch Clapham, *Error on the Right Hand, through a Preposterous Zeal* (1608), pp. 18, 52.
8 See David R. Como, 'The Family of Love and the Making of English Revolutionary Religion: The Confession and "Conversions" of Giles Creech', *Journal of Medieval and Early Modern Studies*, XLVIII/3 (2018), pp. 553–98, 560.
9 Elizabeth Avery, *Scripture-Prophecies Opened* (1647), p. 21. See Sarah Apetrei, *Reformation of the Heart: Gender and Radical Theology in the English Revolution* (Oxford, 2024), pp. 43–4.
10 See Gribben, *God's Irishmen*, pp. 167–8.
11 Thomas Parker, *The copy of a letter written by Mr. Thomas Parker, pastor of the church of Newbury in New-England, to his sister, Mrs Elizabeth Avery, sometimes of Newbury in the county of Berks, touching sundry opinions by her professed and maintained* (1650), pp. 5–20.
12 Zachary Crofton, *Bethshemesh Clouded* (1653), p. 187. See Gribben, *God's Irishmen*, pp. 153–4.
13 John Rogers, *Ohel, or Beth-shemesh* (1653), pp. 464–5.
14 Gribben, *God's Irishmen*, p. 172.
15 Avery, *Scripture-Prophecies Opened*, f. A3v.
16 Clapham, *Error on the Right Hand*, pp. 44, 48–9.
17 Gribben discusses Avery's shifting uses of the woman clothed with the sun, suggesting that she was becoming progressively more moderate in the theological content of her writing, *God's Irishmen*, p. 170.
18 Avery, *Scripture-Prophecies Opened*, pp. 1–46. On doctrines of heavenly flesh as well as Avery's take on this idea, see Apetrei, *Reformation of the Heart*, pp. 26–44.
19 Avery, *Scripture-Prophecies Opened*, f. A3v, p. 37.

ELEVEN: ANNE WENTWORTH

1 On Wentworth and domestic violence, see Warren Johnston, 'Prophecy, Patriarchy, and Violence in the Early Modern Household: The Revelations of Anne Wentworth', *Journal of Family History*, XXXIV/4 (2009), pp. 344–68.

2 Anne Wentworth, *Englands Spiritual Pill* (c. 1679), in Curtis W. Freeman, *A Company of Women Preachers: Baptist Prophetesses in Seventeenth-Century England* (Waco, TX, 2011), pp. 752, 724; Anne Wentworth, *A True Account of Anne Wentworth* (1676), pp. 7–9, 12; Anne Wentworth, *A Vindication of Anne Wentworth* (1677), pp. 4–5.

3 *True Account*, p. 6; *Spiritual Pill*, p. 749; *Vindication*, p. 2; *True Account*, p. 15.

4 *True Account*, pp. 16–17; *Spiritual Pill*, pp. 752, 725; *True Account*, p. 18; *Spiritual Pill*, pp. 737, 751.

5 *Spiritual Pill*, pp. 739–40, 745.

6 CSPD 1677–8, pp. 434–5.

7 *Spiritual Pill*, p. 743.

8 *True Account*, p. 4; *Vindication*, p. 13.

9 *Spiritual Pill*, pp. 744, 752, 720–21.

10 *Vindication*, p. 12; *Revelation*, p. 6. On Wentworth and the woman clothed with the sun, see Johnston, 'Prophecy, Patriarchy, and Violence', p. 358, and Rachel Adcock, *Baptist Women's Writings in Revolutionary Culture, 1640–1680* (London, 2015), p. 186.

11 Anne Wentworth, *The Revelation of Jesus Christ* (1679), p. 1. Johnston comments on Wentworth's use of apocalyptic language in 'Prophecy, Patriarchy, and Violence', p. 358.

12 *True Account*, pp. 4, 20.

13 *Vindication*, p. 1; *Spiritual Pill*, pp. 748–9; *Revelation*, p. 9.

14 *Vindication*, p. 2; *Spiritual Pill*, p. 736; *Revelation*, p. 9.

15 *Revelation*, pp. 19–20; *Vindication*, p. 8.

16 CSPD 1677–8, pp. 411, 279.

17 *True Account*, p. 5; *Spiritual Pill*, pp. 749–50; *Vindication*, pp. 5–6.

18 CSPD 1677–8, pp. 411, 478.

19 Rachel Adcock, 'Women and Gender', in *The Oxford History of Protestant Dissenting Traditions*, vol. I, ed. John Coffey (Oxford, 2020), pp. 464, 466.

20 See Adcock, 'Women and Gender', p. 465, and Natasha Simonova, 'New Evidence for the Reading of Sectarian Women's Prophecies', *Notes and Queries*, LX/1 (2013), pp. 66–70.

21 Sarah Apetrei and Hannah Smith, eds, *Religion and Women in Britain, c. 1660–1760* (London, 2014), pp. 4–5.

TWELVE: JANE LEAD

1 Jane Lead, *The Wars of David* (1700), 'Preface of the Publisher'; Jane Lead, *The Heavenly Cloud Now Breaking* (1681), p. 39.
2 Henry Dodwell, Dr Williams's Library MS 24.109.7–9, ff. 5r-7v; cited in Liam Peter Temple, *Mysticism in Early Modern England* (Martlesham, 2019), p. 144; Lead, *Wars of David*, 'Preface of the Publisher'.
3 See Ariel Hessayon, ed., *Jane Lead and Her Transnational Legacy* (London, 2016), pp. 1–4.
4 On Blake's echoes of Lead, see E. P. Thompson, *Witness Against the Beast: William Blake and the Moral Law* (Cambridge, 1994), pp. 37–9, and Paula McDowell, 'Enlightenment Enthusiasms and the Spectacular Failure of the Philadelphian Society', *Eighteenth-Century Studies*, XXXV/4 (2002), p. 521.
5 Sarah Apetrei, *Women, Feminism, and Religion in Early Enlightenment England* (Cambridge, 2010), p. 195; Nigel Smith, 'Pregnant Dreams in Early Modern Europe: The Philadelphian Example', in *The Intellectual Culture of Puritan Women, 1558–1680*, ed. Johanna Harris and Elizabeth Scott-Baumann (Basingstoke, 2010), p. 195.
6 See Julie Hirst, *Jane Leade: Biography of a Seventeenth-Century Mystic* (London, 2005), pp. 114–16.
7 Bernard McGinn defines mysticism as 'a special consciousness of the presence of God that by definition exceeds description and results in a transformation of the subject who receives it', *The Presence of God: A History of Western Christian Mysticism*, vol. III: *The Flowering of Mysticism* (New York, 1998), p. 26.
8 See Temple, *Mysticism*, p. 139. Warren Johnston notes that the 'perceived decline of apocalyptic beliefs after 1660 . . . has been greatly overstated by historians': 'Jane Lead and English Apocalyptic Thought in the Late Seventeenth Century', in *Jane Lead and Her Transnational Legacy*, ed. Hessayon, p. 120. See also Sara S. Poor and Nigel Smith, eds, *Mysticism and Reform, 1400–1750* (Notre Dame, IN, 2015).
9 Lead, *Wars of David*, Preface.
10 Jane Lead, 'The Life of the Author' (1696), trans. Leigh T. I. Penman, in *Early Modern Prophecies in Transnational, National and*

Regional Contexts, vol. III, ed. Lionel Laborie and Ariel Hessayon (Leiden, 2020), pp. 86–7.

11 Boehme notes that 'Thou wilt find no better book, in which the Divine Wisdom can be found, than a green and blooming meadow', *Three Principles*, 8:12, cited in B. J. Gibbons, *Gender in Mystical and Occult Thought: Behmenism and Its Development in England* (Cambridge, 1996), p. 62.

12 See Gibbons, *Gender in Mystical and Occult Thought*, p. 113.

13 Jane Lead, *A Fountain of Gardens*, vol. 1 (1696), p. 15.

14 On Pordage, see Smith, 'Pregnant Dreams in Early Modern Europe', p. 191.

15 See Joad Raymond, 'Radicalism and Mysticism in the Later Seventeenth Century: John Pordage's Angels', in *Conversations with Angels: Towards a History of Spiritual Communication, 1100–1700*, ed. Joad Raymond (Basingstoke, 2011).

16 Lead, 'Life of the Author', pp. 87–8; *Fountain of Gardens*, vol. I, pp. 328–31.

17 See McDowell, 'Enlightenment Enthusiasms', pp. 515–33.

18 Jane Lead, 'Propositions', from *A Message to the Philadelphian Society*, printed in *Theosophical Transactions of the Philadelphian Society* (1697), vol. II, pp. 87–9; *Theosophical Transactions*, vol. III, pp. 196–7.

19 See *The Vindication and Justification of The Philadelphian Society* (1702), cited in McDowell, 'Enlightenment Enthusiasms', p. 523.

20 Lambeth Palace Library, MS 1048a, ff. 146–9, 163, cited in Hessayon, *Jane Lead and Her Transnational Legacy*, p. 81; McDowell, 'Enlightenment Enthusiasms', p. 516.

21 Jane Lead, *The Enochian Walks with God* (1694), 2nd edn, p. 2; *Fountain of Gardens*, vol. I, pp. 6–7.

22 Jane Lead, *Wonders of God's Creation*, pp. 62–4.

23 Lead, *Fountain of Gardens*, vol. II, p. 166.

24 Lead, *Enochian Walks*, p. 33.

25 Plotinus, *The Enneads*, 4th edn, trans. Stephen Mackenna (London, 1969), 4.8.1.1–11; 4.8.8.1–3.

26 Jane Lead, *Heavenly Cloud*, p. 21; *The Revelation of Revelations* (1683), p. 59; *Fountain of Gardens*, vol. II, p. 264; *Wonders of God's Creation*, p. 80. Hirst describes Lead as a 'spiritual alchemist', *Jane Leade*, p. 9.

27 On radical religious women and the doctrine of universal salvation, see Sarah Apetrei, *Reformation of the Heart: Gender and Radical Theology in the English Revolution* (Oxford, 2024), pp. 55–77.

28 Jane Lead, *The Ascent to the Mount of Vision* (1699), pp. 19, 25; *Enochian Walks*, Preface.

29 Lead, *Revelation of Revelations*, pp. 2–3, 1, 127, 5.

30 Jane Lead, *A Living Funeral Testimony* (1702), pp. 25–31.

31 On the fusion of flesh and spirit in the mystical thought of this era, see Sarah Apetrei, 'Prophecy and Mysticism in Seventeenth-Century Britain', in *Exploring Lost Dimensions in Christian Mysticism: Opening to the Mystical*, ed. Louise Nelstrop and Simon D. Podmore (London, 2021), p. 202.

32 Lead, *Fountain of Gardens*, vol. I, pp. 55, 63–4; *Fountain of Gardens*, vol. II, p. 167.

33 Jacob Boehme, *Mysterium Magnum* (1656), pp. 83, 85.

34 Lead, *Revelation of Revelations*, pp. 105–6, 39.

35 Lead, *Fountain of Gardens*, vol. I, pp. 341–6.

36 See Smith, 'Pregnant Dreams in Early Modern Europe', pp. 190–201.

37 Lead, *Revelation of Revelations*, pp. 2, 6, 39.

38 On the passivity of Sophia in Boehme's thought, see Lucinda Martin, 'Jacob Boehme and the Anthropology of German Pietism', in *An Introduction to Jacob Boehme: Four Centuries of Thought and Reception*, ed. Ariel Hessayon and Sarah Apetrei (London, 2013), p. 131. See also Gibbons, *Gender in Mystical and Occult Thought*, p. 112.

39 On Lead's distinctive emphasis on Sophia as a mother, see Stefania Salvadori, 'The Restitution of "Adam's Angelical and Paradisiacal Body": Jane Lead's Metaphor of Rebirth and Mystical Marriage', in *Jane Lead and Her Transnational Legacy*, ed. Hessayon, pp. 156–7.

40 Lead, *Fountain of Gardens*, vol. II, p. 12; vol. I, p. 124. On Lead and Sophia, see Phyllis Mack, *Visionary Women: Ecstatic Prophecy in Seventeenth-Century England* (Berkeley, CA, 1992), p. 410, and Hirst, *Jane Leade*, pp. 57–70.

41 Lead, *Fountain of Gardens*, vol. II, p. 117.

42 Ibid., vol. I, p. 66. Hirst argues that Lead identifies herself with Sophia in this passage, *Jane Leade*, p. 60.

43 See Elizabeth Bouldin, *Women Prophets and Radical Protestantism in the British Atlantic World, 1640–1730* (Cambridge, 2015), pp. 89, 111–12.

44 Johnston, 'Jane Lead and English Apocalyptic Thought', pp. 120–21, 135–6.

45 Lead, *Fountain of Gardens*, vol. II, pp. 468–71.

46 Lead, *Ascent*, pp. 28–33; see Smith, 'Pregnant Dreams in Early Modern Europe', pp. 190–201.

47 Gibbons notes that Lead was identified in German pietist circles as the apocalyptical mother of Revelation 12 but rejects the idea that Lead identified herself in such terms. He links the idea to the

'patently absurd story' that she gave birth to a baby in Bayreuth, naming this child a son of Christ, *Gender in Mystical and Occult Thought*, p. 151.

48 Lead, *Fountain of Gardens*, vol. ii, pp. 121–32. See Bouldin, *Women Prophets*, p. 112.

49 Lead, *Revelation of Revelations*, pp. 27, 14–17, 7, 26.

50 Mack, *Visionary Women*, p. 410.

51 Lead, *Ascent*, pp. 28, 39.

52 Lead, *Fountain of Gardens*, vol. ii, pp. 520–21.

53 Jane Lead, *The Laws of Paradise* (1695), p. 50; *Fountain of Gardens*, vol. ii, 137, 170.

AFTERWORD

1 Naomi Pullin, *Female Friends and the Making of Transatlantic Quakerism, 1650–1750* (Cambridge, 2018), p. 261.

2 Ronald A. Knox, *Enthusiasm: A Chapter in the History of Religion* (Oxford, 1950), p. 20, quoted in Keith Thomas, 'Women and the Civil War Sects', *Past and Present*, 13 (1958), p. 50.

3 Sarah Apetrei, *Reformation of the Heart: Gender and Radical Theology in the English Revolution* (Oxford, 2024), p. 22.

4 Anon., *Mr Turbulent; or, The Melanchollicks* (1682), p. 60; cited ibid., p. 194.

5 Thomas, 'Women and the Civil War Sects', p. 48.

6 Apetrei, *Reformation of the Heart*, p. 197.

FURTHER READING

GENERAL

Adcock, Rachel, *Baptist Women's Writings in Revolutionary Culture,*
1640–1680 (London, 2015)

Apetrei, Sarah, *Reformation of the Heart: Gender and Radical Theology*
in the English Revolution (Oxford, 2024)

Bouldin, Elizabeth, *Women Prophets and Radical Protestantism in the*
British Atlantic World, 1640–1730 (Cambridge, 2015)

Bradstock, Andrew, *Radical Religion in Cromwell's England: A Concise*
History from the English Civil War to the End of the Commonwealth
(London, 2011)

Capp, Bernard, *The Fifth Monarchy Men: A Study in Seventeenth-Century*
English Millenarianism (London, 1972)

Curelly, Laurent, and Nigel Smith, eds, *Radical Voices, Radical Ways:*
Articulating and Disseminating Radicalism in Seventeenth- and
Eighteenth-Century Britain (Manchester, 2016)

Davies, Stevie, *Unbridled Spirits: Women of the English Revolution,*
1640–1660 (London, 1998)

Feroli, Teresa, *Political Speaking Justified: Women Prophets and the English*
Revolution (Newark, NJ, 2006)

Font, Carme, *Women's Prophetic Writings in Seventeenth-Century Britain*
(London, 2017)

Freeman, Curtis W., *A Company of Women Preachers: Baptist Prophetesses*
in Seventeenth-Century England (Waco, TX, 2011)

Frick, Deborah, *Authority and Authorship in Medieval and Seventeenth-*
Century Women's Visionary Writings (Bielefeld, 2021)

Gill, Catie, *Women in the Seventeenth-Century Quaker Community:*
A Literary Study of Political Identities, 1650–1700 (London, 2005)

Gillespie, Katherine, *Domesticity and Dissent in the Seventeenth Century:*
English Women Writers and the Public Sphere (Cambridge, 2009)

Gray, Catharine, *Women Writers and Public Debate in Seventeenth-Century Britain* (Basingstoke, 2008)

Harris, Johanna, and Elizabeth Scott-Baumann, eds, *The Intellectual Culture of Puritan Women, 1558–1680* (Basingstoke, 2010)

Hill, Christopher, *The World Turned Upside Down: Radical Ideas During the English Revolution* (Harmondsworth, 1975)

Hinds, Hilary, *God's Englishwomen: Seventeenth-Century Radical Sectarian Writing and Feminist Criticism* (Manchester, 1996)

Hobby, Elaine, *Virtue of Necessity: English Women's Writing, 1646–88* (Ann Arbor, MI, 1988)

Keay, Anna, *The Restless Republic: Britain Without a Crown* (London, 2022)

Longfellow, Erica, *Women and Religious Writing in Early Modern England* (Cambridge, 2009)

Lynch, Kathleen, *Protestant Autobiography in the Seventeenth-Century Anglophone World* (Oxford, 2012)

McDowell, Nicholas, *The English Radical Imagination: Culture, Religion, and Revolution, 1630–1660* (Oxford, 2003)

McGregor, J. F., and Barry Reay, eds, *Radical Religion in the English Revolution* (Oxford, 1984)

Mack, Phyllis, *Visionary Women: Ecstatic Prophecy in Seventeenth-Century England* (Berkeley, CA, 1992)

Morton, Timothy, and Nigel Smith, eds, *Radicalism in British Literary Culture, 1650–1830: From Revolution to Revolution* (Cambridge, 2002)

Poole, Kristen, *Radical Religion from Shakespeare to Milton: Figures of Nonconformity in Early Modern England* (Cambridge, 2000)

Pullin, Naomi, *Female Friends and the Making of Transatlantic Quakerism, 1650–1750* (Cambridge, 2018)

Purkiss, Diane, 'Producing the Voice, Consuming the Body: Women Prophets of the Seventeenth Century', in *Women, Writing, History, 1640–1740*, ed. Isobel Grundy and Susan Wiseman (Athens, GA, 1992)

——, *The English Civil War: A People's History* (London, 2006)

Salzman, Paul, *Reading Early Modern Women's Writing* (Oxford, 2006)

Smith, Nigel, *Perfection Proclaimed: Language and Literature in English Radical Religion, 1640–1660* (Oxford, 1989)

Tarter, Michele Lise, and Catie Gill, eds, *New Critical Studies on Early Quaker Women, 1650–1800* (Oxford, 2018)

Thomas, Keith, 'Women and the Civil War Sects', *Past and Present*, XIII/I (1958), pp. 42–62

Warren, Nancy Bradley, *The Embodied Word: Female Spiritualities, Contested Orthodoxies and English Religious Cultures, 1350–1700* (Notre Dame, IN, 2010)

Wiesner-Hanks, Merry, *Women and the Reformations: A Global History*
 (New Haven, CT, 2024)
Wilcox, Helen, et al., eds, *Her Own Life: Autobiographical Writings by
 Seventeenth-Century Englishwomen* (London, 1989)
Wiseman, Susan, *Conspiracy and Virtue: Women, Writing, and Politics
 in Seventeenth-Century England* (Oxford, 2006)
—, '"Unsilent Instruments and the Devil's Cushions": Authority in
 Seventeenth-Century Women's Prophetic Discourse', in *New
 Feminist Discourses*, ed. Isobel Armstrong (London, 1992),
 pp. 176–96

ELIZABETH ATTAWAY

Kerr, Jason A., 'Elizabeth Attaway, London Preacher and Theologian,
 1645–46', *Seventeenth Century*, XXXVI/5 (2021), pp. 733–54

ELIZABETH AVERY

Coolahan, Marie-Louise, *Women, Writing, and Language in Early
 Modern Ireland* (Oxford, 2010)
Gribben, Crawford, *God's Irishmen: Theological Debates in Cromwellian
 Ireland* (Oxford, 2007)

ELIZABETH BARTON

Longfellow, Erica, 'Prayer and Prophecy', in *The Oxford Handbook of
 Early Modern English Literature and Religion*, ed. Andrew Hiscock
 and Helen Wilcox (Oxford, 2017)
Warren, Nancy Bradley, *Women of God and Arms: Female Spirituality
 and Political Conflict, 1380–1600* (Philadelphia, PA, 2005)
Watt, Diane, 'Reconstructing the Word: The Political Prophecies
 of Elizabeth Barton (1506–34)', *Renaissance Quarterly*, L/1 (1997),
 pp. 136–63
—, *Secretaries of God: Women Prophets in Late Medieval and Early
 Modern England* (Woodbridge, 1997)

HESTER BIDDLE

Hobby, Elaine, '"Oh Oxford Thou Art Full of Filth": The Prophetical
 Writings of Hester Biddle, 1629(?)–1696', in *Feminist Criticism:
 Theory and Practice*, ed. Susan Sellers (Hemel Hempstead, 1991)

KATHARINE EVANS AND SARAH CHEEVERS

Fabrizio, Andrea, 'Women Writing Their Faith: Doctrine, Genre and Gender in *This is a Short Relation of some of the Cruel Sufferings (for the Truth's Sake) of Katharine Evans and Sarah Cheevers* (1662)', *Clio*, XLII/3 (2013), pp. 309–29

Gertz, Genelle, *Heresy Trials and English Women Writers, 1400–1670* (Cambridge, 2012)

Gill, Catie, 'Evans and Cheevers's *A Short Relation* in Context: Flesh, Spirit, and Authority in Quaker Prison Writing', *Huntington Library Quarterly*, LXXII/2 (2009), pp. 257–72

—, 'Bad Catholics: Anti-Popery in *This is a Short Relation*', in *Expanding the Canon of Early Modern Women's Writing*, ed. P. Salzman (Newcastle, 2010)

Palmer, Russell, 'Contextualizing the *Cruel Sufferings (For the Truths Sake) of Katharine Evans and Sarah Cheevers*: A Historical Materialist Perspective', *ANQ: A Quarterly Journal of Short Articles, Notes and Reviews*, XXXI/1 (2017), pp. 11–17

Wiseman, Susan, 'Read Within: Gender, Cultural Difference and Quaker Women's Travel Narratives', in *Voicing Women: Gender and Sexuality in Early Modern Writing*, ed. K. Chedgzoy, M. Hanson and S. Trill (Edinburgh, 1996)

MARY FISHER

Andrea, Bernadette, *Women and Islam in Early Modern English Literature* (Cambridge, 2009)

Brown, Sylvia, 'The Radical Travels of Mary Fisher: Walking and Writing in the Universal Light', in *Women, Gender, and Radical Religion in Early Modern Europe*, ed. Sylvia Brown (Leiden, 2007)

JANE LEAD

Apetrei, Sarah, *Women, Feminism, and Religion in Early Enlightenment England* (Cambridge, 2010)

Bowerbank, Sylvia, 'God as Androgyne: Jane Lead's Rewriting of the Destiny of Nature', *Quidditas*, 24 (2003), pp. 5–23

Engelhardt, Juliane, '"We shall be the Mother of Jesus": Visions of Power among Radical Religious Women in Northern Europe, 1690–1760', *Intellectual History Review*, XXXI/1 (2021), pp. 73–90

Gibbons, B. J., *Gender in Mystical and Occult Thought: Behmenism and its Development in England* (Cambridge, 1996)

Hessayon, Ariel, ed., *Jane Lead and Her Transnational Legacy* (London, 2016)

Hirst, Julie, *Jane Leade: Biography of a Seventeenth-Century Mystic* (Aldershot, 2005)

—, '"Mother of Love": Spiritual Maternity in the Works of Jane Lead', in *Women, Gender, and Radical Religion in Early Modern Europe*, ed. Sylvia Brown (Leiden, 2007)

McDowell, Paula, 'Enlightenment Enthusiasms and the Spectacular Failure of the Philadelphian Society', *Eighteenth-Century Studies*, xxxv/4 (2002), pp. 515–33

Smith, C. F., 'Jane Lead: Mysticism and the Woman Clothed with the Sun', in *Shakespeare's Sisters: Feminist Essays on Woman Poets*, ed. Sandra Gilbert and Susan Gubar (Bloomington, IN, 1979)

ELIZABETH POOLE

Brod, Manfred, 'Politics and Prophecy in Seventeenth-Century England: The Case of Elizabeth Poole', *Albion*, xxxi/3 (1999), pp. 395–412

Nevitt, Marcus, 'Elizabeth Poole Writes the Regicide', *Women's Writing*, ix/2 (2002), pp. 233–48

—, *Women and the Pamphlet Culture of Revolutionary England, 1640–1660* (London, 2006)

ROSE THURGOOD

Baker, Naomi, *Scripture Women: Rose Thurgood, 'A Lecture of Repentance' and Cicely Johnson, 'Fanatical Reveries'* (Nottingham, 2005)

—, 'Rose Thurgood and Cicely Johnson', in *Encyclopedia of English Renaissance Literature*, ed. Garrett A. Sullivan Jr and Alan Stewart (London, 2011)

—, 'Counterfeiting Nature: Constructing Agency in the Life Writings of Rose Thurgood and Cicely Johnson', *Women's Writing*, xi/3 (2004), pp. 331–46

—, 'The Devil and the Debt Bill: Poverty, Theology, and the Self in Rose Thurgood's "A Lecture of Repentance" (1636–7)', *Literature and Theology*, xvii/3 (2003), pp. 324–40

Lynch, Kathleen, 'Conversion Narratives in Old and New England', in *The Oxford Handbook of Literature and the English Revolution*, ed. Laura Lunger Knoppers (Oxford, 2012)

ANNA TRAPNEL

Ambrose, Laura Williamson, 'Moved by God: Mobility and Agency in Anna Trapnel's *Report and Plea*', *Renaisssance Studies*, xxxiii/4 (2019), pp. 609–23

Baker, Naomi, 'Anna Trapnel', in *Encyclopedia of English Renaissance Literature*, ed. Garrett A. Sullivan Jr and Alan Stewart (London, 2011)

——, '"Break down the walls of flesh": Anna Trapnel, John James, and Fifth Monarchist Self-Representation', in *Women, Gender, and Radical Religion in Early Modern Europe*, ed. Sylvia Brown (Leiden, 2007)

Burrage, Champlin, 'Anna Trapnel's Prophecies', *English Historical Review*, xxvi/103 (1911), pp. 526–35

Chedgzoy, Kate, 'Female Prophecy in the Seventeenth Century: The Instance of Anna Trapnel', in *Writing and the English Renaissance*, ed. William Zunder and Suzanne Trill (London, 1996)

Gillespie, Katharine, 'Prophecy and Political Expression in Cromwellian England', in *The Oxford Handbook of Literature and the English Revolution*, ed. Laura Lunger Knoppers (Oxford, 2012)

Hinds, Hilary, 'Anna Trapnel: *Anna Trapnel's Report and Plea*', in *A Companion to Early Modern Women's Writing*, ed. Anita Pacheco (London, 2002)

——, 'Soul-Ravishing and Sin-Subduing: Anna Trapnel and the Gendered Politics of Free Grace', *Renaissance and Reformation*, xxv/4 (2001), pp. 117–37

——, 'The Transvaluation of Body and Soul in the Spiritual Autobiographies of Anna Trapnel', in *Paradigms, Poetics, and Politics of Conversion*, ed. J. Bremmer, W. J. van Bekkum and A. L. Molendijk (Leuven, 2006)

——, ed., *Anna Trapnel's Report and Plea* (Tempe, AZ, 2016)

Holstun, James, *Ehud's Dagger: Class Struggle in the English Revolution* (London, 2000)

Killeen, Kevin, '"People of a deeper speech": Anna Trapnel, Enthusiasm, and the Aesthetics of Incoherence', in *The Oxford Handbook of Early Modern Women's Writing in English, 1540–1700*, ed. Elizabeth Scott-Baumann, Danielle Clarke and Sarah C. E. Ross (Oxford, 2023)

Nevitt, Marcus, *Women and the Pamphlet Culture of Revolutionary England* (London, 2006)

Prineas, Matthew, 'The Discourse of Love and the Rhetoric of Apocalypse in Anna Trapnel's Folio Songs', *Comitatus: A Journal of Medieval and Renaissance Studies*, xxviii/1 (1997), pp. 90–110

Wray, Ramona, 'What say you to [this] book? [...] Is it yours?': Oral and Collaborative Narrative Trajectories in the Mediated Writings of Anna Trapnel', *Women's Writing*, xvi/3 (2009), pp. 408–24

ANNE WENTWORTH

Adcock, Rachel, *Baptist Women's Writings in Revolutionary Culture, 1640–1680* (London, 2015)

Gillespie, Katharine, 'Anne Wentworth', in *The Palgrave Encyclopedia of Early Modern Women's Writing*, ed. P. Pender and R. Smith (London, 2021)

Johnston, Warren, 'Prophecy, Patriarchy, Violence in the Early Modern Household: The Revelations of Anne Wentworth', *Journal of Family History*, XXXIV/4 (2009), pp. 344–68

Searle, Alison, 'Women, Marriage and Agency in Restoration Dissent', in *Religion and Women in Britain, c. 1660–1760*, ed. Hannah Smith and Sarah Apetrei (London, 2014)

Smith, William E., 'Anne Wentworth's Apocalyptic Marriages: Bigamy, Subjectivity and Religious Conflict', in *Marriage in Premodern Europe*, ed. J. Murray (Toronto, 2012), pp. 357–72

SARAH WIGHT

Baker, Naomi, 'Sarah Wight', in *Encyclopedia of English Renaissance Literature*, ed. Garrett A. Sullivan Jr and Alan Stewart (London, 2011)

Camden, Vera J., 'Attending to Sarah Wight: "Little Writer" of God's Wonders', *Bunyan Studies*, 11 (2003–4), pp. 94–131

Chedgzoy, Kate, 'Other Maids: Religion, Race, and Relationships Between Girls in Early Modern London', in *Literary Cultures and Medieval and Early Modern Childhoods*, ed. N. J. Miller and D. Purkiss (London, 2019)

Dailey, Barbara Ritter, 'The Visitation of Sarah Wight: Holy Carnival and the Revolution of the Saints in Civil War London', *Church History*, LV/4 (1986), pp. 438–55

Scott-Luckens, Carola, 'Propaganda, or Marks of Grace? The Impact of the Reported Ordeals of Sarah Wight in Revolutionary London, 1647–52', *Women's Writing*, IX/2 (2002), pp. 215–32

Acknowledgements

My greatest debt in writing this book is to Nigel Smith, who first inspired me as an undergraduate student to investigate these remarkable women and who has provided much encouragement ever since. John Stachniewski and Jeremy Maule also offered inspirational help and guidance when I first researched radical religious women's writing, as did Gerald Hammond and Jacqueline Pearson. My former and current editors at Reaktion Books, Dave Watkins, David Hayden and Martha Jay, have been patient and enthusiastic supporters of the project. I am very grateful to Emily Rowe for her meticulous research assistance. Many thanks also to my father Bruce Baker and to Nat Baker, Will Gibson and John Gibson, all of whom generously read draft chapters. And thank you to my friends and colleagues Anke Bernau, Deirdre Boleyn, Felicity Bradley, Jo Carruthers, Debbie Dallmeyer, Lesel Dawson, Jerome de Groot, Zoë Kinsley, Rachel Kirkwood, David Matthews, Annie O'Donnell, James Paz, Eithne Quinn, Chi-ann Rajah, Angela Roberts, Fred Schurink, Martin Thompson and Natalie Zacek for many enjoyable conversations about related topics. This book is dedicated to my wonderful daughters, Isabel and Florence.

Photo Acknowledgements

The author and publishers wish to express their thanks to the sources listed below for illustrative material and/or permission to reproduce it. Some locations of works are also given below, in the interest of brevity:

AdobeStock: p. 205 (*top*; Anibal Trejo); Beinecke Rare Book and Manuscript Library, Yale University, New Haven, CT: pp. 110, 110–11; Boston Public Library: p. 39; Bridgeman Images: p. 106 (British Library Archive); The Courtauld, London (Samuel Courtauld Trust): p. 104; Houghton Library, Harvard University, Cambridge, MA: pp. 158, 222; courtesy John Rylands Research Institute and Library, The University of Manchester (Eng MS 875, fols. 201r and 214r): pp. 52, 53; Lewis Walpole Library, Yale University, Farmington, CT: p. 60; The National Archives, Kew, London (SP 29/103, fol. 99): pp. 178, 179; National Galleries of Scotland, Edinburgh: p. 143; National Gallery of Art, Washington, DC: pp. 166, 221; The New York Public Library: p. 197; Rijksmuseum, Amsterdam: p. 92; Shutterstock.com: pp. 203 (Sergey-73), 205 (*bottom*; Nikitich Viktoriya); Wellcome Collection, London (MS 2492): p. 252; Dr Williams's Library, London, photo Internet Archive: p. 264; The Women's Library, London School of Economics and Political Science: p. 161; Yale Center for British Art, New Haven, CT: p. 195.

Index

Page numbers in *italics* refer to illustrations